GERM
WARRIORS

STORIES OF MEN AND WOMEN FIGHTING
THE WORLD'S WORST PLAGUES

GERM WARRIORS

STORIES OF MEN AND WOMEN FIGHTING
THE WORLD'S WORST PLAGUES

EDITED BY CLINT WILLIS

Thunder's Mouth Press
New York

GERM WARRIORS: STORIES OF MEN AND WOMEN FIGHTING THE WORLD'S WORST PLAGUES

Compilation copyright © 2003 by Clint Willis
Introductions copyright © 2003 by Clint Willis

Published by
Thunder's Mouth Press
An Imprint of Avalon Publishing Group Incorporated
245 West 17th St., 11th floor
New York, NY 10011

Library of Congress Cataloging-in-Publication Data is available.

ISBN 1-56025-560-9

Book design: Sue Canavan
Printed in the United States of America
Distributed by Publishers Group West

For Lee Schwamm

contents

Introduction

The emergence of new diseases is a threat to our species. AIDS alone—already the fourth-leading cause of death in the world—could claim an additional 65 million lives by 2020. Meanwhile, old plagues are resurfacing in the United States and elsewhere, often in newly virulent forms. Most citizens of the world's industrialized nations assume that scourges such as malaria, tuberculosis and cholera have been relegated to history's dustbin—but nothing could be further from the truth. For example, there are more than two million new cases of tuberculosis each year in India, where the disease kills 1,000 people a day.

The United States and other developed countries have been spared the worst ravages of these diseases. Yet there are clear signs that our relative immunity will not last forever—that it may be ending even now.

AIDS remains an enormous and growing public health problem in the United States. The recent SARS outbreak was a reminder of how quickly a new virus can spread from the developing world to the streets of a North American city. The spectacularly frightening Ebola virus surfaced in a Washington, D.C. suburb a few years ago—and there is no telling where it will surface next. Meanwhile, some old-fashioned illnesses are making a comeback in the United States, where growing numbers of mostly poor patients are suffering from treatment-resistant tuberculosis and other maladies.

The stories in this collection are about such threats and our collective response to them. That response has been woefully inadequate, in both human and practical terms. We are content to ignore an illness as long as it is mostly contained within the borders of a distant continent (say, Africa) or a fringe population (say, gay men). This is an ethical failure easily comparable to the decision of a previous generation to ignore the Holocaust.

Worse, our greed and our complacency help to create the conditions for much of the suffering caused by disease. This can happen when we finance a civil war that destroys a nation's fledgling economy, leading to conditions that foster the emergence of new strains of illness. Likewise, we ask for trouble when we destroy a species that once sheltered a virus, which may adapt by jumping to a human host. So-called compassionate conservatives who gut government health and welfare programs help create the conditions for the emergence of dangerous new strains of tuberculosis in our cities.

Such behavior amounts to a crime against our planet, and punishment may be in store for us. When we ignore or cause the suffering of our fellow human beings in Africa and elsewhere, we contribute to the conditions that are likely to lead to our own suffering. AIDS came from the developing world—where it emerged amid conditions of poverty and ecological devastation. The same is true of Ebola and other, even more frightening plagues that eventually could threaten even the world's most affluent countries.

Some people—researchers, writers, doctors, nurses, aid workers, political activists—are facing the threat that germs pose to our collective welfare. Their stories and their ideas are at the heart of this book. Their work reflects imaginative insights: the understanding that borders are abstractions; that human beings share the world with each other and with the rest of creation; that no person—and indeed, no species—is an island.

We don't know how long our species will survive. The answer to that question depends in part on how well we adapt to problems we have created. These stories suggest that courage and compassion offer our most successful adaptive response to the forces of greed and complacency that may yet destroy us all.

—Clint Willis

from Dangerous Medicine
by Tom Clynes

Journalist Tom Clynes joined a team of doctors and researchers responding to an Ebola outbreak. His report ran in National Geographic Adventure *(June 2001).*

After the sun sets, a distant clanging begins. It starts faintly, a rhythmic din that gets closer and louder. Soon it's joined by deeper drumbeats. At the beginning of the outbreak, the drumming—on pots and pans as well as drums—became a nightly ritual to chase away the Ebola demon. After a few weeks it diminished as the local population began to feel more secure. Now the drumming is back.

Dr. Anthony Sanchez got the news on a Sunday afternoon in mid-October when he stopped by his lab at the Centers for Disease Control and Prevention (CDC), in Atlanta. Sanchez was surprised to find his boss, Pierre Rollin, in the office.

Rollin began by telling Sanchez that he could decline the

assignment. After all, Sanchez had a four-month-old daughter at home.

"Feel free to say no, Tony," Rollin said. "But I'm putting together a team to go over and set up a lab; we could use you." This was the first Sanchez had heard that Ebola, after a four-year respite, had resurfaced, this time in northern Uganda.

Sanchez, 47, had spent much of his career researching the Ebola virus, often in the CDC's maximum-containment lab, protected by a space suit. But he had never seen it operate in a human epidemic. Once, a few years ago, he wondered if he had missed his chance, if it would ever come again.

Now the agency was spread thin, with a team in Saudi Arabia trying to contain an epidemic of Rift Valley fever. And an on-site laboratory could give the Ebola containment operation a tremendous advantage. Sanchez walked to his office and picked up the phone. He dialed his home number and told his wife that there was something he needed to talk about when he got home, something important. The line was silent for several long seconds, and then:

"I'm not going to be happy about this, am I?"

The old Czech prop plane lurches to a halt at the side of the military airstrip; the doctors unfurl their stiff legs, disembark, and begin unloading. They shift 47 boxes—a metric ton of laboratory gear—onto a truck and drive toward town, trailing a spiral of orange dust as they pass army checkpoints and outsize churches, roadside vendors, and crowds of people listening to radios, talking, and singing.

The most surprising thing is how ordinary it all looks, at first. Set in the middle of a fertile, if unrelieved, savanna, the town of Gulu, Uganda, could be any other East African provincial center. Everywhere, people are on the move, some pedaling bikes, others riding on the fringed rear seats of bicycle taxis, most just walking. They walk upright, with stone-straight posture, some carrying babies on their backs, some balancing loads on their heads, some barefoot, others in sandals. They walk—and the doctors drive—past the field where the pope once spoke; past the turnoff that leads to the witch doctor's house; past another road that leads to a small village near the forest, where, maybe, it all started.

It takes a few minutes, as if their eyes were getting used to a new light, before hints begin to emerge that life here is far from normal: There are none of the usual swarms of school-children in uniform. White trucks drive through town, emblazoned with the red crosses and acronyms—UN, WHO, MSF—that portend crisis. The hospital building, where the doctors pull up, is wrapped in white plastic sheeting; a hand-lettered sign warns "No entrance without permission." The sign is illustrated with a crude human figure with an X drawn over it.

Five weeks into the crisis, a crowd of foreigners occupies a government office room in a yellow concrete-block building on the north side of Gulu. Doctors and scientists hunch over notebook computers and speak into walkie-talkies. Amid the babble of languages and accents, an American woman's voice talks into a satellite telephone: "We've got more Ebola-positives in Pabo now—we've got to get on top of this."

Whenever a serious epidemic is confirmed anywhere in the world, an alert goes out to members of the Global Outbreak Alert and Response Network, and scores of doctors, scientists, and humanitarian workers start packing bags and booking flights. The international disease-fighting team assembled to combat the Ebola outbreak in Uganda ultimately numbers more than a hundred professionals from a dozen countries, plus more than a thousand Ugandans. Among them are epidemiologists and virologists, physicians and nurses, laboratory workers, logistics specialists, and educators. Later, they'll be joined by researchers eager to take advantage of a rare opportunity to learn more about a virus that has baffled scientists for 25 years.

The Ebola virus is named after the river in Zaire (now called the Democratic Republic of the Congo) where it was first identified in 1976, during an outbreak that killed 280. Since that epidemic, and a concurrent outbreak in Sudan, the disease has struck in Côte d'Ivoire, again in Sudan and Congo, and three times in Gabon. Ebola is one of the deadliest, most infectious pathogens known to man; once in the bloodstream, it wipes out the immune system within a matter of days, causing high fever, vomiting, diarrhea, and, in a small but well-publicized number of cases, uncontrolled bleeding. There is no cure and no effective treatment. No one knows its natural host—the organism it usually infects—and no one knows why or how it sometimes leaps into the human realm.

Right now, though, the focus is not on solving Ebola's mysteries. Right now, everyone in this room has only one goal: to stop the epidemic.

The woman on the satellite phone, Cathy Roth, a 47-year-old physician with the World Health Organization (WHO), is currently coordinating the containment operation. She hangs up, and I walk over to introduce myself. When I extend my hand, she throws both of hers over her head in a "Don't shoot!" gesture.

"Uh, we're not actually doing that anymore," Roth says, smiling down at my retreating hand. Ebola is spread through contact with bodily fluids, including sweat. And although it's unlikely that either of us is carrying the virus, people are avoiding handshakes like . . . well, like the plague.

A dozen or so exhausted-looking professionals trudge in for Roth's afternoon update meeting. "Everyone's getting really tired now," she tells me. "We were thinking we had it under control, and I was thinking about giving the mobile teams a Sunday off. After five weeks of 24-7, they're at risk of making mistakes and they need rest." But now Roth is worried that the illness is flaring up again, threatening to break through the containment operation.

In the past, Ebola has struck only in rural areas, and the disease's rapid death sequence has actually worked in favor of containment, since infected people couldn't travel far before they succumbed. But the Gulu area is densely populated, with transport links to East Africa's major cities—and, from there, to anywhere in the world. No one in this room is interested in finding out what might happen if they were to give the virus a chance to take advantage of these more favorable conditions.

CDC medical epidemiologist Scott Harper begins the meeting with bad news from Pabo, a refugee camp north of Gulu. "A woman came into the clinic last Sunday and miscarried, and there was a lot of hemorrhaging," he says. "No one knew she was Ebola-positive, and she spent at least two days in the maternity ward, bleeding."

His colleague Marta Guerra picks up the story: "She had five women in the maternity ward with her, plus at least 15 visitors. Eleven nurses and other workers were exposed before they got her isolated. So far, we've taken blood from all but one."

Roth tucks her hair behind her ears. "This thing has the potential to blow up into a huge problem," she says.

A few blocks from the international team's headquarters, a

teenage boy motions for me to follow him. "Miracle," he says, and he leads me into a crowd gathered at a gate, peering into a brown-dirt courtyard. In the shade of a sprawling tree, a woman sits in a plastic chair, her head arched backward. Eyes wide and teary, she stares into the branches while another woman cuts her hair, felling the thin braids with slow, deliberate snips of the scissors.

A preacher stands in front of her, aiming a video camera with his outstretched left hand, rocking back and forth as he calls out a surreal narration: "She was mentally deranged for 12 years," he says. "She was possessed by evil powers. The family took her to many witch doctors, but the demon inside would not relent."

He turns toward the crowd. "We prayed and we urged her to surrender her witch doctor gadgets. And now, look at her!" The woman smiles and sobs silently as her braids fall. "Look at her!" the preacher says, his voice rising. "The Lord has rescued her from demonic oppression!"

Watching the faces in the crowd, I have no doubt that everyone wants to believe that a miracle—be it religion, witchcraft, or science—could defeat a demon. But the woman's gaze remains unsettled, and her eyes dart tentatively, searching among the branches.

Dr. Simon Mardel enters the dressing room outside the isolation ward at St. Mary's Lacor Hospital and pulls a full-length surgical smock over his head. He stretches a first layer of gloves over the top of the smock's tight elastic cuffs, then he pulls knee-high gum boots over his feet and tucks in his pants. He puts on a paper shower cap and a thick plastic surgical apron, then a second pair of gloves and a mask. Just before he walks through the first of two disinfectant boot baths, he places the final protective barrier—goggles—over his eyes.

An expert in emergency and refugee health care, Marcel had taken a leave of absence from his duties as an emergency room physician in England's Lake District to assist at a recent epidemic of another highly contagious hemorrhagic fever—Marburg—in Congo. He was on his way home in October when he was diverted to Gulu. A few years earlier, during the war in Bosnia, Mardel hiked into Srebrenica to treat wounded civilians while the city was under siege—a heroic action that earned him the Order of the British Empire for humanitarianism.

Mardel arrived in Gulu with the first WHO team and took charge of the isolation wards, calmly demonstrating barrier-nursing techniques to terrified hospital workers. "Remember," the clear-eyed 43-year-old told a group of nurses and nuns, "the system is only as strong as its weakest moment."

Mardel enters the suspect ward, set aside for people who are symptomatic but unconfirmed as Ebola-positive. In one corner of the room, a male patient lies sideways on a bed, coughing and moaning. He holds a wad of tissues to his nose, which streams with black blood. He seems utterly indifferent to the doctor's presence.

"We'll get some blood from him," Mardel says, and the patient offers his arm weakly to the needle.

The Lacor hospital is well endowed and well equipped by African standards, and its wood-trimmed wards and array of diagnostic equipment stand in contrast to the bare concrete of the government-run Gulu Hospital, across town, where doctors scrounge for basic supplies. In the mission-hospital tradition, Lacor's care is intensive and hands-on. Because of the vomiting, diarrhea, and hemorrhaging, Ebola patients need massive care; at Lacor, nurses and nuns are responsible for everything from mopping up to helping patients die with as much dignity as possible.

Inside the isolation ward, health workers are fully enveloped in protective gear; their goggled eyes are their only semirecognizable features. To aid identification, many have scrawled their names with markers on the fronts of their white plastic surgical aprons.

Mardel spots an apron across the room labeled "Dr. Matthew" and heads over to a corner where Matthew Lukwiya is treating an Ebola-stricken nurse. Lukwiya, 42, Lacor's medical superintendent, had been on leave in Kampala, 200 miles south of Gulu, where he received word of "a strange new illness" making its way through the hospital's wards. He immediately left his wife and five children in the capital and drove up to Gulu. Within two days of his arrival, 17 people—including three nurses—were dead or dying with the same dire symptoms.

"At first it looked like some sort of super-malaria," he says. "But the patients did not respond to quinine treatment, and it was killing people very quickly." He began flirting with the possibility that one of the rare diseases of the filovirus family, Ebola or the somewhat less deadly Marbug, might have come in from Sudan or Congo. However unlikely this diagnosis— Ebola had never been seen in Uganda—he sent samples off to a laboratory in Johannesburg. Three days before the results were due, Lukwiya concluded that all signs were pointing to the worst possible scenario—Ebola—and that he needed to act immediately. He stayed up all night reading a manual titled "Infection Control for Viral Hemorrhagic Fevers in the African Health Care Setting," downloaded from the Internet. In the morning, he and his staff started setting up a barrier-nursing environment, using whatever resources were on hand. They built hands-free boot removers from scrap wood and constructed an incinerator out of a 55-gallon drum. They fashioned aprons from duct tape and plastic sheeting and converted a hospital pavilion into an isolation ward. Then, from behind these crude protective layers, they began nursing Ebola patients.

Through the goggles, Mardel's eyes meet Lukwiya's, which are heavy with concern. The nurse he is treating is in critical condition.

"If she dies," Lukwiya says, "she will be our seventh."

In the morning, volunteer James Kidega reports to the Red Cross office, where a map hangs on one wall, dotted with pushpins: green for refugee camps, red for land mine sites, pink for recent ambushes. Since the mid-1980s, a nebulous guerrilla force known as the Lord's Resistance Army (LRA), whose stated objective is to carve a Christian state out of Uganda, has terrorized the region's civilian population. To protect their children at night, when the rebels usually operate, most of the rural population has moved into refugee camps near Ugandan army barracks. Every day since the containment operation began, scores of Red Cross volunteers have fanned out to these "protected villages" to follow up on Ebola rumors, call for ambulances, educate the populace, and relay information about hospitalized relatives and neighbors.

Before the epidemic hit, the 25-year-old Kidega had worked at a charitable agency that helps children who have escaped from the rebels. Because of his extensive contacts in the villages and his polished demeanor—he is rarely seen without a clean shirt and necktie—Kidega was recruited as a volunteer leader.

Today, he will lead a team that will visit two villages north of Gulu. With red-and-white flags flying, two trucks set out. As Kidega guides the trucks north, he recalls the first few days of the epidemic. At Gulu's two hospitals, he says, many nurses and orderlies stopped coming to work, fearing that they might be assigned to the isolation wards, and some international agencies based in Gulu left town. In the villages surrounding Gulu, rumors of sorcery circulated as entire families were wiped out. In Rwot Obilo village, the virus moved through one family so quickly that a dying woman told her young grandson, moments after his mother's death, "Suck your mother's last milk so you, too, can die—there is no one here to look after you now."

"It felt like being on a sinking ship," Kidega says. "You can't believe the fear." Some victims swarmed the hospitals; others ran away in panic as nurses fell ill all around them. Even the rebels were spooked; the LRA released 40 prisoners, fearing that they might be carrying the virus.

When the trucks pull into Akwayugi, villagers look up from their work of sifting maize and wheat. This isn't as bad as sub-Saharan Africa gets, but there's serious squalor here. About a fifth of the children have the bulging bellies that indicate severe malnutrition.

The Red Cross volunteers divide into four-person teams and move through the village, asking questions of the small crowds that gather wherever they go: Has anyone had a fever? Has anyone had bloody diarrhea or vomit? Was there a sudden death?

The team has a "reintegration kit" for two girls who survived Ebola after they lost their mother to the disease. They find them with their father, Charles Odongo, outside the family's round, mud-brick hut. Two weeks earlier, Odongo returned from the fields to find his wife in the hut with a headache and a high fever. "It took six hours for the ambulance to get here," he says. "By the time they arrived, she had died." When he sees the kit—cooking pots, blankets, soap, salt, and clothing—he smiles gratefully. "Immediately after we left for the hospital with my wife's body, our things were burned by the neighbors," he says.

Although the Ebola-Zaire strain can kill nearly 90 percent of its victims, the Gulu virus is similar to the less lethal Sudan strain, which has a mortality rate of about 50 percent. Odongo's three-year-old daughter, Skovia, survived the disease that killed her mother. "You should not fear her," a volunteer says to a circle of onlookers. "This is not a contagious little girl." The motherless girl seems to brighten when she sees the dress the team has brought for her, but her nine-month-old sister, Geoffrey, clings to her father listlessly. She's severely malnourished, weakened by the disease, and silent except for an occasional phlegmy cough. It's hard to imagine her making it to her first birthday.

On the way back to town, Kidega stops by his mother's house for a cup of tea. "James," his mother asks him, putting the kettle on the stove, "why so many coffins passing by here today?"

"It's going up again," Kidega says. "We were beginning to think it was nearly over, that they would reopen the schools, but I think now they will wait. People are hiding the facts. They think they will be shunned."

"Why don't they put the coffins inside when they transport them?" she asks. "This is making people very nervous." As she pours the tea, her 20-year-old niece, Sarah, walks in.

"This Ebola, I wish we could see it," Sarah says, clucking her tongue. "If we could see it, then we could beat it to death, with a stick."

Later, Kidega's radio crackles. A teenage girl has run into the clinic in Pabo, terrified of bleeding that would turn out to be nothing more than her first menstrual period. There's gunfire on the road near the Lacor hospital. And north of Gulu, a soldier in an armored personnel carrier has broken out in a fever and is vomiting red inside the vehicle. The other soldiers have run away.

"Can you send an isolation ambulance?" the military commander pleads.

Saturday morning at the hospital guest house, Tony Sanchez and Pierre Rollin are finishing breakfast in the dining room, getting ready to suit up for the lab. Since arriving in Gulu, they've been occupied controlling the outbreak; they're hoping to soon shift their focus to research.

"You can't do productive field research on Ebola when it vanishes," says Rollin. "So you need to get the information when you can."

Researchers at the National Institutes of Health recently announced progress in developing an Ebola vaccine that works in monkeys, but the virus's underlying logic is still beyond the reach of science. Since coming to the world's attention in 1976, the disease has baffled a generation of researchers, who have collected hundreds of thousands of specimens from plants, animals, and insects. Humans are what research virologists like Sanchez and Rollin call "accidental hosts" for the Ebola virus. "We don't know where it hides," Rollin says. "It may turn out to be something right under our noses. There are different schools of thought. Some say it is carried by rodents, or insects, or bats. . . ."

At that moment, as if summoned, Bob Swanepoel strides into the dining room, decked out in a khaki bush-hunter outfit. Swanepoel is a bat man. The director of the Special Pathogens Unit of the South African Institute for Virology in Johannesburg, the goateed, 64-year-old veterinarian has made a career out of tramping into Africa's remote jungles, looking for the natural reservoirs of Ebola and other hemorrhagic fevers.

"He's at every outbreak," says Rollin. Over the past 20 years, the 47-year-old Rollin and Swanepoel have developed a bond that's fed by a shared fascination for viral diseases. When they're not working together at an outbreak, they communicate over the phone, from Atlanta to Johannesburg, at least once a week.

Swanepoel was in Saudi Arabia at the Rift Valley-fever epidemic when the first samples of Ebola-infected blood, sent by Lukwiya, arrived at his Johannesburg lab. Now he has finally made it to Gulu, along with two assistants and several bundles of nets and poles. "Pierre told me not to come," he says, settling in at Rollin's table. "He said there is nothing here, that we're too far downstream in the epidemic. But what do you do when you hear that? Do you stay home? No, you have to see for yourself."

Swanepoel is eager to do some reservoir hunting, but his bat-nabbing nets remain bundled outside his room. "Right now," he says, "there are several hurdles. First, I need to know the focal point before I start trapping. Did one person get it first, or were there a lot of people who separately picked up this thing from nature? It's the Sudan strain of Ebola, but was it brought in by a rebel from Sudan, or did it start near here? Northern Uganda and southern Sudan have roughly the same terrain and ecology, and the entire region is like a Bermuda

Triangle of filoviruses. We're close to the Ebola River, to Durba, Mount Elgon, Kitum Cave—all the hotbeds of Marburg and Ebola.

"The second hurdle is, I need approval. You go out in a place like this without approval, and the next thing you know you're into ten kinds of sh—. We got arrested in Congo, and it took half a day before they tracked down the colonel to vouch for us. He was at a brothel.

"Third, there are security issues. It's best to work at night, but . . ."

Rollin finishes Swanepoel's sentence: "But if you put a net up at night, you're more likely to catch a rebel than a reservoir."

Rollin often raises an eyebrow when he talks, which gives him a wryly comical look. "What I would like to know," Rollin says, "is did somebody do something in the bush that people don't normally do? Something seemed to be happening in September, before Matthew arrived. There was a lot of diarrhea, and rumors about some unusual malaria in a certain village. What you want to find is, was there a village where it started? But because of stigma, and because so much time has passed and so many people are dead, you don't get the straight story."

As Rollin talks, a dark spot forms above his left eyebrow. No one says anything, but in a minute Rollin feels the liquid as it starts to run down his forehead. He wipes it with his index finger.

"Hmm. It's blood. Very strange. I don't think I cut myself here. And I haven't shaved my forehead lately."

He wipes it away. When it keeps coming, he gets up and grabs a tissue. He succeeds in stanching the flow and sits back down. All conversation has stopped.

"Maybe I have started to bleed with Ebola a new way," he says, smiling as he raises an eyebrow. And everyone laughs.

Nervously.

After breakfast, Tony Sanchez walks out of the Lacor guest house, toward the lab. An ambulance pulls around the corner, and Sanchez averts his eyes as an Ebola suspect is led into the ward.

"What we don't experience up in Atlanta is the wards, the bleeding," he says. "I talked to Pierre about what to expect, but to tell you the truth, I've never seen large numbers of people dead and dying before—and the way they suffer. . . . During the day, you're doing your job, and you don't think about it. But at night, you see their faces. Your subconscious comes up with questions you can't answer."

Brother Elio Croce calls Sanchez's name and trots over. A Verona missionary who runs Lacor's technical and transportation services, Brother Elio, 54, is a plump Sean Connery look-alike with a compassionate demeanor that's balanced by a cranky sanctimoniousness.

"Tony, I need to take you out to Bardege Village," Elio says, "to get blood and a skin sample for a biopsy from a little girl who just died. We need to get there before they bury her."

I introduce myself to Elio and extend my hand—it's amazing just how reflexive the custom is. Before I realize my mistake, Elio reaches out, grabs my hand, and looks me straight in the eye. "We're not shaking hands here anymore," he says, shaking my hand. "There's an Ebola epidemic going on here you know."

Actually, the Gulu epidemic was initially spread more by contact with the dead than with the living. According to local ritual, a dead body stays in the house for a day or two while extended family and friends wash the corpse, eat and drink, and wash hands in a communal basin. Then they bury the body next to the house. ("For you, the dead take care of themselves," James Kidega says. "For us, we take care of the dead.")

The viral count is at its peak in a just expired body, but despite the risk and despite an aggressive education campaign, it's been extremely difficult to get people to stop customs that have been entrenched for generations. For that reason, health workers have encouraged residents to report deaths in neighboring families.

Sanchez grabs his gear, and we jump into a truck with Elio. As the clergyman drives, he talks nonstop in a singsongy Italian accent that seems incongruous with the content of his monologue: "The nurse, Grace Akulu, died. She was conscious until the very end—it's not true that everyone is demented in the final stages. She died singing; she never feared to encounter our Lord. We buried her behind the hospital in a beautiful ceremony. I have tape-recorded the singing. I will play it for you later."

"I thought it was supposed to be slowing down," Sanchez says.

"I do not think it is slowing down now," Elio says. "Tomorrow, we have to dig more graves."

With the isolation ambulance trailing, Elio turns off the road and drives through the elephant grass, following a single-track trail that terminates in a tidy dirt courtyard surrounded by a half dozen round mud-brick huts with thatched roofs.

The deceased girl's name is Sunday Onen; she was two years old. Her mother sits next to two other women, who are nursing young children; her grandfather, Peter Ola, talks to Sanchez and Elio.

"The child was healthy," Ola says incredulously. "She ate breakfast around nine, then she had a fever and began vomiting.

When her diarrhea became bloody, my daughter began to carry her to the hospital. But midway, she did not cry out any longer, so she brought her back here."

Ebola doesn't usually work that quickly, but there are enough Ebola symptoms that it must be treated as a suspect case. The villagers watch in silence as Sanchez suits up; the three ambulance crew members stand in the sun, sweating inside their protective clothing.

As Sanchez bends down and leans into the hut, Brother Elio pulls out his tape recorder and begins a peculiar commentary.

"He's down on one knee, entering the hut. Yes, that's it, careful."

Encumbered by the hut's darkness and his layers of protective gear, Sanchez draws blood and cuts a skin sample from the tiny corpse. It takes longer than it should, because the lab has run out of biopsy punches, devices that work like high-tech cookie cutters to neatly remove a small patch of skin. He has to tug the girl's skin up, then make the cut with surgical scissors, working slowly, with full awareness of the consequences of even the smallest nick to his hands.

"He's down on both knees now," Elio continues. "Respect. Respect."

Sanchez backs out of the hut and straightens up, breathing hard through his surgical mask. He walks to the center of the clearing and lays out a sheet of white cloth, then he kneels down to pack the specimens. An ambulance crew member comes over with a garden-pump dispenser of disinfectant and sprays the bottoms of Sanchez's feet. Then the sprayer follows the other two crew members into the hut. Sanchez stands up just as the crew emerges, carrying a small white bundle.

"My God," Sanchez says. "I thought this was going to be an easy day." His right hand is twitching.

As the body is brought to the ambulance, the villagers suddenly become agitated. They gather around Brother Elio, talking to him in the Acholi language. Elio approaches Sanchez.

"See the problem now, Tony," he says, "there's been a misunderstanding. They thought that we would come out and test the girl, and if it wasn't Ebola, we would leave her here for them to bury her according to tradition."

Sanchez does his best to explain that he needs to bring the blood back to the lab to test for the Ebola antibody. The test takes several hours, and it may not be conclusive. They need to send the skin samples away for testing in Atlanta. In the meantime, the whole village may be vulnerable to infection until the body is taken away and buried at the isolation graveyard.

After a few minutes, the villagers stop talking; they just stare at Sanchez, the white man in the white suit insisting that their loved one be sent off to the afterlife unprepared, buried as if she had never lived at all. There is no actual threat—apart from the threat of having to remember these faces for the rest of a lifetime.

Sanchez takes Elio aside, and the two men's roles flip-flop. Sanchez, the scientist, wants to compromise, to humanize the rules. The body was in good condition, he says. It may not have been Ebola. Maybe it was a snakebite. . . .

"But the grandfather said she did not cry out," Elio says sharply. Sanchez's hand twitches again.

"What are we going to do?" he asks.

"We're not going to do anything," Elio snaps. His face is pinched, and the words come out that way, in a clipped staccato. "We can't let them bury her here. They will not do it the way we want."

Sanchez and Elio move toward the truck, and the villagers

follow, forming a crescent around the front of the vehicle, continuing to stare as the two men get in.

It feels as if the air has been sucked out of the sky.

Elio starts the truck and shifts it into reverse. He begins to let out the clutch—then he stops.

"Hey," he says, looking at Sanchez. "What do you think? We let them bury her here. We stay, we supervise, they dig the grave very fast. It's more human, no?"

In an instant, they're out of the truck. Elio makes the announcement, and the dirt starts flying, with Sunday's father, who can't be more than 17 years old, leading the dig. A half hour later, the hole is completed, six feet deep. The ambulance crew lowers Sunday Onen's body gently into the ground.

Saturday evening, the team gathers in the courtyard at the Acholi Inn, tucked behind the roofless carcass of a burned-out building on the northern edge of town. Under a canopy of trees thick enough to block a light rain, a waitress runs back and forth with food and rounds of the local beer, Nile Special, politely requesting that the foreigners not lean back on the rear legs of the fragile plastic chairs. As the shadows lengthen, monkeys and an occasional rat scurry around the garden's perimeter; after sunset, bats swoop among the overhead branches.

Even the Nobel Peace Prize–winning Doctors Without Borders (Médecins Sans Frontières) is perennially short of recruits who are willing to turn their backs on comfortable, lucrative careers to come to needy places like Gulu, where the patient-to-doctor ratio approaches 18,000 to 1. (In the United States, it's around 400 to 1.) Yet despite the high stress and low comfort, despite the sound of machine gun fire in the night, everyone seems to feel privileged to be here.

"I had been wanting to do something like this since I was a teenager," says Patricia Campbell, an American physician with Doctors Without Borders. "I saw medicine as a passport to the world. But then I got married and had children, so I had to put it off until my kids were older." Now in her mid-60s, Campbell says she's "addicted."

"I go home to Scarsdale [New York], and I wonder how anyone can stand it, treating rich kids for tonsillitis. After a few weeks, I'm saying, 'Get me out of here!'"

The obvious question: Are you afraid?

"No," Campbell says flatly. "You follow protocol. Unless you're in direct contact with body fluids, you won't get Ebola."

Murmurs of agreement wash over the table. "If there was that high of a risk," says Simon Mardel, "I wouldn't be here."

Of course, playing down the risks is a coping mechanism, a way of keeping panic at bay. Like cigarette smoking or gallows humor, denial keeps you functioning effectively in the presence of danger and death—whether you're a doctor in a plague zone or a soldier in a battle zone.

For all the talk about managing risk, though, the odds don't look very good for medical people in their ongoing battle with the Ebola virus. In the 1995 Ebola outbreak in Congo, 80 medical workers became infected; 63 died. Hospitals—especially deprived African hospitals—provide an ideal environment for the virus to prosper, and health workers are vulnerable targets because of their close contact with bodily fluids. Ebola does not forgive even the smallest mistake.

On Sunday morning, grief takes a holiday. James Kidega walks through the double doors of Christ Church and joins the congregation in the throes of a full-blown dance party. At the front of the low altar, a band of musicians strum on stringed gourd instruments; they're nearly drowned out by a platoon of drummers, whacking away in a polyrhythmic fury. Around the musicians and into the back pews, people of all ages pogo up and down, driven in a raucous call-and-response by a young woman croaking through a distorted sound system.

"The love of Jesus has taken away the sins of the people," she sings.

"Evil can't touch us!" the dancers cry.

Outside his guest room in a wooded corner of the Lacor hospital compound, Bob Swanepoel slouches in a chair, flinging pebbles into the trees with a wrist-rocket slingshot. Nearby Pierre Rollin sits on the concrete floor of the patio, his back against the door, his legs stretched in front of him. Someone brings over a straw-colored fruit bat killed by a local boy, and Swanepoel perks up.

"These things are vicious," Swanepoel says, spreading the bat's wings. "Look at these teeth, and these claws—they're like razors. They'll go after you like a dog." He asks one of his researchers to put it in the refrigerator, along with a cobra that was killed on the Lacor grounds yesterday after menacing some nurses.

Swanepoel's bat-trapping expedition has been approved, but he's pessimistic about what the fieldwork might turn up. If you don't know where the epidemic started, he says, "it's a shot in the dark."

"Also," he says, "we've learned that the caves in the Kalak Hills aren't what we thought they were. Apparently, there are lots of very narrow caves that are difficult and dangerous to navigate. Maybe we can go up to the top and drop the nets— I don't know."

Elio rides up on his bike. He wants Rollin to test him for Ebola.

"That will be the third time you've been tested," says Rollin. "You keep thinking you're infected."

"We lost another nurse today," Elio says. "That makes eight, plus a nurse's boyfriend. We can't figure out how the boyfriend was exposed, since the nurse did not get Ebola. He was a young man, and strong. At the end, he told me he wanted to get married before he died, so I got the priest and sent for the girl. But as she was on her way here, we realized that we had time only to give him his last sacraments. When she arrived, the father went out to meet her." Elio pauses.

"He told her that he had already left for the long safari."

At headquarters, Cathy Roth comes outside and announces that she's "canceled the cancellation of this afternoon's meeting." Everyone troops inside.

There have been five deaths today so far. The CDC's Scott Harper reports that six people were admitted yesterday, and they aren't on any contact lists. "People seem to be hiding family members," he says. "The system seems to be breaking down. In Atiak, a suspect was buried, and no one got a specimen."

In Pabo, some recovering patients have been lost. At Gulu Hospital, an Ebola-positive patient "escaped" last night. (He later turned up at Lacor.) As for the infected woman who miscarried, there are now 32 contacts, including 11 health-care workers. After her procedure, two deliveries were performed on the same table.

Dr. Paul Onek, the district health director, gives voice to everyone's frustration. "If we have escaped patients, if we are not even able to take specimens from deceased people, then we are back to square one." He is silent for half a minute, then he speaks. "Yesterday, we breathed a sigh of relief. But now . . ." He purses his lips and sighs. There's no relief in it.

• • •

After the church service, James Kidega travels past the field where the pope spoke. He approaches a cluster of huts. The witch doctor, Abodtu, is in, although the authorities ordered him to remove his "traditional African healing" banner after a witch doctor in Rwot Obilo treated—and possibly infected—up to 30 people before dying of Ebola.

But Abodtu doesn't claim to cure Ebola—at least, not yet.

"Right now, I have no medicine for this," he says, lighting a candle inside his hut. "I cure people who are lame or berserk. I make the leg stop swelling and the brain start working. Or I send death to someone who has done wrong to your family.

"As for the white man's medicine and the white man's religion, I do not cross there. *This* is what I know." He sweeps his eyes over his altar—a clutter of beads and bones, snake skins and rattles, jugs and strings of shells.

Where does Ebola come from?

"I have asked my bad-thing where it came from. The spirit tells me to wait for instructions, then to go to the forest and look up to a special big tree. This tree has the answer; it will tell me where it comes from." He inhales deeply. "I will look up to the tree, and I will learn from the tree how to stop it."

Dr. Mike Ryan arrives from London, and three-quarters of the international team and seemingly half the town converge in the headquarters' parking lot within minutes to welcome him. A WHO medical officer, Ryan, 36, led the first team to hit the ground in Gulu, and he spent the next four weeks coordinating the operation before being summoned to London to represent the WHO at an infectious-disease conference. Now he's back, and with his long red sideburns bursting out from under his baseball cap he jumps from a rented van and immediately starts greeting people with big handshakes and bear hugs.

Suddenly, the energy seems cranked up.

"We managed to convince ourselves that it was under control," Ryan says, torching a cigarette as he addresses a group of mobile-team members. "Everyone's getting lethargic and exhausted. But we've got 17 people in the hospital now, and four new ones already today. We've got 45,000 people living in Pabo, and we can't afford to let it go. We can't take our eyes off the ball."

Waving his arms and bellowing, Ryan manages to get his audience guffawing, then he springs onto the porch. Just before dashing into the room, he turns and yells back at the group, loud enough for the entire parking lot to hear: "Let's keep our boots down on the neck of this bastard!"

At noon, Bob Swanepoel's team finally rolls out of Gulu for the Kalak Hills, escorted by 13 soldiers and an armored personnel carrier. They drive along the dirt roads, between walls of eight-foot-tall elephant grass, dodging bicyclists and pedestrians. Arriving at the refugee camp of Guruguru, Swanepoel negotiates with the villagers—two of whom say they dined on bats earlier that day—and sets out with a team of bat hunters and porters. In a scene that's vaguely reminiscent of some Great White Hunter epic, Swanepoel's party—soldiers, hunters, porters, and scientists—trudges over the hills toward the Kalak caves, trailed by an enthusiastic swarm of village children.

"It's very unlikely that we'll turn anything up," Swanepoel says, wiping sweat off his forehead as he walks. "You could test 100,000 bats for a virus before you find it; that's the sort of job we face."

Swanepoel decided a few years ago to shift his gaze upward, to arboreal virus carriers such as bats and canopy-dwelling insects, after exhaustive tests on ground-dwelling animals failed to reveal anything conclusive.

"At several points," he says, "bats have figured prominently in outbreaks of Ebola and Marburg. In some of those incidents, so have monkeys and chimps—but they died just like humans, so they can't be the reservoir. It has to be something that can carry Ebola without coming to harm. In the lab, when we injected Ebola into bats, we found that it could grow to a very high concentration, but it did not kill them. In fact, some of them excreted virus in their feces."

Arriving at the caves, Swanepoel assembles the lab on a large rock. The caves are narrow and steep, and the locals have been climbing in on rope ladders and using thorny branches to hook bats. But it's dangerous work; in the past year, more than ten residents of Guruguru have died in the caves, most by falling off the ladders. It's agreed that the bat hunters will work only in the most accessible caves to lessen the chance of anyone getting hurt. They head into the caverns, outfitted with nets and instructions to bring the animals back alive.

In Congo, Swanepoel used huge nets mounted on bamboo poles; in Gabon, he hunted with slingshots and live traps; in Côte d'Ivoire, he ascended elaborate walkways built in the treetops. He has used UV-light traps and fogging machines to collect insects. But today the expedition is decidedly low-tech, with teenage hunters wielding simple nets. As they bring in the bats, Swanepoel extracts vials of blood and puts the bodies in a freezer box for later dissection.

After four hours, the sun is moving toward the horizon, and the army commander indicates that it's time to go. The hunters have collected only nine bats, and Swanepoel is clearly disappointed. "To do this properly, you need hundreds, and you should really work at night. Like I said, it's a shot in the dark. I doubt we'll find anything—but we'll be back."

When the convoy pulls into town at dusk, Ryan and Kidega come out to the office parking lot, looking relieved. All afternoon, they've monitored radio reports of an ambush near where the expedition was working. The rebels attacked a vehicle, blowing it up with a rocket-propelled grenade, killing three people.

Just past sunset, most of the team gathers in the Acholi Inn courtyard. After dinner, they linger under the trees, drinking Nile Specials and occasionally getting scolded for leaning on the hind legs of the chairs. The talk gets around to the first few days of the epidemic.

"This is the one that could have gotten away," Ryan says. "And it still might. But if we manage to contain it, we've got Matthew [Lukwiya] to thank. By the time we got here he was already mobilizing the community and building a containment operation, and that gave us a head start we haven't had in other outbreaks."

Looking back, Ryan says he's amazed by Lukwiya's instincts: "Ebola isn't the first thing you'd think about here; it's not even the tenth thing. But Matthew put two and two together—and he got *shite* for an answer. Had he not taken action when he did, I don't know what would have happened."

By all accounts, though, the first few days were shambolic. When Ryan arrived, he found Gulu in the grip of panic. Immediately, he began coordinating the multiagency, multilingual war against the virus, cracking jokes and chainsmoking cigarettes, winning the confidence and support of local health officials and military personnel. "We needed to train, to get equipment, to get people off 24-hour shifts," he says. "We stopped all IV interventions and cut down admissions to only the most life threatening. We needed to get simple things right, like standardizing disinfectant mixes and training people to use the protective gear."

Ryan orders another round. "When we arrived," he says, "there were bodies piling up at the morgue. It's an old brick building that sits in the middle of a field on the outskirts of town, like something out of a 19th-century horror story."

Once an isolation graveyard was established, several military personnel were assigned the grim, dangerous task of burying the highly contagious bodies.

"The first guys," says Simon Mardel, "when they saw us coming with the bodies, they ran away. We were yelling, 'Hey, at least leave your shovels!'"

"They were terrified," says Ryan. "They were convinced they'd get Ebola if they got anywhere within an arse's roar of the virus. Simon and I realized that we couldn't expect them to do it if we weren't willing to do it ourselves. So we suited up and jumped in with the shovels. We were trying to joke with the fellows—saying things like, 'Hey, you just volunteered for the graveyard shift'—but they were pretty grim at first. In the end, though, they became the Olympic burial team; we wouldn't have had a prayer without them."

The next day, Mardel joins Lukwiya for rounds in the Lacor isolation ward. The two play a "good cop, bad cop" routine as they urge the more coherent patients to drink their rehydrating fluid. The majority of Ebola victims die of shock due to fluid loss; aggressive hydration is the only real treatment available for the disease.

Among the most serious cases on the ward are several nurses. Despite efforts to improve staff safety procedures and reduce fatigue, Lacor's nurses continue to get infected. But Marcel has a plan, and he tries to convince Lukwiya to buy into it.

"From now on, how about if we have the mobile teams bring all the new cases from the community to Gulu Hospital, to give your people a rest? We could still treat existing patients at Lacor, until they die or recover, and let self-referrals choose their hospital. That way, we keep all avenues of admission open."

Lukwiya says he'll consider it, but the following morning dawns with more bad news. Two nurses and a nun have died during the night, and the surviving medical-ward nurses walk out in frustration, grief, and terror. They assemble in a meeting hall and send for Lukwiya.

Lukwiya is calm and resolute as he walks into the room. For the past 17 years, he has been the stabilizing force at Lacor, the gentle but unyielding leader who has refused to let a civil war, a lack of resources, or anything else get in the way of helping his patients. A few years ago, on Good Friday, a band of rebels came to the hospital to take nurses as hostages. Lukwiya stepped forward and persuaded the guerrillas to take him instead. He spent a week on the move with them, treating their wounded soldiers, before they let him go.

Lukwiya tells the nurses of the plan to shift the bulk of the isolation work to Gulu Hospital and of his efforts to convince the government to provide hardship pay and compensation to the families of fallen nurses. He reemphasizes the need for full vigilance and adherence to the barrier-nursing techniques, especially at night, when tired workers are more likely to let down their guard.

"Those who want to leave, can leave," he finally says. "As for me, I will not betray my profession."

Lukwiya's words and the afternoon funerals, which take

place in a downpour with lots of singing and praying, have a calming effect. The nurses return to work.

Lukwiya has seen more than a hundred Ebola patients, but none have developed the relatively rare severe hemorrhagic form of Ebola. Unfortunately, one of his nurses, 32-year-old Simon Ojok, is the first. Sanchez, who had begun to think that the stories of spectacular bleeding were "a bunch of crap," now sees it with his own eyes.

Ojok's condition deteriorates quickly, and in the middle of the night he starts thrashing in his bed, pulling off his oxygen mask and spraying bright-red, oxygen-saturated blood all around him. He stumbles out of bed, and, as night-shift nurse Stanley Babu pleads with him to stay put, Ojok walks out of the room, tearing away from his IV tube. Agitated and mumbling, Ojok stands in the hallway, coughing infectious blood and mucous onto the walls and floor. Terrified, Babu runs to Lukwiya's quarters and wakes him.

"Blood is pouring from his eyes and nose like tap water," Babu tells Lukwiya. "He is confused, fighting death. We are afraid to take him back to bed because he seems violent."

Lukwiya sprints across the compound and hurries into the dressing room. He can hear the commotion through the wall as he pulls on his gown, his boots, his apron. Then his mask, his cap, his two pairs of gloves. He does not put on his goggles.

When Lukwiya enters the room, Ojok has stumbled back into bed and is gasping for breath, wrapped in his blood-soaked gown and sheets. Lukwiya props him up to help him breathe and changes his gown and bedding. Just past dawn, as Lukwiya is mopping the floor, Ojok dies.

A few days later, Lukwiya sends for Rollin and Sanchez. Could they please come to his office—and could they bring their blood-sampling gear?

When they arrive, Lukwiya is calm. "I've developed a fever," he says. Rollin tells him that it's probably just the flu or malaria, nothing to worry about.

Rollin draws Lukwiya's blood, then heads to the lab, where he changes into a respirator suit with a battery-powered filter unit. He centrifuges the blood and generates a master plate, then dispenses a measured amount of the sample into the dimpled well of the plate. Pausing often to wipe the sweat from his face with the inside of his cloth hood, he deposits and rinses the various agents—among them are mouse and rabbit antibodies, horseradish peroxidase, and skim milk—in a strict order. Finally, some five hours after he began, he positions the pipette tip over the sample well and adds the final reagent, the telltale chemical that will turn green if the sample contains Ebola. The mixture doesn't turn green.

"Tony, he's negative," Rollin says. There's no sign of Ebola.

That night, Lukwiya vomits and develops a headache. When Rollin draws blood the next morning, Lukwiya's eyes are a ghostly gray. This time, the reagent turns a weak green.

OK, Rollin thinks, there's a 50 percent chance that he'll make it. The viral count is still low. Maybe he'll develop a mild case.

But the next day, the test goes a solid green, and Lukwiya asks to be taken to the isolation ward. "If I die," he tells the hospital's administrator, Dr. Bruno Corrado, "I only pray that I am the last."

He requests that his wife, Margaret, be told just that he has a fever and that she should not come up from Kampala. She comes anyway, of course, not letting herself imagine where she will be led when she walks through the hospital's front gate. Then it's as if she had practiced walking toward the building covered in plastic, practiced suiting up, practiced being strong and cheerful as she enters the ward to see her husband, dying of Ebola.

"Look here, Margaret," Lukwiya says when he sees her. "It is dangerous in here. Don't even come in." Then: "If you must come in, please stay for just one minute."

Wearing protective clothing, Margaret sees him twice a day for the next two days, unable to embrace or even touch him. Once, she breaks down.

"If you cry," Lukwiya says, "you'll rub your face, which won't be safe. Cool down, Margaret—and stand firm. Keep praying."

Simon Mardel and a Lacor doctor, Yoti Zabulon, team up to treat him, experimenting with aggressive interventions. As Lukwiya's breathing becomes more and more labored, they decide to artificially ventilate him.

His pulse returns to near normal, and his fever comes down. A second round of chest X-rays looks better, and the hospital announces that his condition has begun to improve. But later that night, he hemorrhages into his airway, and the doctors realize that what is happening to their friend is beyond their power to arrest, or even influence.

"There's nothing more anyone can do," Mike Ryan says. "Except say good-bye."

On December 5, at 1:20 a.m., Matthew Lukwiya, who fought so hard to keep the statistics down, joins the numbers himself, the 156th recorded victim of the outbreak.

The next afternoon, he is buried—in a tightly sealed coffin, with pallbearers wearing head-to-toe protective gear—in the shade beneath a mango tree in the Lacor hospital courtyard.

"I don't think he would regret this," Margaret Lukwiya says

at the memorial service. "He knew the risk. He saw what was needed for his patients and he did it. That was him. Matthew was not for worldly desires."

Bruno Corrado says he sees Lukwiya's death as a symbol of defeat—a defeat made more painful by the hospital's initial success in containing the outbreak's first wave. "We all wanted Matthew to survive, not only because he was our colleague and friend but as living proof that this disease could be defeated," Corrado says. "We wanted to be able to declare that we fought against this thing together, and we won. But this is not the case. We did not defeat it."

Yet, by the time of Lukwiya's death, the epidemic was on the wane, largely due to his efforts during the first days of the outbreak. After a brief flareup, admissions slowed to just a handful each day, all of whom were now directed to Gulu Hospital. And although several workers temporarily left as a result of Lukwiya's death, the majority stayed on, inspired by his dedication. True to his hopes, Lukwiya was the last of the hospital staff to die.

On January 23, Uganda's last known Ebola patient was discharged, and the virus retreated back to nature, taking its secrets—including when it will come again—along with it. The international team scattered back to families and routines, in Geneva, Tokyo, Johannesburg.

In Atlanta, months later, Gulu already seems to Tony Sanchez like another life in another universe, a place that exists in flashes of memory and unaccountable longings—for that place where he dealt with things as they were, not as he wished they were; where he felt at once close to death and unimaginably alive. Sometimes, the place comes back in dreams, images piled one atop the other. In one, he is in the isolation ward, treating a terrified little girl not much older than his own daughter, whom he was afraid to touch for a few days after he returned. In the dream, sometimes, one girl becomes the other, and he's helpless—he can't soothe her with his touch, and he can't save her life.

But there are good memories, too. One night at the Acholi Inn, as bats swooped overhead, Mike Ryan held forth on one subject after another, a font of vinegar and piss. The waitress came out and scolded him for leaning back in his chair, and he apologized. Then he settled back squarely on the chair and requested another round of Nile Specials.

"Ah, the source of the Nile," he said when she returned. And he smiled mischievously and rocked back in the chair again, unthinkingly. And she smiled back, and said nothing.

A few minutes later, Simon Mardel and Cathy Roth said good night, and Ryan leaned back with his hands clasped behind his neck and let out a big sigh. "What a bloody ride this is," he said, looking up into the dark foliage overhead.

Like the woman and her exorcist, like the witch doctors in the villages and all the churchgoers in Gulu, like the doctors and nurses and virus hunters, Ryan imagined that there might be answers up there in the trees. But until someone manages to coax those answers out of the darkness, he and the others will be there to stanch the blood.

The truth is, you can't always slay the dragon. But sometimes, if you manage to keep your boot down on its neck long enough, you can quiet it.

The Case of the Red Leg
by Atul Gawande

Atul Gawande writes about medical issues for the New
Yorker. *His work undercuts the notion that doctors
know just what they are doing. This piece appeared in
Gawande's recent book,* Complications: A Surgeon's
Notes on an Imperfect Science.

Seeing patients with one of the surgery professors in his
clinic one afternoon, I was struck by how often he had to
answer his patients' questions, "I do not know." These
are four little words a doctor tends to be reluctant to
utter. We're supposed to have the answers. We want to have the
answers. But there was not a single person he did not have to
say those four little words to that day.

There was the patient who had come in two weeks after
an abdominal hernia repair: "What's this pain I feel next to
the wound?"

There was the patient one month after a gastric-bypass
operation: "Why haven't I lost weight yet?"

There was the patient with a large pancreatic cancer: "Can you get it out?"

And to all, the attending gave the same reply: "I do not know."

A doctor still must have a plan, though. So to the hernia patient, he said, "Come back in a week and let's see how the pain's doing." To the gastric-bypass patient, "It'll be all right," and asked her to come back in a month. To the cancer patient, "We can try to get it out"—and although another surgeon thought he shouldn't (given the tumor's appearance on a scan, an operation would be futile and risky, the colleague said), and he himself thought the odds of success were slim at best, he and the patient (who was only in her forties, with still-young children at home) decided to go ahead.

The core predicament of medicine—the thing that makes being a patient so wrenching, being a doctor so difficult, and being a part of a society that pays the bills they run up so vexing—is uncertainty. With all that we know nowadays about people and diseases and how to diagnose and treat them, it can be hard to see this, hard to grasp how deeply the uncertainty runs. As a doctor, you come to find, however, that the struggle in caring for people is more often with what you do not know than what you do. Medicine's ground state is uncertainty. And wisdom—for both patients and doctors—is defined by how one copes with it.

This is the story of one decision under uncertainty.

It was two o'clock on a Tuesday afternoon in June. I was in the middle of a seven-week stint as the senior surgical resident in the emergency room. I had just finished admitting someone with a gallbladder infection and was attempting to sneak out for a bite to eat when one of the emergency room physicians stopped me with yet another patient to see: a twenty-three-year-old, Eleanor Bratton, with a red and swollen leg. (The names of patients and colleagues have been changed.) "It's probably only a cellulitis"—a simple skin infection—"but it's a bad one," he said. He had started her on some intravenous antibiotics and admitted her to the medical service. But he wanted me to make sure there wasn't anything "surgical" going on—an abscess that needed draining or some such. "Would you mind taking a quick look?" Groan. No. Of course not.

She was in the observation unit, a separate, quieter ward within the ER where she could get antibiotics pumped into her arm and wait for admitting to find her a bed upstairs. The unit's nine beds are arrayed in a semicircle, each separated by a thin blue curtain, and I found her in Bed 1. She looked fit, athletic, and almost teenage, with blond hair tight in a pony-tail, nails painted gold, and her eyes fixed on a television. There did not seem anything seriously ill about her. She was lying comfortably, a sheet pulled up to her waist, the head of the bed raised. I glanced at her chart and saw that she had good vital signs, no fever, and no past medical problems. I walked up and introduced myself: "Hi, I'm Dr. Gawande. I'm the senior surgical resident down here. How are you doing?"

"You're from surgery?" she said, with a look that was part puzzlement and part alarm. I tried to reassure her. The emergency physician was "only being cautious," I said, and having me see her to make sure it was nothing more than a cellulitis. All I wanted to do was ask a few questions and look at her leg. Could she tell me what had been going on? For a moment she said nothing, still trying to compute what to think about all this. Then she let out a sigh and told me the story.

That weekend she had gone back home to Hartford, Con-necticut, to attend a wedding. (She had moved to Boston with some girlfriends the year before, after graduating from Ithaca College, and landed work planning conferences for a downtown law firm.) The wedding had been grand and she had kicked off her shoes and danced the whole night. The morning after, however, she woke up with her left foot feeling sore. She had a week-old blister on the top of her foot from some cruddy sandals she had worn, and now the skin surrounding the blister was red and puffy. She didn't think too much of this at first. When she showed her foot to her father, he said he thought it looked like a bee sting or maybe like she'd gotten stepped on dancing the night before. By late that afternoon, however, riding back to Boston with her boyfriend, "my foot really began killing me," she said. The redness spread, and during the night she got chills and sweats and a fever of one hundred and three degrees. She took ibuprofen every few hours, which got her temperature down but did nothing for the mounting pain. By morning, the redness reached halfway up her calf, and her foot had swelled to the point that she could barely fit it into a sneaker.

Eleanor hobbled in on her roommate's shoulder to see her internist that afternoon and was diagnosed with a cellulitis. Cellulitis is your garden-variety skin infection, the result of perfectly ordinary bacteria in the environment getting past the barrier of your skin (through a cut, a puncture wound, a blister, whatever) and proliferating within it. Your skin becomes red, hot, swollen, and painful; you feel sick; fevers are common; and the infection can spread along your skin readily—precisely the findings Eleanor had. The doctor got an X ray to make sure the bone underneath was not infected. Satisfied that it was not, she gave Eleanor a dose of intravenous antibiotics in the office, a tetanus shot, and a prescription for a week's worth of antibiotic pills. This was generally sufficient treatment for a cellulitis, but not always, the doctor warned. Using an indelible black marker, she traced the border of the redness on Eleanor's calf. If the redness should extend beyond this line, the doctor instructed, she should call. And, regardless, she should return the next day for the infection to be checked.

The next morning, Eleanor said—this morning—she woke up with the rash beyond the black line, a portion stretching to her thigh, and the pain worse than ever. She phoned the doctor, who told her to go to the emergency room. She'd need to be admitted to the hospital for a full course of intravenous antibiotic treatment, the doctor explained.

I asked Eleanor if she had had any pus or drainage from her leg. No. Any ulcers open up in her skin? No. A foul smell or blackening of her skin? No. Any more fevers? Not since two days ago. I let the data roll around in my head. Everything was going for a cellulitis. But something was pricking at me, making me alert.

I asked Eleanor if I could see the rash. She pulled back the sheet. The right leg looked fine. The left leg was red—a beefy, uniform, angry red—from her forefoot, across her ankle, up her calf, past the black ink line from the day before, to her knee, with a further tongue of crimson extending to the inside of her thigh. The border was sharp. The skin was hot and tender to the touch. The blister on the top of her foot was tiny. Around it the skin was slightly bruised. Her toes were uninvolved, and she wiggled them for me without difficulty. She had a harder time moving the foot itself—it was thick with edema up through the ankle. She had normal sensation and pulses throughout her leg. She had no ulcers or pus.

Objectively, the rash had the exact appearance of a cellulitis, something antibiotics would take care of. But another possibility lodged in my mind now, one that scared the hell out of me. It was not for logical reasons, though. And I knew this perfectly well.

• • •

Decisions in medicine are supposed to rest on concrete obser-
vations and hard evidence. But just a few weeks before, I had
taken care of a patient I could not erase from my mind. He was
a healthy fifty-eight-year-old man who had had three or four
days of increasing pain in the left side of his chest, under his
arm, where he had an abrasion from a fall. (For reasons of
confidentiality, some identifying details have been changed.)
He went to a community hospital near his home to get it
checked out. He was found to have a small and very ordinary
skin rash on his chest and was sent home with antibiotic pills
for cellulitis. That night the rash spread eight inches. The following morning he spiked a fever of one hundred and two
degrees. By the time he returned to the emergency room, the
skin involved had become numb and widely blistered. Shortly
after, he went into shock. He was transferred to my hospital
and we quickly took him to the OR.

He didn't have a cellulitis but instead an extremely rare and
horrendously lethal type of infection known as necrotizing
fasciitis (fa-shee-EYE-tiss). The tabloids have called it a disease
of "flesh-eating bacteria" and the term is not an exaggeration.
Opening the skin, we found a massive infection, far worse
than what appeared from the outside. All the muscles of the
left side of his chest, going around to his back, up to his
shoulder, and down to his abdomen, had turned gray and soft
and foul with invading bacteria and had to be removed. That
first day in the OR, we had had to take even the muscles
between his ribs, a procedure called a birdcage thoracotomy.
The next day we had to remove his arm. For a while, we actually thought we had saved him. His fevers went away and the
plastic surgeons reconstructed his chest and abdominal wall
with transfers of muscle and sheets of Gortex. One by one,

however, his kidneys, lungs, liver, and heart went into failure, and then he died. It was among the most awful cases I have ever been involved in.

What we know about necrotizing fasciitis is this: it is highly aggressive and rapidly invasive. It kills up to 70 percent of the people who get it. No known antibiotic will stop it. The most common bacterium involved is group A *Streptococcus* (and, in fact, the final cultures from our patient's tissue grew out precisely this). It is an organism that usually causes little more than a strep throat, but in certain strains it has evolved the ability to do far worse. No one knows where these strains come from. As with a cellulitis, they are understood to enter through breaks in the skin. The break can be as large as a surgical incision or as slight as an abrasion. (People have been documented to have gotten the disease from a rug burn, a bug bite, a friendly punch in the arm, a paper cut, a blood draw, a toothpick injury, and chicken pox lesions. In many the entry point is never found at all.) Unlike with a cellulitis, the bacteria invade not only skin but also deep underneath, advancing rapidly along the outer sheaths of muscle (the fascia) and consuming whatever soft tissue (fat, muscle, nerves, connective tissue) they find. Survival is possible only with early and radical excisional surgery, often requiring amputation. To succeed, however, it must be done early. By the time signs of deep invasion are obvious—such as shock, loss of sensation, widespread blistering of the skin—the person is usually unsalvageable.

Standing at Eleanor's bedside, bent over examining her leg, I felt a little foolish considering the diagnosis—it was a bit like thinking the ebola virus had walked into the ER. True, in the early stages, a necrotizing fasciitis can look just like a cellulitis, presenting with the same redness, swelling, fever, and high white blood cell count. But there is an old saying taught in medical school: if you hear hoofbeats in Texas, think horses not zebras. Only about a thousand cases of necrotizing fasciitis occur in the entire United States each year, mainly in the elderly and chronically ill—and well over *three million* cases of cellulitis. What's more, Eleanor's fever had gone away; she didn't look unusually ill; and I knew I was letting myself be swayed by a single, recent, anecdotal case. If there were a simple test to tell the two diagnoses apart, that would have been one thing. But there is none. The only way is to go to the operating room, open the skin, and look—not something you want to propose arbitrarily. Yet here I was. I couldn't help it. I was thinking it.

I pulled the sheets back over Eleanor's legs. "I'll be back in a minute," I said. I went to a phone well out of her earshot and paged Thaddeus Studdert, the general surgeon on call. He called back from the OR and I quickly outlined the facts of the case. I told him the rash was probably just a cellulitis. But then I told him there was still one other possibility that I couldn't get out of my head: a necrotizing fasciitis.

The line went silent for a beat.

"Are you serious?" he said.

"Yes," I said, trying not to hedge. I heard an epithet muttered. He'd be right up, he said.

As I hung up the phone, Eleanor's father, a brown-and-gray-haired man in his fifties, came around with a sandwich and soda for her. He had been with her all day, having driven up from Hartford, but when I was seeing her, it turned out, he had been gone getting her lunch. Catching sight of the food, I jumped to tell him not to let her eat or drink "just yet" and with that the cat began crawling out of the bag. It was not the best way to introduce myself. He was immediately taken aback, recognizing that an empty stomach is what we require for patients going to surgery. I tried to smooth matters over, saying that holding off was merely "routine procedure" until we had finished our evaluation. Nonetheless, Eleanor and her father looked on with new dread when Studdert arrived in his scrubs and operating hat to see her.

He had her tell her story again and then uncovered her leg to examine it. He didn't seem too impressed. Talking by ourselves, he told me that the rash looked to him only "like a bad cellulitis." But could he say for sure that it was not necrotizing fasciitis? He could not. It is a reality of medicine that choosing to *not* do something—to not order a test, to not give an antibiotic, to not take a patient to the operating room—is far harder than choosing to do it. Once a possibility has been put in your mind—especially one as horrible as necrotizing fasciitis—the possibility does not easily go away.

Studdert sat down on the edge of her bed. He told Eleanor and her dad that her story, symptoms, and exam all fit with cellulitis and that that was what she most likely had. But there was another, very rare possibility, and, in a quiet and gentle voice, he went on to explain the unquiet and ungentle effects of necrotizing fasciitis. He told them of the "flesh-eating bacteria," the troublingly high death rate, the resistance to treatment by antibiotics alone. "I think it is unlikely you have it," he told Eleanor. "I'd put the chances"—he was guessing here—"at well under five percent." But, he went on, "without a biopsy, we cannot rule it out." He paused for a moment to let her and her father absorb this. Then he started to explain what the procedure involved—how he would take an inch or so of skin plus underlying tissue from the top of her foot, and perhaps from higher up on her leg, and then have a pathologist immediately look at the samples under the microscope.

Eleanor went rigid. "This is crazy," she said. "This doesn't make any sense." She looked frantic, like someone drowning. "Why don't we just wait and see how the antibiotics go?" Studdert explained that this was a disease that you cannot sit on, that you had to catch it early to have any chance of treating it. Eleanor just shook her head and looked down at her covers.

Studdert and I both turned to her father to see what he might have to say. He had been silent to this point, standing beside her, his brow knitted, hands gripped behind him, tense, like a man trying to stay upright on a pitching boat. He asked about specifics—how long a biopsy would take (fifteen minutes), what the risks were (a deep wound infection was the biggest one, ironically), whether the scars go away (no), when it would be done if it were done (within the hour). More gingerly, he asked what would happen if the biopsy were positive for the disease. Studdert repeated that he thought the chances were less than 5 percent. But if she had it, he said, we'd have to "remove all the infected tissue." He hesitated before going on. "This can mean an amputation," he said. Eleanor began to cry. "I don't want to do this, Dad." Mr. Bratton swallowed hard, his gaze fixed somewhere miles beyond us.

In recent years, we in medicine have discovered how discouragingly often we turn out to do wrong by patients. For one thing, where the knowledge of what the right thing to do exists, we still too frequently fail to do it. Plain old mistakes of execution are not uncommon, and we have only begun to recognize the systemic frailties, technological faults, and human inadequacies that cause them, let alone how to reduce them. Furthermore, important knowledge has simply not made its way far enough into practice. Among patients recognized as having heart attacks, for example, it is now known that an aspirin alone will save lives and that even more can be saved with the immediate use of a thrombolytic—a clot-dissolving drug. A quarter of those who should get an aspirin do not, however; and half who should get a thrombolytic do not. Overall, physician compliance with various evidence-based guidelines ranges from over 80 percent of patients in some parts of the country to less than 20 percent in others. Much of medicine still lacks the basic organization and commitment to make sure we do what we know to do.

But spend almost any amount of time with doctors and patients, and you will find that the larger, starker, and more painful difficulty is the still abundant uncertainty that exists over what should be done in many situations. The gray zones in medicine are considerable, and every day we confront situations like Eleanor's—ones in which clear scientific evidence of what to do is missing and yet choices must be made. Exactly which patients with pneumonia, for example, should be hospitalized and which ones sent home? Which back pains treated by surgery and which by conservative measures alone? Which patients with a rash taken to surgery and which just observed on antibiotics? For many cases, the answers can be obvious. But for many others, we simply do not know. Expert panels asked to review actual medical decisions have found that in a quarter of hysterectomy cases, a third of operations to put tubes in children's ears, and a third of pacemaker insertions (to pick just three examples), the science did not exist to say whether the procedures would help those particular patients or not.

In the absence of algorithms and evidence about what to do, you learn in medicine to make decisions by feel. You count on experience and judgment. And it is hard not to be troubled by this.

A couple weeks before seeing Eleanor, I had seen an arthritic and rather elderly woman (she was born before Woodrow Wilson was president) who had come in complaining of a searing abdominal pain that radiated into her back. I learned that she had recently been found to have an aortic aneurysm in her abdomen and instantly my alarm bells went off. Examining her gingerly, I could feel the aneurysm, a throbbing and tender mass just deep to her abdominal muscles. She was stable, but it was on the verge of rupturing, I was convinced. The vascular surgeon I called in agreed. We told the woman that immediate surgery was the only option to save her. We warned her, however, that it was a big surgery, with a long recovery in intensive care and probably in a nursing home afterward (she still lived independently), a high risk that her kidneys would not make it, and a minimum 10 to 20 percent chance of death. She did not know what to do. We left her with her family to think on the decision, and then I returned fifteen minutes later. She said she would not go ahead with surgery. She just wanted to go home. She had lived a long life, she said. Her health had long been failing. She had drawn up her will and was already measuring her remaining days in coffee spoons. Her family was devastated, but she was steady-voiced and constant. I wrote out a pain medication prescription for her son to fill for her, and half an hour later she left, understanding full well that she would die. I kept her son's number and, when a couple weeks had passed, called him at home to hear how he had weathered the aftermath. His mother, however, answered the telephone herself. I stammered a hello and asked how she was doing. She was doing well, she said, thank you. A year later, I learned, she was still alive and living on her own.

Three decades of neuropsychology research have shown us numerous ways in which human judgment, like memory and hearing, is prone to systematic mistakes. The mind overestimates vivid dangers, falls into ruts, and manages multiple pieces of data poorly. It is swayed unduly by desire and emotion and even the time of day. It is affected by the order in which information is presented and how problems are framed. And if we doctors believed that, with all our training and experience, we escape such fallibilities, the notion was dashed when researchers put us under the microscope.

A variety of studies have shown physician judgment to have these same distortions. One, for example, from the Medical College of Virginia, found that doctors ordering blood cultures for patients with fever overestimated the probability of infection by four- to tenfold. Moreover, the highest overestimates came from the doctors who had recently seen *other* patients with a blood infection. Another, from the University of Wisconsin, found evidence of a Lake Wobegon effect ("Lake Wobegon: where the women are strong, the men are good-looking, and all the children are above average"): the vast majority of surgeons believed the mortality rate for their own patients to be lower than the average. A study from Ohio University and Case Western Reserve Medical School examined not just the accuracy but also the confidence of physicians' judgments—and found no connection between them. Doctors with high confidence in a judgment they made proved no more accurate than doctors with low confidence.

David Eddy, a physician and expert on clinical decision making, reviewed the evidence in an unflinching series of articles published over a decade ago in the *Journal of the American Medical Association*. And his conclusion was damning. "The plain fact is," he wrote, "that many decisions made by physicians appear to be arbitrary—highly variable, with no obvious explanation. The very disturbing implication is that this arbitrariness represents, for at least some patients, suboptimal or even harmful care."

But in the face of uncertainty, what other than judgment does a physician have—or a patient have, for that matter? Months after seeing Eleanor that spring afternoon, I spoke with her father about the events that had unfolded.

"It felt like it was five minutes from having a swollen foot to being told that she could possibly be losing her life," Mr. Bratton said.

A chef who had owned his own delicatessen for seventeen years and now taught at a culinary arts school in Hartford, he knew no one in Boston. He knew our hospital was affiliated with Harvard, but he knew enough to realize that this did not necessarily mean we were anything special. I was just the resident on duty that day; Studdert was likewise just the surgeon on call. Eleanor had left things to her father now, and he tried to take stock. Some clues were encouraging. Studdert's being in scrubs and an operating hat, having just come from the OR, seemed to suggest experience and know-how. Indeed, it turned out he had seen a number of patients with necrotizing fasciitis before. He was also self-assured, without being bullying, and took time to explain everything. But Bratton was shocked at how young he appeared. (Studdert was, in fact, just thirty-five.)

"This is my daughter we are talking about," Bratton remembered thinking at the time. "Isn't there anybody better than you?" Then he knew what to do. He turned to Studdert and me and spoke softly.

"I'd like another opinion," was what he said.

• • •

We agreed to the request, and it did not upset us. We were not oblivious to the conundrums here. Eleanor's fever had gone away; she didn't look unusually ill; and likely the biggest reason I had thought of flesh-eating bacteria was that terrible case I had seen a few weeks before. Studdert had put a numeric estimate on the chances of the disease—"well under five percent" he had said—but we both knew it was a stab in the dark (a measure of probability and confidence, but how good is that?) and a vague one at that (how *much* less than 5 percent?). Hearing what someone else might think seemed useful, we both thought.

But, for the Brattons, I had to wonder how useful it would be. If opinions disagreed, then what? And if they did not, wouldn't the same fallibilities and questions remain? Furthermore, the Brattons did not know anyone to call and had to ask if *we* had any ideas.

We suggested calling David Segal, a plastic surgeon on staff who like Studdert had seen such cases before. They agreed. I called Segal and filled him in. He came down within minutes. In the end what he gave Eleanor and her father was mainly confidence, from what I could see.

Segal is a rumpled and complexly haired man, with pen stains on his white coat and glasses that seem too large for his face. He is the only plastic surgeon I know who looks like he has a Ph.D. from M.I.T. (which, as it happens, he does). But he seemed, as Bratton later put it, "not young." And he did not disagree with what Studdert had said. He listened to Eleanor's story and looked carefully at her leg and then said that he too would be surprised if she turned out to have the bacteria. But he agreed that it could not be ruled out. So what else was there but to biopsy?

Eleanor and her dad now agreed to go ahead. "Let's get it

over with," she said. But then I brought her the surgical consent form to sign. On it, I had written not only that the procedure was a "biopsy of the left lower extremity" but also that the risks included a "possible need for amputation." She cried out when she saw the words. It took her several minutes alone with her father before she could sign. We had her in the operating room almost immediately after. A nurse brought her father to the family waiting area. He tracked her mother down by cell phone. Then he sat and bowed his head, and made some prayers for his child.

There is, in fact, another approach to decision making, one advocated by a small and struggling coterie in medicine. The strategy, long used in business and the military, is called decision analysis, and the principles are straightforward. On a piece of paper (or a computer), you lay out all your options, and all the possible outcomes of those options, in a decision tree. You make a numeric estimate of the probability of each outcome, using hard data when you have it and a rough prediction when you don't. You weigh each outcome according to its relative desirability (or "utility") to the patient. Then you multiply out the numbers for each option and choose the one with the highest calculated "expected utility." The goal is to use explicit, logical, statistical thinking instead of just your gut. The decision to recommend annual mammograms for all women over age fifty was made this way and so was the U.S. decision to bail out Mexico when its economy tanked. Why not, the advocates ask, individual patient decisions?

Recently, I tried "treeing out" (as the decision buffs put it) the choice Eleanor faced. The options were simple: to biopsy or not biopsy. The outcomes quickly got complicated, however. There was: not being biopsied and doing fine; not being biopsied, getting diagnosed late, going through surgery, and surviving anyway; not being biopsied and dying; being biopsied and getting only a scar; being biopsied and getting a scar plus bleeding from it; being biopsied, having the disease and an amputation, but dying anyway; and so on. When all the possibilities and consequences were penciled out, my decision tree looked more like a bush. Assigning the probabilities for each potential twist of fate seemed iffy. I found what data I could from the medical literature and then had to extrapolate a good deal. And determining the relative desirability of the outcomes seemed impossible, even after talking to Eleanor about them. Is dying a hundred times worse than doing fine, a thousand times worse, a million? Where does a scar with bleeding fit in? Nonetheless, these are the crucial considerations, the decision experts argue, and when we decide by instinct, they say, we are only papering this reality over.

Producing a formal analysis in any practical time frame proved to be out of the question, though. It took a couple of days—not the minutes that we had actually had—and a lot of back and forths with two decision experts. But it did provide an answer. According to the final decision tree, we should *not* have gone to the OR for a biopsy. The likelihood of my initial hunch being right was too low, and the likelihood that catching the disease early would make no difference anyway was too high. Biopsy could not be justified, the logic said.

I don't know what we would have made of this information at the time. We didn't have the decision tree, however. And we went to the OR.

The anesthesiologist put Eleanor to sleep. A nurse then painted her leg with antiseptic, from her toes up to her hip. With a small knife, Studdert cut out an inch-long ellipse of skin and tissue from the top of her foot, where the blister was, down to her tendon. The specimen was plopped into a jar of sterile saline and rushed to the pathologist to look at. We then took a second specimen—going deeper now, down into muscle—from the center of the redness in her calf, and this was sent on as well.

At first glance beneath her skin, there was nothing apparent to alarm us. The fat layer was yellow, as it is supposed to be, and the muscle was a healthy glistening red and bled appropriately. When we probed with the tip of a clamp inside the calf incision, however, it slid unnaturally easily along the muscle, as if bacteria had paved a path. This is not a definitive finding, but enough of one that Studdert let out a sudden, disbelieving, "Oh shit." He pulled off his gloves and gown to go see what the pathologist had found, and I followed right behind him, leaving Eleanor asleep in the OR to be watched over by another resident and the anesthesiologist.

An emergent pathology examination is called a frozen section, and the frozen section room was just a few doors down the hallway. The room was small, the size of a kitchen. In the middle of it stood a waist-high laboratory table with a black slate countertop and a canister of liquid nitrogen in which the pathologist had quick-frozen the tissue samples. Along a wall was the microtome that he had used to slice micron-thin sections of the tissue to put on glass slides. We walked in just as he finished preparing the slides. He took them to a microscope and began scanning each one methodically, initially under low power magnification and then under high power. We hovered, no doubt annoyingly, awaiting the diagnosis. Minutes passed in silence.

"I don't know," the pathologist muttered, still staring through the eyepieces. The features he saw were "consistent with necrotizing fasciitis," he said, but he wasn't sure he could clinch the diagnosis. He said he would have to call in a dermatopathologist, a pathologist who specializes in looking at skin and soft tissue. It took twenty minutes before the specialist arrived and another five before he could make his call, our frustration growing. "She's got it," he finally announced grimly. He had detected some tiny patches where the deep tissue had begun to die. No cellulitis could do that, he said.

Studdert went to see Eleanor's father. When he walked into the crowded family waiting area, Bratton caught the expression on his face and began yelling, "Don't look at me like that! *Don't look at me like that!*" Studdert took him to a private side room, closed the door behind them, and told him that she appeared to have the disease. He would have to move fast, he said. He was not sure he could save her leg and he was not sure if he could save her life. He would need to open her leg up, see how bad things were, and then go from there. Bratton was overcome, crying and struggling to get out words. Studdert's own eyes were wet. Bratton said to "do what you have to do." Studdert nodded and left. Bratton then called his wife. He told her the news and then gave her a moment to reply. "I will never forget what I heard on the other end of the line," he later said. "Something, some sound, I cannot and will never be able to describe."

Decisions compound themselves, in medicine like in anything else. No sooner have you taken one fork in the road than another and another come upon you. The critical question now was what to do. In the OR, Segal joined Studdert to offer another set of hands. Together they slit open Eleanor's leg, from the base of her toes, across her ankle, to just below her knee, to get a full view of what was going on inside. They pulled the opening wide with retractors.

The disease was grossly visible now. In her foot and most of her calf, the outer, fascial layer of her muscles was gray and dead. A brownish dishwater fluid was seeping out with a faint smell of decay. (Tissue samples and bacterial cultures would later confirm that this was toxic group A *Streptococcus* advancing rapidly up her leg.)

"I thought about a BKA," a below-knee amputation, Studdert says, "even an AKA," an above-knee amputation. No one would have faulted him for doing either. But he found himself balking. "She was such a young girl," he explains. "It may seem harsh to say, but if it was a sixty-year-old man I would've taken the leg without question." This was partly, I think, a purely emotional unwillingness to cut off the limb of a pretty twenty-three-year-old—the kind of sentimentalism that can get you in trouble. But it was also partly instinct again, an instinct that her youth and fundamentally good health might allow him to get by with just removing the most infested tissue (a "debridement") and washing out her foot and leg. Was this a good risk to take, with one of the deadliest bacteria known to man loose in her leg? Who knows? But take it he did.

For two hours, using scissors and electrocautery, he and Segal cut and stripped off the necrotic outer layers of her muscle, starting from the webbing of her toes, going up to the tendons of her calf. They took out tissue going three-quarters of the way around. Her skin hung from her leg like open coat flaps. Higher up, inside the thigh, they reached fascia that looked pink-white and fresh, very much alive. They poured two liters of sterile saline through the leg, trying to wash out as much of the bacteria as possible.

At the end, Eleanor seemed to be holding steady. Her blood

pressure remained normal. Her temperature was ninety-nine degrees. Her oxygen levels were fine. And the worst-looking tissue had been removed from her leg.

But her heart rate was running a bit too fast, one hundred and twenty beats a minute, a sign that the bacteria had provoked a systemic reaction. She was requiring large amounts of intravenous fluid. Her foot looked dead. And her skin was still burning red with infection.

Studdert stood firm with his decision not to take more, but you could see he was uneasy about it. He and Segal conferred and thought of one other thing they could try, an experimental therapy called hyperbaric oxygen. It involved putting Eleanor in one of those pressure chambers they put divers in when they get the bends—a perhaps kooky-sounding notion but not a ludicrous one. Immune cells require oxygen to kill bacteria effectively and putting a person under double or higher atmospheric pressure for a few hours a day increases the oxygen concentration in tissue tremendously. Segal had been impressed by results he had gotten using the therapy in a couple of burn patients with deep wound infections. True, studies had not proven that it would work against necrotizing fasciitis. But suppose it could? Everyone latched onto the treatment immediately. At least it made us feel as if we were doing something about all the infection we were leaving behind.

We did not have a chamber at our hospital, but a hospital across town did. Someone got on the phone and within a few minutes we had a plan for ambulancing Eleanor over with one of our nurses for two hours under 2.5 atmospheres of pressurized oxygen. We left her wound open to drain, laid wet gauze inside it to keep the tissues from desiccating, and wrapped her leg in white bandages. Before sending her over, we wheeled her from the OR to intensive care, where we could make sure she would be stable enough for the trip.

It was eight o'clock at night now. Eleanor woke up nauseated and in pain. But she was sharp-witted enough to surmise from the crowd of nurses and doctors around her that something was wrong.

"Oh God, my leg."

She reached down to find it, and for a few panicked moments she wasn't sure she could. Slowly, she convinced herself that she could see it, touch it, feel it, move it. Studdert put his hand on her arm. He explained what he had found, what he had done, and what more there would be to do. She took the information with more grit and fight than I knew she had. Her whole family had now arrived to be with her, and looked as though an SUV had hit them. But Eleanor pulled the sheet back over her leg, took in the monitors flashing their green and orange lights and the IV lines running into her arms, and said, simply, "OK."

The hyperbaric chamber that night was, as she describes it, "like a glass coffin." She lay inside it on a narrow mattress with nowhere to put her arms except straight down or folded across her chest, a panel of thick plexiglass a foot from her face, and an overhead hatch sealed tight with turns of a heavy wheel. As the pressure increased, her ears kept popping, as if she were diving down into a deep ocean. Once the pressure reached a certain point, she would be stuck, the doctors had cautioned. Even if she should start throwing up, they could not get to her, for the pressure could only be released slowly or it would give her the bends and kill her. "One person had a seizure inside," she remembered them telling her. "It took them twenty minutes to get to him." Lying there enclosed, more ill than she'd ever imagined one could be, she felt far away and almost totally alone. It's just me and the bacteria in here, she thought to herself.

The next morning, we took her back to the operating room, to see if the bacteria had spread. They had. The skin over most of her foot and front of her calf was gangrenous and black and had to be cut off. The edges of fascia we had left behind were dead and had to be excised as well. But her muscle was still viable, including in her foot. And the bacteria had not killed anything up in her thigh. She had no further fevers. Her heart rate had normalized. We repacked her wound with wet gauze and sent her back for more hyperbaric oxygen—two hours twice a day.

We ended up operating on her leg four times in four days. At each operation, we had to take a little more tissue, but each time it was less and less. At the third operation, we found the redness of her skin had finally begun to recede. At the fourth operation, the redness was gone and we could see the pink mossy beginnings of new tissue in the maw of her wound. Only then was Studdert confident that not only had Eleanor survived, but her foot and leg had, too.

It is because intuition sometimes succeeds that we don't know what to do with it. Such successes are not quite the result of logical thinking. But they are not the result of mere luck, either.

Gary Klein, a cognitive psychologist who has spent his career observing people who deal routinely with uncertainty, tells the story of a fire commander he once studied. The lieutenant and his team had pulled up to fight an ordinary-seeming fire in a one-story home. He led the hose crew in through the front and encountered the fire in the back kitchen area. They tried dousing it with water. But the flames came right back at them. They tried spraying the fire again but, once more, found little effect. The team retreated a couple of steps to plan another line of attack. Then suddenly, to the bafflement of his men, the lieutenant ordered them out of the building immediately. Something—he didn't know what—didn't feel right. And as soon as they exited, the floor they'd been standing on collapsed. The seat of the fire turned out to be in the basement, not the back. Had they stayed just a few seconds longer, they would have plunged into the fire themselves.

Human beings have an ability to simply recognize the right thing to do sometimes. Judgment, Klein points out, is rarely a calculated weighing of all options, which we are not good at anyway, but instead an unconscious form of pattern recognition. Reviewing the events afterward, the commander told Klein that he had not thought once about the different possibilities in that house. He still had no idea what made him get his crew out of there. The fire had been difficult, but not to a degree that had ever made him flee before. The only explanations seemed either luck or ESP. But questioning him closely about the details of the scene, Klein identified two clues the lieutenant had taken in without even realizing it at the time. The living room had been *warm*—warmer than he was used to for a contained fire in the back of a house. And the fire was *quiet*, when what he had expected was the fire to be loud and noisy. The lieutenant's mind appeared to have recognized in these and perhaps other clues a dangerous pattern, one that told him to give the all-out order. And, in fact, thinking very hard about the situation could well have undermined the advantage of his intuition.

It is still not apparent to me what the clues were that I was registering when I first saw Eleanor's leg. Likewise, it is not obvious what the signs were that we could get by without an amputation. Yet as arbitrary as our intuitions seem, there must have been some underlying sense to them. What there is no sense to is how anyone could have known that, how anyone can reliably tell when a doctor's intuitions are heading down the right track or spinning wildly off.

For close to thirty years, Dartmouth physician Jack Wennberg has studied decision making in medicine, not up close, the way Gary Klein has, but from about as high up as you can get, looking at American doctors as a whole. And what he has found is a stubborn, overwhelming, and embarrassing degree of inconsistency in what we do. His research has shown, for example, that the likelihood of a doctor sending you for a gallbladder-removal operation varies 270 percent depending on what city you live in; for a hip replacement, 450 percent; for care in an intensive care unit during the last six months of your life, 880 percent. A patient in Santa Barbara, California, is five times more likely to be recommended back surgery for a back pain than one in the Bronx, New York. This is, in the main, uncertainty at work, with the varying experience, habits, and intuitions of individual doctors leading to massively different care for people.

How can this be justified? The people who pay for the care certainly do not see how. (That is why insurers bug doctors so constantly to explain our decisions.) Nor might the people who receive it. Eleanor Bratton, without question, would have been treated completely differently depending on where she went, who she saw, or even just when she saw me (before or after that previous necrotizing fasciitis case I'd seen; at 2 a.m. or 2 p.m.; on a quiet or a busy shift). She'd have gotten merely antibiotics at one place, an amputation at another, a debridement at a third. This result seems unconscionable.

People have proposed two strategies for change. One is to shrink the amount of uncertainty in medicine—with research, not on new drugs or operations (which already attracts massive amounts of funding) but on the small but critical everyday decisions that patients and doctors make (which gets shockingly little funding). Everyone understands, though, that a great deal of uncertainty about what to do for people will always remain. (Human disease and lives are too complicated for reality to be otherwise.) So it has also been argued, not unreasonably, that doctors must agree in advance on what should be done in the uncertain situations that arise—spell out our actions ahead of time to take the guesswork out and get some advantage of group decision.

This last goes almost nowhere, though. For it runs counter to everything we doctors believe about ourselves as individuals, about our personal ability to reason out with patients what the best course of action for them is. In all the confusion of different approaches that different doctors take to a given problem, somebody must get it right. And each of us—used to making decisions under uncertainty every day—remains convinced that that somebody is me. For however many times our judgment may fail us, we each have our Eleanor Bratton, our great improbable save.

It was a year before I saw Eleanor again. Passing through Hartford, I called in on her at her family's home, a roomy, spic-and-span, putty-colored colonial with a galumphy dog and beds of flowers outside. Eleanor had moved back home to recover following her twelve days in the hospital, intending to stay only temporarily but instead finding herself nestling in. Returning to a normal life, she said, was taking some getting used to.

Her leg had taken time to heal, not surprisingly. In her final operation, done during her last days in the hospital, we had needed to use a sixty-four-square-inch skin graft, taken from her thigh, to close the wound. "My little burn," she called the result, rolling up the leg of her sweatpants to show me.

It wasn't anything you'd call pretty, but the wound looked remarkably good to my eye. In final form, it was about as broad as my hand and ran from beneath her knee to her toes. Inevitably, the skin color was slightly off, and the wound edges were heaped up. The graft also made her foot and ankle seem wide and bulky. But the wound had no open areas, as there sometimes can be. And the grafted skin was soft and pliant, not at all tight or hard or contracted. Her thigh where the graft had been taken was a bright, cherry red, but still fading gradually.

Recovering the full use of her leg had been a struggle for her. At first, coming home, she found she could not stand, her muscles were so weak and sore. Her leg would collapse right under her. Then, when she'd built the strength back, she found she still could not walk. Nerve damage had given her a severe foot drop. She saw Dr. Studdert and he cautioned her that this was something she might always have. With several months of intense physical therapy, however, she trained herself to walk heel-toe again. By the time of my visit, she was actually jogging. She'd also started back working, taking a job as an assistant at one of the big insurance company headquarters in Hartford.

A year on, Eleanor remained haunted by what happened to her. She still had no idea where the bacteria came from. Perhaps the foot soak and pedicure she had gotten at a small hair-and-nail shop the day before that wedding. Perhaps the grass, outside the wedding reception hall, that she'd danced barefoot through with a conga line. Perhaps somewhere in her own house. Any time she got a cut or a fever, she was stricken with mortal fear. She would not go swimming.

She would not immerse herself in a bath. She would not even let the water in the shower cover her feet. Her family was planning a vacation to Florida soon, but the idea of traveling so far from her doctors frightened her.

The odds—the seeming randomness—were what disturbed her most. "First, they say the odds of you getting this are nothing—one in two hundred fifty thousand," she said. "But then I got it. Then they say the odds of my beating it are very low. And I beat those odds." Now, when she asked us doctors if she could get the flesh-eating bacteria *again*, we told her, once more, the odds are improbably low, one in two hundred fifty thousand, just like before.

"I have trouble when I hear something like that. That means nothing to me," she said. She was sitting on her living room sofa as we talked, her hands folded in her lap, the sun rippling through a bay window behind her. "I don't trust that I won't get it again. I don't trust that I won't get anything else that's strange or we've never heard of, or that anyone we know isn't going to get such a thing."

The possibilities and probabilities are all we have to work with in medicine, though. What we are drawn to in this imperfect science, what we in fact covet in our way, is the alterable moment—the fragile but crystalline opportunity for one's know-how, ability, or just gut instinct to change the course of another's life for the better. In the actual situations that present themselves, however—a despondent woman arrives to see you about a newly diagnosed cancer, a victim bleeding from a terrible injury is brought pale and short of breath from the scene, a fellow physician asks for your opinion about a twenty-three-year-old with a red leg—we can never be sure whether we have such a moment or not. Even less clear is whether the actions we choose will prove either wise or helpful. That our efforts succeed at all is still sometimes a shock to me. But they do. Not always, but often enough.

My conversation with Eleanor wandered for a while. We talked about the friends she'd gotten to see now that she was back in Hartford and her boyfriend, who was something called a "fiber-optic electrician" (though what he actually wanted to do, she said, was "high voltage"), about a movie she had recently gone to, and about how much less squeamish she's discovered herself to be after going through her whole ordeal.

"I feel a lot stronger in some ways," she said. "I feel like there is some kind of purpose, like there has to be some sort of reason that I'm still here.

"I think I am also happier as a person"—able to see things in perspective a bit more. "Sometimes," she went on, "I even feel safer. I came through all right, after all."

That May she did go to Florida. It was windless and hot, and one day, off the eastern coast above Pompano, she put one bare foot in the water and then the other. Finally, against all her fears, Eleanor jumped in and went swimming in the ocean.

The water was beautiful, she says.

from Yellow Fever, Black Goddess
by Christopher Wills

Christopher Wills' 1996 book includes a discussion of the Black Plague, which has killed perhaps 200 million human beings.

Between March and July of the year in question . . . it is reliably thought that over a hundred thousand human lives were extinguished within the walls of the city of Florence[.] Yet before this lethal cata-strophe fell upon the city, it is doubtful whether anyone would have guessed it contained so many inhabitants.

Giovanni Boccaccio, *The Decameron*
(tr. G. H. McWilliam)

In the summer of 1986, a Canadian government helicopter was carrying out a routine aerial survey that included some flights over remote Banks Island. This island, covered with low tundra vegetation, lies in the Northwest Territories, far above the Arctic Circle. In previous years, dead and dying muskoxen had often been spotted by aerial surveys. But now, as the helicopter flew over the peaceful landscape, the pilot suddenly saw the bodies of almost sixty wild muskoxen, scattered over several square miles. Had they been wantonly shot by airborne hunters? Veterinarians who were helicoptered to the site found that the truth was even more unnerving. All were discovered to have died, within the space of a few days, from acute respiratory infections.

During that summer, 122 sick and dead animals were found over an area of 1000 square kilometres. Muskoxen, which were driven to local extinction on the island a century ago by overhunting, have rebounded to a population size of 25,000, a size that has remained fairly stable. Before these dead and dying animals were examined, it had been assumed that shortage of food was now limiting the size of this recovered population.

Microscopic investigation of various tissues showed that their deaths were caused by the bacillus *Yersinia pseudotuberculosis*. This organism is a relative of the far more infamous bacterium *Y. pestis* which is responsible for human bubonic plague. The animals were riddled with infection, which had been as devastating to this herd of muskoxen as the great plagues of Europe have been to our own species. And this was not an isolated incident. Occasional fatal outbreaks of *Yersinia* have been recorded among different species of animals in many parts of North America, Europe and Asia, and it seems certain that innumerable similar incidents have gone unrecorded.

Most of us probably assume that such plagues are visited on

the human species alone. Of course this is not true. Plagues are an important part of the natural world, though most of them are easy to ignore because they have no direct effect on us. Each kind of plague can be seen as an evolutionary detective story, complete with a vast assortment of clues. In a classic detective story the criminal has some weakness or failing that can eventually lead to his or her downfall. The same is true of the organisms that cause plagues, and the trick is to find it, though sometimes the clues are buried very deeply.

No trail of clues is more devious or fascinating than the one that has led to our current understanding of bubonic plague. This horrendous disease has, by one estimate, been responsible for as many as 200 million human deaths during our recorded history. To comprehend the plague in all its aspects, and to probe for any weaknesses that it might have, we must tell four stories. The first shows how it has affected our own species, the second recounts its effect on other species of animals, the third is the tale of the plague bacillus itself, and the fourth is an account of the precarious interaction of the bacillus with fleas, showing the desperate lengths to which the bacillus must go to perpetuate itself. By the end of this chapter and its four stories you will be able to make connections between the events that happened to our own species in previous centuries (and are still happening to us today in places as different as New Mexico, Tanzania and India) and the disease that struck down those innocent muskoxen on the tundra a few years ago.

The Human Tale

In the year 542, the Byzantine Empire was in its usual state of upheaval, pursuing war on many fronts. General Belisarius, the head of its armies, was fighting an indecisive war in Persia.

The campaign was something of a distraction for him, sand-wiched between two much more successful campaigns against the fierce armies that occupied the remains of the Western Roman Empire. He was labouring to accomplish the simple but sweeping goal of his master, the Emperor Justinian, which was nothing less than to re-establish the Roman Empire in all its glory.

Suddenly, in the midst of Belisarius' attempt to execute Justinian's grand design, a disaster overtook Byzantium. A plague of huge proportions swept out of Egypt, carved its way through the eastern Mediterranean, and went on to devastate the rest of the known world.

The historian Procopius was an eyewitness to the effects of the pestilence when it arrived in Constantinople. Groping for an explanation, he could only attribute it to God, for 'it embraced the entire world, and blighted the lives of all men, though differing from each other in the most marked degree, respecting neither sex nor age.' He thought that the plague could not have been transmitted by anything other than the capricious will of the Deity, for he observed that many nurses and physicians were unaffected even though they were working in the midst of those who had been felled.

Procopius described the symptoms of the pestilence vividly, so we can be pretty certain that it was in fact bubonic plague. He recounted the panic that the plague caused among super-stitious people—many of the victims, he reported, claimed that they had been visited by demons even before the disease's onset. This might have been due to the general hysteria of the time, or simply have been hallucinations brought on by the fever as it developed. But there were no mystical trappings to Procopius' account of the course of the disease itself, which is clinically accurate—the great swellings called buboes that appeared in the groin and the armpits as the lymph nodes became engorged, the delirium and frantic restlessness suffered by some victims and the comatose state of others. He observed, accurately, that if the buboes broke open there was a chance the victims would recover, though they were sometimes crippled. Otherwise death almost certainly ensued within a few days.

The plague raged in the city for three months, and so numerous were the corpses that many of them were simply cast into the hollow towers of some uncompleted fortifications in nearby Galata, across the Golden Horn. Procopius calculated that as many as 300,000 inhabitants died, which may be an exaggeration since the total population of the city has been estimated by modern historians to be smaller than that. But, as Boccaccio later observed during the time of the Black Death, it was easier to count corpses than it was to count the living poor who infested the ancient alleyways of crowded medieval cities. Procopius' estimate may have been right. Whatever the exact numbers, there is no doubt that, as with other outbreaks of bubonic plague, the mortality was very high. Yet in spite of the disaster, Justinian (who according to Procopius was himself briefly ill with the plague but recovered) immediately took advantage of the devastation in nearby regions to invade Armenia. So powerful were the military machines of Byzantium and the states that surrounded it that warfare continued unabated both during and after the ravages of the plague.

Yet this and previous pestilences had helped to change the balance of history. All of Europe was affected by the Plague of Justinian—five years after it first appeared in Constantinople, the disease had swept west three thousand kilometres to Ireland. While other, less well-documented epidemics had preceded this pandemic during the decline of the Roman Empire, they might have been anthrax or typhus rather than plague. There have been many speculations that Justinian's Plague was the event that precipitated the final collapse of the tattered remnants of the Western Roman Empire and the advent of the Dark Ages.

Without this disaster, history might have gone in quite a different direction. Before the plague struck, Belisarius and others of Justinian's generals had won a series of victories, both in North Africa and Italy to the west and in the countries of the Levant. The growing Byzantine Empire had been strong, healthy and well-populated—perhaps, just perhaps, if the plague had not taken place Justinian might indeed have re-established the elusive glory of Rome.

The plague continued to be an important factor in frustrating the plans of Justinian and his successors, for not only did it sweep through his realm in the three years following 542, but it recurred at intervals, sometimes no more than three or four years apart, for decades thereafter. Its malign effects extended well into the seventh century. And the longer the intervals between subsequent epidemics, the greater the mortality among young people, since many unexposed children were born in the lulls between the outbreaks.

These repeated epidemics knocked the population down faster than it could recover. The historian Josiah Russell has estimated that the proportional impact on the population of Europe may have been even greater than it was during the later Black Death. The population of western Europe may have been reduced by as much as fifty per cent by the year 600.

The periodicity of the outbreaks, which was also seen in the Black Death some eight hundred years later, is now suspected to mirror the rise and fall of populations of rats and other rodents in the affected areas. As rats increased in number, the plague bacillus would begin to spread among them, so that both the rats and the people who lived in close association with them would be decimated. If the rat population fell dramatically, it might be a decade or more before it could recover, but when it did the plague would reappear. If the rats were not as severely affected, their population could rebound in three or four years. All this had, it might be supposed, relatively little to do with the humans involved, who seem merely to have been hapless victims caught on the perimeter of this rodent-bacillus population cycle. But is that really true?

We must begin by asking where Justinian's Plague came from, and why it appeared when it did. There is general agreement, among observers at the time as well as present-day historians, that the much later Black Death of the fourteenth century originated in central Asia. We can never be sure, but there is also a growing feeling among historians that the earlier plague of Justinian's time had its origin elsewhere. Procopius claimed that it originated in Egypt. Arab physicians of the time, who had themselves been confronted with some of the repeated outbreaks of plague that soon followed its first appearance in 542, thought that the disease had originated further south, in the uncharted regions of Abyssinia. Indeed, fragmentary historical accounts suggest that the plague has been endemic for many centuries in that remote country, where it was called *jaghalah*. An early Arabic medical compendium, published in the year 850, placed the origin further to the west, in the Sudan, where the Nile would have provided an easy route for the disease to spread into Egypt.

None of these early accounts implicates Asia. Indeed, there is even some evidence that plague was rare or unknown in central Asia at the time. After the death of Procopius, the

Byzantine historian Theophylact Simocattes continued his mentor's task of recording the history of the Eastern Empire. Simocattes told of Turkish potentates from central Asia, visiting the Byzantine court soon after Justinian's time, who boasted that the plague and other contagious diseases were quite unknown in their part of the world.

So, an African rather than an Asian origin of the Plague of Justinian is a very real possibility. At the present time there are known to be foci of plague among the rodents of eastern Africa, and outbreaks of the disease have been traced unmistakably to that area since the sixteenth century. Possibly the plague that lurks there now could have been a recent introduction to Africa, from other known foci in Asia perhaps, at some time subsequent to the sixth century. But this seems unlikely, for so many different rodents native to East Africa are currently involved, and the situation is so complicated, that it seems certain that the plague bacillus and its many rodent hosts have had a long and complex evolutionary history in Africa.

The records of such a distant time are never unequivocal, however. Asia cannot be ruled out as a source of Justinian's Plague. Large populations of rodents have swarmed in central Asia since long before humans first moved into the region a million or more years ago. Some of these rodents came in close contact with humans, and were hunted for food and even for their skins. Marco Polo, relaying tales of the region of Tartary that lay to the north of China, says: ' . . . there are various small beasts of the marten or weasel kind, and those which bear the name of Pharaoh's mice. The swarms of the latter are incredible, but the Tartars employ such ingenious devices for catching them, that none can escape their hands.' The term 'Pharaoh's mice' had originally been applied to the mongooses of Egypt, so it is a little unclear which rodents

Marco Polo meant, but the little animals he had seen in such numbers were probably tarbagans or Manchurian marmots, about the size of a squirrel. They have been shown by Russian microbiologists to harbour the plague bacillus, and yet Marco Polo does not mention disease among the Tartars.

Just as in Africa, the rodent population of the steppes of central Asia is a diverse one, and there's an astounding number of different rodents living there that carry many different strains of the plague bacillus and of allied bacterial strains. In central Asia, as in Africa, plague has had a long and complex evolutionary history. The disease certainly goes back to a time long before there were any humans in the region.

In spite of the prevalence of plague among the wild rodents, we have only fragmentary evidence for early outbreaks of bubonic plague affecting the human populations of Asia. Chinese historians kept careful records, starting in 244 BC, of plagues and pestilences that devastated the country repeatedly. The numbers of such events are astonishing—from AD 37 to 1718 there were 234 recorded outbreaks. Chroniclers recorded one every three years on the average during the sixteenth and seventeenth centuries, when records were probably quite complete. They noted the provinces affected, and gave some account of the numbers of people who perished, but unfortunately they almost never made note of the plagues' symptoms—many of them could have been, and probably were, typhoid, smallpox or something else. Two accounts, however, do mention 'malignant buboes' and other symptoms that sound suspiciously like plague, one dating from AD 610 and the other from AD 642. If the plague was really that old in China, then it might by whatever devious route have been the source of Justinian's Plague. As we saw earlier, equally equivocal references to plague in India can be traced back, through the chronicle of the *Bhagvata Purana,* to as long ago as 1500 BC, suggesting that plague may be much older than the earliest Chinese records.

Whatever its origins, one thing seems plain. When we disturb its various ancient haunts, the plague bacillus comes forth. Human disturbances of this status quo in the ancient world were, like those of modern times, primarily due to trade and the movement of peoples. In the days of Justinian there was little contact with Asia, but Arab traders were beginning to penetrate Abyssinia and the even more remote regions further south in search of gold, slaves and ivory. They may have found more than they bargained for.

Yet in the centuries that followed Justinian's Plague, bubonic plague essentially vanished from the West. Many other dreadful diseases afflicted the inhabitants of Europe as they shuffled blindly through the very nadir of the Dark Ages. But bubonic plague died out in spite of what would appear to be ideal conditions for its persistence. Did this have something to do with the fact that the plague had so dramatically reduced the European population?

It is almost certainly not coincidental that eight centuries later, when bubonic plague re-emerged in what would later be known as the Black Death, this new scourge happened just when the population was beginning to increase and the outside world was again starting to impinge on the isolated European peninsula. Traders were venturing in substantial numbers along the Silk Road that stretched across Turkestan and central Asia to the empire of the Great Khan. They were lured not only by silk but by spices, and by the astounding tales of wonders brought back by Marco Polo. Like a monster in a horror film that seems to lie around every corner, the plague waited for them there as well.

Oddly, it appears that it was refugees from the Byzantine Empire who may have been the first to fall victim to this second great plague pandemic. In the fifth century, shortly before the Plague of Justinian, there had been a considerable religious upheaval (one of many) in Byzantium. The followers of Nestorius, bishop of Constantinople, were driven from the main body of the Orthodox Church because of their refusal to acknowledge Mary as the mother of God. Fiercely persecuted, they established settlements in the remotest parts of Asia, and some of them eventually came under the protection of Kublai Khan. As a result of this forced diaspora, communities of Nestorian Christians have persisted on the remote edges of the known world for centuries.

In the year 1338, an outbreak of a devastating disease killed many members of one of these communities, which was located on the shores of Lake Issyk-Kul not far from what is now the Kazakh-Chinese border. These deaths were quite unremarked at the time, and their cause was only discovered early in this century by the Russian archaeologist Daniel Abramovich Chwolson, who translated some headstones and found that the victims had probably died of bubonic plague.

This event has usually been cited as the beginning of the second great plague pandemic, which later became known as the Black Death. It may or may not have been, of course. The plague may have originated further to the east in China—or perhaps even in Africa. The trail of evidence is tenuous to say the least, and has grown cold in the intervening 650 years. Whatever its origin, and whatever the trigger may have been for its new spread, the plague found fertile ground.

At the beginning of the twelfth century, throughout Europe and the Mediterranean, populations had begun to grow after the dreadful stasis of the Dark Ages. During the 'little

Renaissance' of that century political stability grew, new crops were introduced, and a middle class made its first tentative appearance. Agriculture began to improve—not much, but enough to make a difference. One of the reasons Europe had remained mired in the Dark Ages for so long was the pitiful yield of crops—on average, one seed had to be planted for every three obtained, which might seem to make agriculture an almost pointless exercise. Such dismal harvests actually persisted in Russia well into the nineteenth century, and helped foment the political discontent that eventually led to revolution. But elsewhere in Europe things began to get better as windmills, water wheels, horseshoes, the horse collar, and the mouldboard plough came into widespread use during and after the twelfth century. These inventions permitted land that had been allowed to revert to forest or marsh during the Dark Ages to be cleared and drained again.

Trade employing money rather than barter became widespread for the first time since the fall of the Roman Empire, and with this new prosperity towns began to grow. Both the towns and the countryside became surprisingly densely populated—Leopold Genicot writing in the Cambridge Economic History has estimated that many parts of rural France had populations that would not be surpassed until the beginning of the twentieth century. German towns, too, grew until the middle of the fourteenth century, achieving sizes that would not be seen again until the nineteenth.

However, so tenuous was this gradual emergence from the long intellectual night, so dependent was it on everything going well, that there were soon setbacks. The climate began to change for the worse in the late thirteenth century, and the cold winters and rainy summers wreaked havoc with crops throughout Europe. In spite of technological improvements, agriculture could not keep up with the growing population. In the early fourteenth century, devastating famines occurred every few years right up to the time of the Black Death.

The result, as always, was the spread of poverty and misery. Most of the towns became overcrowded and filthy. War also played a role in societal breakdown. The Hundred Years War, which broke out in 1337 over the English King Edward III's efforts to claim the kingdom of France, quickly degenerated into an endless series of raids and looting parties. English knights ravaged the French countryside and carried what they could back to England, founding rich dynasties there with their booty while at the same time sowing centuries of hatred between the two countries. All in all, as the historian Barbara Tuchman has vividly pointed out, the fourteenth century was not a good time to be alive.

Things very quickly got much worse. Plague swept through the land of the Uzbeks in central Asia in late 1346. Although the apocalyptic hyperbole that was so beloved of medieval chroniclers makes it difficult to be certain, this may have formed part of an outbreak of the disease that devastated India and China a year or two earlier. As with other natural disasters of the time, tales about the plague were quickly embroidered. Earthquakes, rains of fire and other phenomena were said to have accompanied the onset of disease, but of course the plague itself was bad enough. It soon spread west towards the Black Sea.

In 1346, a small Italian trading colony in the Crimean port of Kaffa was besieged by a Muslim army. When the disease appeared among the besiegers, they catapulted the bodies of its victims over the walls into the city. It is unclear whether this early attempt at germ warfare worked, but either because of this or for other reasons plague soon appeared among the defenders. Remarkably, they were still able to escape from the siege. Some of them, fleeing in ships with their remaining treasures, spread the plague to Constantinople and then to Messina in Sicily. By late 1347, the plague was breaking out everywhere along the Mediterranean coast. We associate the year 1348 with the Black Death because that was the year it spread through Italy, France and England, but in fact the mortality in the Middle East in the preceding two years was at least as devastating.

The plague engendered extreme behaviour. Whole families of victims were nailed up inside their houses and left to starve. Bands of flagellants, endlessly inflicting tortures on themselves, roamed the countryside. These bands started as religious mendicants, but quickly degenerated into a rabble of looters. In many parts of Europe, Jews were accused of bringing on plague by poisoning the water supply, and these baseless rumours started vicious pogroms more terrible than any that were to be seen in Europe before the rise of Hitler. Tens of thousands of Jews were burned to death in cities and towns throughout Spain, Germany, Switzerland and France. These pogroms were sometimes initiated by the flagellants. Although Pope Clement VI and the emperor Charles IV, along with the medical faculties of the universities of Paris and Montpellier, all announced that the Jews were innocent of wrongdoing, their weak protests had no effect because they were not backed by any concrete action. Only King Casimir of Poland managed to prevent pogroms in his country, perhaps because of the entreaties of his Jewish mistress.

Fifty-six thousand people were said to have died of the plague in Marseilles, and many other towns suffered similarly. Almost everywhere, the first wave of plague killed between twenty per cent and fifty per cent of the people in the communities that it swept through. The mortality was worst in the coastal towns, and indeed some of those that were inland managed to evade its greatest impact. A few city governments instituted sensible regulations. Milan, in particular, vested its board of public health with broad powers and enforced strict sanitation laws. But Milan was an exception.

The plague changed the face of Europe in many ways, both physically and intellectually. In 1348 the city of Siena was about to triple the size of its cathedral, intending that its grandeur would exceed that of St Peter's in Rome. This immense project was stillborn when Siena's population was decimated by the plague. Petrarch's Laura perished, as did many members of the intellectual and artistic élite. And while there was no great upsurge of disbelief in the efficacy of organized religion, like that which would be sparked by the earthquake in Lisbon in 1755, the obvious helplessness of the Church in the face of this apparent act of God began to raise questions that would help to sow the seeds of the Reformation a century and a half later.

The plague spread by both sea and land with amazing rapidity, just as it had 800 years earlier in the time of Justinian. One odd feature, which has puzzled historians of disease ever since, is that it struck down people in remote farms and tiny villages as readily as it did those in the big cities. Even monasteries, those most isolated of communities, were not immune. All the members of an Austin Friars monastery near Avignon and of a Franciscan monastery near Marseilles succumbed.

The Animals' Tale

> In 1665 no one was left alive—
> In 1666 London was burned to sticks.
>
> Children's rhyme

How could even these isolated communities have been affected so severely? We now know, though medieval scholars and doctors did not, that rats and their fleas, and even on occasion the fleas of humans, are important vectors of the plague, but that it can sometimes spread more directly. Certainly rats must have had a role in the spread of the disease by ship. But it is unclear how much of a role they played in its spread across the land.

Of the two major species of rat associated with humans, the black rat, *Rattus rattus,* is by far the more dangerous. Because it originated in the tropics, when it migrates to the temperate zones it naturally gravitates to warm houses and barns. In addition to plague, it carries typhus, rabies and trichinosis. The brown rat, *Rattus norvegicus,* which despite its name originated in the temperate zone of Asia, rarely carries plague and does not live in close association with humans.

We tend to think of rats as coming to live with our remote ancestors when they were still inhabiting caves. Indeed, a few remains of black rats, dated to 17,000 years ago, have been found in a cave in Bavaria, and the excavators of Egyptian tombs have occasionally discovered the dried bodies of black rats that were accidentally sealed inside. Because black rats are tropical animals, they can only survive in numbers in Europe in the houses, granaries and barns built by humans. These provide them with a precarious niche that protects them from the full force of winter. As such structures were crude and sparse during the Dark Ages, black rats were not particularly common.

At the present time, humans provide rats with an abundance of food and shelter. Brown rats, better adapted to a temperate climate, have largely displaced black rats in the cities of the north. Twentieth-century civilization has proved ideal for rats. There is a growing tendency for the inhabitants of New York and other large cities to eat food in the subways and other public areas. This, coupled with the widespread use of plastic garbage bags instead of metal bins with lids, has given rats greater opportunities than ever. While tales of rats reaching the size of cats are probably exaggerations, the largest brown rat on record weighed 1.6 kilograms and was over half a metre long. Tellingly, urban brown rats tend to be much larger than those from rural areas, suggesting that they have actually been selected for increased size in places where there is plenty of food. The largest rats will be the most successful at competing for mates, and in a food-rich environment they will suffer no disadvantage. Undoubtedly, if there was a rat population explosion in medieval times following the Dark Ages, it must also have been driven by the growing amounts of food as agriculture improved.

Dead and dying black rats are often seen at the beginning of plague outbreaks, as they were in 1994 in the Beed district in India. In both India and China, folk wisdom made a connection between rat plague and human plague long before the discovery of the actual bacillus—when the rats started dying, it was time to flee.

But could black rats, even if they exploded locally into large populations, have accounted for the firestorm of infections during Justinian's Plague and the Black Death? To some authorities this has seemed very doubtful, to the point indeed that it has actually been suggested that neither of these pandemics was bubonic plague at all, but something else like outbreaks of anthrax.

We do not need to go so far—the coincidence of symptoms is too great for either plague to have been anything but bubonic plague. None the less, the question of why the disease spread so rapidly, even in the cold and thinly settled regions of northern Europe with their sparse populations of black rats far from their native tropics, continues to nag at historians and epidemiologists.

Rats and fleas are chancy vectors. When the first cases of plague appear, the human victims have almost certainly acquired the bacteria from rat fleas. The disease, which takes a few days to develop, constitutes the classic bubonic plague with its swellings due to infected lymph nodes. But the plague can spread like wildfire if the bacteria reach the lungs, for there they multiply furiously. Victims cough and spit blood, spewing bacteria into the air with every breath. Anyone near them will breathe in enormous concentrations of bacilli, setting up their own lung infections in turn. So rapid is the progression of this pneumonic form of the disease—untreated victims die in three days, while victims of the bubonic form take five days to die— that the buboes or lymph node swellings that are normally characteristic of the plague have no chance to form. But the plague bacillus does not survive for long outside the body, which means that for even pneumonic plague to spread people must be crowded together. Then why did plague spread so effectively in the countryside as well?

Boccaccio tells an odd tale of his experience of the plague in Florence. He watched two pigs rooting in the discarded rags of a plague victim, and saw them —within minutes—writhe, collapse and die. Later writers have assumed that this event had nothing to do with the plague, but his tale may have been too hastily dismissed. We have had no recent experience with a real plague outbreak—the last substantial ones took place in China and India during the first quarter of this century, and while they were disastrous they were not quite as catastrophic as the medieval plagues. We have no idea of what the dynamics of a truly fulminating epidemic might be. During such a plague the bacterial count might reach astronomical proportions in places where people and animals are closely confined. In view of the fact that plague and plague-like bacilli can infect a variety of animals, not just rodents, it may be that a temporary infection of large domestic animals could add fuel to the plague wildfire.

We do not know, after a lapse of centuries, what combination of susceptibilities of humans, rodents, farm animals, and their various fleas might have resulted in the plague that spread with terrible swiftness, not just through the cities and towns, but through the countryside. We do know that a surprising range of animals are susceptible to plague, including dogs and cats (though dogs do not die). When cats are fed infected mice, many of them develop fully-fledged symptoms of plague, complete with buboes.

Animals other than rats may be involved in more recent outbreaks as well. In August 1994, the small 'ratfall' seen by the inhabitants of Manila, the small village near Beed in Maharashtra state, took place about three weeks before the first human plague victims appeared. Ken Gage, a member of the World Health Organization team that visited the area soon after the outbreak, told me that some cats in the village had died as well—a good indicator that the outbreak was probably plague. The cats had been buried when the WHO team arrived, but they were able to examine several dogs from the villages and found that they had been exposed to the plague bacillus at some point in the past. Unfortunately, of course, we do not know how many of the millions of dogs wandering India's streets and alleys have been similarly exposed.

Our difficulty in imagining the conditions of a fully-fledged plague is complicated by the fact that the plague itself has changed over time. When the descriptions of Pro-copius, Boccaccio and other eyewitnesses of the earlier plagues are contrasted with the almost casual description of the London plague of 1665 by Samuel Pepys, we are struck by the fact that Pepys seems almost to have been talking about a different disease. The Great Plague of London fol-lowed a series of outbreaks of the disease in that city that had occurred intermittently over the previous century, most recently in 1647. At the Great Plague's peak, at the end of August 1665, the Bills of Mortality show that as many as 10,000 of the inhabitants of London had died in a single week. The royal court, and anyone else who could, fled the city. Pepys himself eventually left reluctantly and lived for some weeks near Greenwich. Yet he returned to London as soon as he was able. Even though his own doctor had died of the plague along with many of Pepys's other acquaintances, his own family had been untouched and he was able to carry on his life as if little had happened—celebrating a great naval victory against the Dutch, conducting business in the Royal Exchange and elsewhere, being naughty with an assortment of ladies, and generally behaving with the smug delight in his own accomplishments and growing wealth that we expect of Pepys:

> Thus I ended this month [July 1665] with the greatest joy that ever I did any in my life, because I have spent the greatest part of it with abundance of joy and honour, and pleasant Journys and brave entertainments, and without cost of money.

After a long spell of hot dry weather broke with heavy rain on 9 September, Pepys note an immediate decline in the number of plague cases, though he did not connect the probable cleansing effects of the rains, with this decline.

In part because of his detachment, Pepys's is one of the very best accounts we have of the plague in London—Daniel Defoe, who was a child at the time, wrote his fictional account *A Journal of the Plague Year* almost sixty years later, and included many incidents that were probably highly embroidered. Pepys does give a few glimpses of the kinds of behaviour people were driven to *in extremis*—recounting for example how people ill with the plague would lean out of their windows and vengefully breathe in the faces of healthy passers-by.

The London plague, dreadful as it was, did not have the full dimensions of horror of the medieval plague three centuries earlier. For Pepys, society continued almost undisturbed. For him and his contemporaries, the toll of the plague was rather like the toll of automobile accidents in society today—regrettable but largely unavoidable.

During the sixteenth and seventeenth centuries, outbreaks of plague in Europe were largely confined to the towns. Repeated waves of plague started every decade or two in London and spread out to the smaller towns over the succeeding two or three years. Sometimes isolated villages, like Eyam in Derbyshire, were devastated as well, but in general simply fleeing into the countryside to avoid the disease, something that had not worked in earlier centuries, began to make a great deal of sense. Isaac Newton did exactly this to avoid the Great Plague of London. And, while the evidence is fragmentary, it seems likely that the mortality due to the plague itself was diminishing, with the outbreaks less severe in the seventeenth than the sixteenth century.

There is another intriguing but fragmentary bit of evidence

that the conditions of the disease were changing. The historian Paul Slack and others have observed that the correlation between plague outbreaks and famine, so striking in earlier centuries, had begun to fade by the sixteenth and seventeenth centuries. By that time, the earlier abject and crushing poverty of much of the countryside had been replaced, if not by prosperity, at least by a less desperate way of life. But this does not explain how the earlier waves of the disease spread even to relatively prosperous isolated communities such as monasteries. One is driven to suppose that the way the disease spread might have changed—in a few short centuries, the agent of plague may have evolved. Or, alternatively, the way people lived had changed so much since the fourteenth century that the plague could not spread as easily. Or, very likely, both. My own guess—and it is only a guess—is that the intimate forced association of poverty-stricken farmers with their animals, so widespread during the Dark Ages and medieval times, was beginning to become less common. Perhaps this reduced the number of available paths of infection between animals and humans. If so, then the options open to the plague bacilli had begun to narrow long before the seventeenth century.

Shortly before the Great Plague of 1665, London's Bills of Mortality recorded three outbreaks of plague, in 1630, 1636 and 1647. The most severe, in 1636, killed 10,400. And plague was always present even between outbreaks—only three out of the 22 years for which the Bills survive had no reported cases of plague. Deaths from the plague peaked dramatically in 1665, with 69,596 plague deaths recorded. The numbers dropped precipitously in 1666, to only 1998. This was, of course, the year of the Great Fire, which razed the teeming warrens of the ancient city, burning 'from Pudding Lane to Pie Corner'. Then, astonishingly, the plague quickly vanished.

Cases dropped to 35 in 1667, to 14 in 1668, then trickled along sporadically with a few cases each year until 1679, when the last two were recorded. Few other cases have appeared in the city in the succeeding centuries, and all seem to have been introduced by foreign visitors.

Is it too much to suppose that before the Great Fire there was some kind of focus of the plague, perhaps lurking in the sewage-filled alleys and tottering houses of Pudding Lane or nearby Thames Street with its rotting wharves? If there was such a focus, then it was somehow activated every decade or two, spreading its effects out to the rest of the towns of England. The nature of the focus can only be speculated about. Perhaps it was a particularly crowded population of rats and their fleas. If so, then they must have been swarming in a small piece of the medieval world that had lasted beyond its time, somehow surviving down to the London of the Restoration. And it was obviously a piece of that world that the people of London could do without. The Great Fire, widely regarded as a disaster, seems instead to have been a much-needed prophylaxis, burning out a canker in the heart of the city. And once that canker disappeared, the cycle of the plague bacillus was broken as well.

Yet if the Great Fire had burned out the only source of the plague, one would expect that the disease would have disappeared immediately. There must have been other sources that gave rise to the few cases that followed the Great Fire, and that were removed as the city gradually left behind the filth and squalor of medieval times.

The plague faded away in the rest of Europe at about the same time, though not all at once and not correlated with so obvious an event as London's Great Fire. The last major outbreak in Italy, involving regions to the north and south of

Rome as well as the city itself, took place in 1656. In France, there was a severe outbreak in the town of Amiens in 1667–8, but oddly none took place in the much more crowded city of Paris. The final French flare-up occurred in Marseilles in 1720, killing 50,000 of its inhabitants, though this was probably an introduction from abroad. Plague had repeatedly devastated the entire Iberian peninsula during the sixteenth and seventeenth centuries, with the most massive outbreak taking place between 1647 and 1652. It contributed greatly to the political upheavals of the time. A less severe outbreak, and the last in the region, took place between 1676 and 1685. And finally there was a severe epidemic in Hungary between 1739 and 1742, the last major one in Europe.

Something was happening during this time throughout Europe, even in its most backward regions, something that broke the cycle of the plague with surprising ease. Why was the plague's grip so tenuous that it could be defeated by almost imperceptible changes in the ways that people lived?

The Bacillus' Tale

Discovery of the agent of plague had to await the remarkable advances of nineteenth-century biological science. Bacteria are tiny rods, spheres and spirals, usually almost colourless, far smaller than the cells of their hosts. Their virtual invisibility even under magnification explains why they remained unnoticed for so long in spite of intense scrutiny of both healthy and diseased tissues by many microscopists of the seventeenth and eighteenth centuries. Their discovery had to await improvements in microscope optics and the invention of specific stains that could be used to colour the bacteria. Once they were found, the next important advance was the realization that these micro-organisms could be grown separately from their hosts in pure culture and reinoculated into new animals. If the same disease resulted from such reinoculation and the organism could be isolated from these animals in turn, then, as the microbiologist Robert Koch pointed out, the likelihood was strong that the causative agent had been found.

The plague bacillus was discovered in the course of the great epidemic that swept through southern China in 1894. Two scientists claimed to have found it, and for a long time there was great confusion about which of them was right. Much of the confusion stemmed from the fact that the microbiological community was split at the end of the nineteenth century into two intensely nationalistic factions, the followers of the Frenchman Louis Pasteur and those of the German Robert Koch.

Alexandre Yersin, a young Swiss medical student who had trained at the Institut Pasteur, was a partisan of the French school. When he began his hunt for the plague bacterium during the last decade of the nineteenth century, he already had impeccable credentials for the search, though he did not realize how impeccable they were. In the late 1880s, working at Pasteur's Institute in Paris, he had succeeded in isolating a bacterium from guinea pigs and rabbits which were suffering from a kind of animal tuberculosis. He showed, using the reasoning that had been pioneered by Koch, that inoculation of healthy animals with this bacillus would give them the disease. The bacillus is now known as *Yersinia pseudotuberculosis,* in Yersin's honour, and it is the same one that killed those muskoxen in the remote northern reaches of Canada. Yersin could not have known that it is an extremely close relative— unnervingly close—of the bacillus that causes bubonic plague.

Although a brilliant career in medicine beckoned, Yersin was then seized by wanderlust. Abandoning his family and friends, he set off for Southeast Asia and a completely different kind of career. He arrived in the part of Indochina that is now Vietnam, and immediately embarked on a series of mapping explorations of the unknown mountain ranges of the interior. It turned out that he was as good a mapmaker as he was a bacteriologist. With Pasteur's help, Yersin obtained some support for his cartographic work from French geographical societies. But he could not avoid getting involved again with disease, for everywhere he went he found cases of the plague. The closer he got to the Chinese border, the commoner the disease became. He wanted to trace it to its source, which he suspected to be adjacent to the northern parts of the province of Tonkin, in the Chinese province of Yunnan, but the colonial governor refused him permission—presumably for fear of what he would find. The governor's reply to his entreaties was: 'There has never been any plague in Yunnan, and if there were I would deny it.'

It soon became obvious that there was indeed plague in Yunnan, however. In 1894 a huge outbreak occurred in the city of Canton, killing perhaps 100,000 people. And the plague soon spread to nearby Hong Kong, where it could no longer be ignored. Yersin pleaded to be sent there, and eventually gained permission, but he was given no official backing.

Plentiful official backing had, however, been provided to Shibasaburo Kitasato, the representative of the Koch school who arrived in Hong Kong at the same time. While he was with Koch in Germany, Kitasato had done important work on vaccines for tetanus and diphtheria. He was also the co-discoverer of antibodies, the proteins that make up a central part of the immune system. He arrived in the city with a large retinue of assistants and mountains of equipment. Welcomed at Hong Kong's hospitals, he swiftly cultured a bacterium from the finger of an autopsied plague victim, then announced that he had found the bacillus of plague.

Yersin was denied access to the hospitals, and indeed during the few times that he and Kitasato met their relationship could be charitably described as one of strained politeness. To obtain material he was forced to bribe the English sailors who were in charge of burying some of the victims. They let him into a cellar where the bodies were kept for a few hours before burial, resting in rough coffins on a bed of lime.

Yersin took a more careful approach than Kitasato's. He cultured his candidate bacillus from the inflamed lymph nodes of the victims, the buboes themselves, which he found to be filled with bacteria that looked like tiny fat ovals. He quickly found that the bacilli were gram-negative—that is, when they were stained with a concoction of crystal violet called Gram stain and then killed, most of the stain could easily be washed out from the dead cells.

Kitasato's bacillus, rounder and fatter, was a coccus, and when he stained it with crystal violet it retained the stain. It was gram-positive.

Robert Koch had clearly set down four rules for determining the causative agent of a disease—his famous postulates. It must be found in the victim, preferably at the site of the disease itself—Yersin's bacillus fit this criterion more closely than Kitasato's, although both strains had certainly come from plague victims. It must be culturable to form a pure strain. Then, when it is inoculated into a healthy host, the new host must come down with the disease. Finally, the presumptive causative agent must then be culturable from the new host. These last two steps were of course impossible to carry out in humans, but Yersin was able to inject his bacillus into rats. It quickly killed them, and he then isolated the same bacillus in large numbers from the dead rats, Kitasato was never able to close this circle of proof using his coccus.

Returning to France, Yersin inoculated his bacillus into horses to produce an antiserum. During another outbreak of the plague in Hong Kong in 1896, he returned and cured several victims with it—the first successful cures for the plague in the history of the world.

After decades of controversy, it is now universally agreed that Yersin and not Kitasato was the discoverer of the plague bacillus. Yersin originally called it *Pasteurella pestis* in honor of his mentor, but it has since been found to be much more closely related to his earlier bacillus that caused tuberculosis in animals than it is to other bacteria of the *Pasteurella* group. It has been renamed *Yersinia pestis.*

Yersin spent most of the rest of his life in Indochina, training doctors from among the local people and defending them against the stupidities of the colonial administration. He also helped to found the rubber industry in the area, and imported cinchona trees for the production of the quinine that was the only specific treatment at the time for malaria. By his death in 1943 he had become a much-admired figure. But during his work in Hong Kong he had missed an important step in understanding how the plague was spread, for he knew nothing about the role of rats or their fleas. This gap was filled in by the physician Masanori Ogata, working in Formosa, and independently by the medical missionary Paul Louis Simond in Bombay. Both observed that rats often came down with symptoms very much like those of human plague, complete with swollen lymph nodes that looked like the characteristic buboes of humans. Further, they found that human victims of the plague had often been bitten by fleas. Both tried some simple experiments to see whether rat fleas might be involved in the disease's spread. They ground up fleas and injected them into healthy rats, and found that the rats quickly developed the unmistakable symptoms of plague. Simond went a step further and discovered that massive plugs of plague bacilli were blocking the guts of the infected fleas. The work of these pioneers was dismissed for some years, until it was finally confirmed in 1905 during a subsequent outbreak of plague in India.

With this discovery, it seemed that the emerging science of microbiology had added another shining prize to its string of triumphs. The causative agent for plague had certainly been found. A successful serum against it had been produced, and the missing link in the spread of the disease, the rat flea, had also been discovered. But the complexity of the story had hardly begun to be explored. The bacteria themselves were still an enigma.

Much of what distinguishes dangerous from benign bacteria revolves around how they invade cells. There is an eerie elegance in the way that plague bacteria and the various kinds of cells that make up the tissues of their hosts interact with each other, each always exploiting the other's weakness.

Yersinia pestis is one of ten species that have been distinguished in the genus *Yersinia,* all closely related. The actual number of species is a bit of a guess—it is much harder to tell various species of bacteria apart than it is to distinguish species of groups such as birds or insects. This is because species of bacteria have far fewer obvious properties that can define them, and often these properties are simple ones like the ability to grow on a certain sugar, to make a particular amino acid, or to elicit a specific antibody in their hosts. Two species of bacteria need not be as distinct as two species of hummingbird, and sometimes bacteriologists discover to their surprise that only a few mutational changes or gene-borrowings are enough to turn one species into something almost identical to another.

Three of the *Yersinia* are pathogenic in animals: *Y. pseudotuberculosis,* the bacterium that Yersin had found back in France, another species called *Y. enterocolitica,* and of course the plague bacillus *Y. pestis.* The first two are ubiquitous in the environment, far commoner than *Y. pestis.* They are often found in wild and domesticated animals. They are also, unlike *Y. pestis,* motile—they can swim about in an aqueous medium using long thin flagella. Just like their more remote relative *Salmonella,* they can enter our digestive tracts through contaminated food. Once there they quickly invade the cells lining the inner walls of the intestines. Sometimes they have little effect, but sometimes, just as with *Salmonella,* severe cases of *Yersinia* infection can cause vomiting and diarrhoea. Occasionally, rampant infection can result in tissue destruction and even death. And if the lungs are infected, the destruction can be very like that caused by tuberculosis. Occasionally, as we saw with the muskoxen, there are outbreaks of *Yersinia* infections that are just as deadly to their animal hosts as plague is to humans.

Ralph Isberg and Stanley Falkow of Stanford University were the first to discover exactly how *Y. pseudotuberculosis* enters the cells of its host. The bacterium manufactures a protein called invasin, molecules of which migrate to its surface in large numbers. Invasin forms a strong attachment to other specific molecules, known as integrins, that have accumulated by a similar process on the surfaces of the host's gut cells. (Integrins are involved in various functions in the host cell, and the bacterial invasin has evolved the ability to cling to these highly visible proteins.) Once a bacterium covered with invasin molecules attaches to a cell of its host, the cell membrane breaks down at the point of attachment and the bacterium can slip inside. But it must do so quickly, before the patrolling white blood cells called macrophages or phagocytes of the host's immune system arrive at the site of the bacterial invasion.

These prowling phagocytes are also covered with a variety of protein molecules that are specialized for different functions. Some of these proteins are the same integrins that the bacteria can attach to. The result is that if the phagocytes arrive quickly enough on the scene, they too readily bind to the bacteria and ingest them—but the crucial difference is that the phagocytes can destroy the bacteria once they have engulfed them, while the gut cells cannot.

In order to survive in its host, *Y. pseudotuberculosis* must therefore be very good at entering gut cells, so good that an appreciable number can hide there before the phagocytes can find them. Usually this hide-and-seek process has few consequences for the host. Once they are safely hidden, the bacteria have a good chance of spreading to other members of the host species, because the cells that they infect are continually being shed from the gut lining. The cells pass out in the faeces, and the bacteria they contain become part of the teeming bacterial population of the soil. There they are able to persist long enough to be picked up by another host animal.

They can increase their chances of being passed on, of course, if they multiply to high numbers in the host, but here is where the game can turn deadly. Strains of *Yersinia* that multiply in the gut in large numbers can cause lesions in the gut lining, which spew out more bacteria and their accompanying toxins. The host animal may vomit and suffer severe diarrhoea. All this upheaval means that far more bacteria can escape into the environment, but at a cost. There is a high probability that this violent reaction will kill the host, since a sick animal is unlikely to survive for long in the wild. In effect, the bacteria have given their host a mild kind of plague, briefly increasing their own chances of survival but only at the host's expense.

Strains of bacteria that take this more risky route are arising all the time. This can happen by mutation, or they may pick up an odd bit of DNA from a kind of dilute brew of DNA molecules that is always present in the host's gut or in the soil. These DNA molecules often come from other, completely different, species of bacteria. They may have escaped from various bacterial cells that have died and broken open, or they may be packaged inside viruses called bacteriophages that are specialized to live on bacteria. *Yersinia* and other bacteria can then pick them up, as if they were sale items in a bargain basement.

If these little bits of DNA confer sufficient virulence, bacteria that acquire them may be aided in their ability to infect the host animal and multiply. But these mutant bacteria are unlikely to survive unless there are many host animals nearby, enabling them to spread even if their immediate host dies as a result of their activities. If this condition is met the result can be an animal plague or *epizootic* (as distinct from a human epidemic). Most such epizootic plagues pass unnoticed because the animals that are affected tend to be small and their demise is hidden from our view. But sometimes, if the animals happen to be large like those muskoxen that died on the Canadian tundra, the effects can be dramatic.

No Boccaccio, Defoe or Pepys has recorded the billions of sad little deaths that have taken place as a result of these animal plagues. The end product of this long grim history, however, has been the evolution of strains of *Yersinia* that are capable of producing a great range of types of infection, all the way from mild and almost unnoticeable invasions of a few gut cells to the explosive and fully-fledged manifestations of the Black Death.

For many years this great variety of responses and abilities tended to cause confusion among microbiologists who worked with *Yersinia*. Strains isolated from nature were often virulent in laboratory animals, but after they were cultured for a few generations their virulence would be lost. It was not until new ways of examining their DNA became available that it was discovered that their virulence resided chiefly in two small 'extra' chromosomes called plasmids.

A bacterium normally has one large chromosome, in the form of a long double-helical strand of DNA that is joined at its ends to form an immense circle. Often, however, it may carry smaller circles of DNA that are not necessary for its survival but which may contain genes not found on the main chromosome. If a cell carrying such a plasmid happens to break open and release its DNA, then the plasmid can actually be picked up by another species of bacterium—the bargain basement effect. The most virulent strains of *Yersinia*, including *Y. pestis*, carry these plasmids, which provide them with extra capabilities. But often, particularly when the bacteria are cultured in the laboratory, the plasmids are lost, and so is the virulence.

The plague that affects humans is so severe, so overwhelming in its symptoms, that one is tempted to suppose that *Y. pestis* must somehow have acquired even more virulence factors than its less fatal brethren. Actually, the opposite is the case. It turns out that the cause of human plague is a crippled bacterium that has had many of its options for escape to a new host closed to it. But, like a wounded animal backed into a corner, *Y. pestis* can still strike back using all its remaining powers.

The tally of these missing capabilities of *Yersinia pestis* became longer and longer the more it was studied. To begin with, as we saw earlier, it has lost the ability to swim about, and must drift passively. In addition, it has lost so many biochemical pathways as a result of mutation that it is unable to survive for long outside the body of its animal host. This means that if *Y. pestis* is carried in faeces from the animal to the soil, it will soon die. One of its most startling defects is a missing step in an absolutely essential part of cellular metabolism known as the Krebs Cycle. This cycle of biochemical reactions is a source of building blocks that are needed to make amino acids and compounds essential for respiration. It is so important that its discovery won the chemist Hans Krebs the Nobel Prize. The *Y. pestis* bacteria that lack part of this cycle are unable to survive for long unless they can obtain the missing compounds from their host. The host might be a human, a rat or a flea, but a host is essential. This is an important reason why these bacteria cannot survive in the soil.

The existence of many of these defects had been known for years. Then, in 1987, Daniel Sikkema and Robert Brubaker of Michigan State University reported the discovery of an even more startling defect, one that has large implications for virulence. They found that, unlike its free-living relatives, *Y. pestis* actually lacks the ability to invade cultures of human cells grown in the laboratory. The defect is connected to a difficulty in taking up iron-containing compounds that it needs to survive. The weakened bacillus must survive by drifting about and obtaining its nourishment from the circulatory fluids.

This inability to hide in the cells of their host should leave the bacteria helpless against attacks from the host's patrolling phagocytes. And if phagocytes are able to catch and eat these poor helpless mutant bacteria, then surely this ought to make them less virulent, not more. Instead, these crippled bacteria actually turn out to be far more virulent than their relatives that are still able to hide in the cells of their hosts.

This discovery spawned a flurry of research. What were the really important genetic differences between *Y. pestis* and its less virulent relatives? Some of the differences were tracked down by scientists working at the University of Umeå in Sweden, 500 kilometres north of Stockholm on the shores of the frigid Gulf of Bothnia. In that remote place, Hans Wolf-Watz and his colleagues have been experimenting for years with both *Y. pseudotuberculosis* and *Y. pestis,* trying to pin down just what distinguishes them.

At the outset, they found that *Y. pestis* did not even make the invasin protein of Isberg and Falkow, which seemed to be one obvious reason why it could not invade host cells. So they next asked what would happen if they destroyed the invasin gene in *Y. pseudotuberculosis.* Their idea was to try to turn it into a kind of imitation *Y. pestis.* It was straightforward for them, using modern molecular biological methods, to destroy this specific gene on the bacterial chromosome, leaving all the rest of the genes intact. They found that *Y. pseudotuberculosis* that had been crippled in this way could no longer invade cultured human cells, so that now it acted more like *Y. pestis.* Other properties had changed too, for the altered bacteria had suddenly become more virulent—it took far fewer of the crippled *Y. pseudotuberculosis* to kill mice. While their modified *Y. pseudotuberadosis* was nowhere near as virulent as *Y. pestis,* they had retraced in the laboratory at least part of the evolutionary path that separated the two bacterial species. And this had been done by destroying a gene rather than by introducing some new virulence factor.

They then went a step further and destroyed another gene

that they suspected from previous work might have an invasin-like function. This gene was found not on the main chromosome but on one of the plasmids. When this second gene was destroyed, the virulence of the crippled bacteria increased ten thousandfold when they were injected beneath the skin of mice, and a thousandfold when they were given orally. These doubly crippled bacteria were now behaving much more like their fierce relatives, Y. pestis.

Wolf-Watz was able to find and clone the equivalent gene in Y. pestis, which was also harboured in a plasmid. He found that this gene, too, had been damaged so that it could no longer work. Y. pestis, then, just like their laboratory strain of Y. pseudotuberculosis, was doubly crippled. The remarkable thing, of course, was that the defective Y. pestis strains had been isolated not from the laboratory but from the real world. The crippling defects of Y. pestis had arisen in nature, at some unknown point in the past.

Wolf-Watz and his colleagues had been able to imitate this double genetic blow by deliberate genetic manipulation of its close relative Y. pseudotuberculosis. They had been able to retrace part of the evolutionary pathway that separated Y. pseudotuberculosis from Y. pestis, a pathway that had already been followed long before in the natural world.

Thus, it appears that some of the genetic differences that separate Y. pestis from Y. pseudotuberculosis are rather simple. It is easy to make a mutation in a gene that will destroy its function, and such mutations are likely to arise very commonly in the natural world as well as in the laboratory. Because of this, Wolf-Watz suggested that there is a real possibility that Y. pestis might have arisen more than once, perhaps from Y. pseudotuberculosis or from some other close relative. Perhaps strains of Y. pestis might have arisen independently centuries ago in both

Asia and Africa, giving rise to those two great plagues that bracketed the Dark Ages.

On the face of it, such an evolutionary situation ought to be highly unlikely. Defective genes arise in natural populations all the time, but only rarely and under unusual circumstances do they spread through an entire population. In order for this to happen, the descendants of the organism in which the defect arose must somehow out-reproduce all the other members of the population, so that the harmful gene will be able to spread. This is particularly improbable if the population is large, as it is in bacteria. And you can see immediately that the more harmful the mutation, the less likely it is to spread in such a fashion.

While it is possible to imagine, barely, that one such mutation might have arisen and spread through the *Y. pestis* population by chance, the likelihood that two independent mutations could have done so is far smaller. The difficulty is compounded when we remember all the other mutations that have helped to make *Y. pestis* so defective, like the one that damaged the Krebs Cycle. There has to be some good reason why these mutant strains of bacteria have been so successful, even though they appear to have decreased capabilities.

More recently, other parts of the story have emerged. Thomas Quan and a group of colleagues at the Centers for Disease Control in Fort Collins, Colorado, have managed to destroy another gene on one of the plasmids that is carried by *Y. pestis*. This gene codes for a protease, which is an enzyme that digests other proteins. They found that *Y. pestis* carrying the destroyed gene were a million times *less* virulent than those that carried the intact gene. So this protease gene contributes to the virulence of *Y. pestis* when it is functional, not when it is mutant, which is quite the opposite of the effects of the genes investigated by Wolf-Watz.

Quan and his colleagues therefore thought that Wolf-Watz must be wrong, that it is not the loss of genes that contributes to the viciousness of *Y. pestis* but rather the acquisition from some unrelated bacterium of a plasmid that carries the protease. Searching among bacteria that are close relatives of *Yersinia,* they found that similar plasmids could be found in *Salmonella* and even in the common gut bacterium *E. coli.* Perhaps, they thought, the virulent *Yersinia* had acquired its protease-gene-carrying plasmid from one of these bacteria.

The two groups of scientists, I suspect, are both right. They have uncovered different parts of the story. There is no doubt that, as Wolf-Watz found, *Y. pestis* is damaged genetically, increasing its virulence. On the other hand, Quan has certainly managed to show that a gene on one of the plasmids it has picked up also helps it to invade and multiply within its host. Remember, though, that the plasmid can be acquired in a single step, so that although *Y. pestis* has gained some of its virulence from a mutation that happened in its invasin gene and more virulence from a plasmid carrying a protease gene, after all this it is still a few simple genetic steps away from being harmless.

If *Y. pestis* is such a terrifying pathogen, then how has it managed to paint itself into such a corner? Why has it acquired all these genetic defects that prevent it from living anywhere except in the host's body? Its vulnerable genotype tells us that it is forced to live in animal hosts most of the time, and yet it rapidly kills those hosts. It can only be transmitted to new hosts if the host population is numerous enough, and if fleas happen to be available. But if hosts are sparse and fleas are few, than it will kill its host too soon and find itself trapped in a rapidly cooling dead body with no means of escape.

The plague bacillus cannot live anywhere but inside its

hosts, but it is so fragile that most of the time it must be cautious. If it behaves with wild abandon and causes the plague, then most of the time it will die as well. To explain all the genetic abilities that *Y. pestis* has lost, we are forced to conclude that most of the time, for whatever reason, it must refrain from causing the plague. Most of the time, *Y. pestis* cannot be—indeed, cannot afford to be—a plague-causing bacillus.

There are, therefore, likely to be less virulent close relatives of *Y. pestis* lurking in our penumbra of diseases. We must remember that the highly virulent laboratory strains of *Y. pestis* were isolated from humans and animals that had actually come down with the plague, and as a result they are hardly typical. They are likely to be a small subset of the universe of *Y. pestis*-like bacteria that are scattered throughout the soil, the water, and the gastrointestinal tracts of many different animals including ourselves.

Another possibility is that *Y. pestis* itself, with all its defects, lives in other animals, but does not for some reason cause the dramatic symptoms of plague. Recent experiments by Quan and his co-workers reinforce this possibility—they deliberately infected black-footed ferrets and Siberian polecats, likely carriers of the plague bacillus, with a highly virulent strain of *Y. pestis* and found that it caused no symptoms. Remarkably, they also discovered that wild ferrets trapped from a Wyoming population were already making high levels of antibodies to *Y. pestis*, which means that they must have been exposed to this bacillus (or a close relative) while they were living in the wild. If so, since *Y. pestis* cannot live in the soil, these strains must be passed directly from animal to animal.

The crippled *Y. pestis* might never have evolved if its relative *Y. pseudotuberculosis* were itself only one or two genetic steps away from being able to cause the plague in humans. This robust organism *can* live in the soil, and *can* be passed easily from one host to another even if the population is sparse. It can occasionally cause something very like the horror of bubonic plague in other animals. So why is the wimpish, genetically damaged *Y. pestis* so much more potentially dangerous to us than the strong *Y. pseudotuberculosis* that has all its faculties intact?

To get at least a glimpse of an answer to this question, we must follow the history of *Y. pestis* in the bodies of its victims, and see how it manages to pass from one human to another.

The Flea's Tale

When *Y. pestis* invades the body of a human or animal host, its defective genes prevent it from entering the host's cells. The bacteria are therefore exposed to the phagocytes that should be able to hunt and destroy them. But they are not helpless victims of these cruising defenders. They have a weapon against them, in the form of the protease that Quan and his colleagues discovered.

Whenever the bacteria come in contact with phagocytes, the protease destroys or damages proteins on the phagocytes' surface. So long as their protease gene is intact, the bacteria can ward off the phagocytes even though they cannot get inside the host's cells. This allows them to multiply relatively unhampered inside the host's body. During a full-fledged *Y. pestis* infection the bacteria are free to gather in great clots under the skin and accumulate in the lymph nodes, because the immune system is helpless to destroy them. The result is the black blotches and swollen buboes of the Black Death.

It is the sheer numbers of these bacteria that kill their hosts, by inducing toxic shock syndrome. They stimulate the host's immune system in a nonspecific and uncontrolled way, producing high fever and choking swelling of the throat.

So immense do the bacterial numbers become that they often manage to invade the lungs, where they immediately begin to break down the delicate tissues. As the lungs literally dissolve under this onslaught, the bacteria are broadcast on the breath, in tiny droplets of fluid. This bacterial destruction of the lungs accounts for the fetid breath of plague victims that figures in all the medieval accounts of the pestilence. And it also accounts for the sudden emergence of pneumonic plague during a bubonic plague infection. Stanley Falkow of Stanford University, who has looked into many old autopsy reports, tells me that about half the victims of bubonic plague show invasion of the lung tissue. Pneumonic plague, it seems, is only a short but catastrophic step away from the bubonic variety. It probably does not require any further mutation of the plague bacilli.

So devastating is the infection that the human or animal host will almost certainly soon die—and when this happens the invading bacteria will die as well. Their immense numbers, however, are their temporary salvation. The great gatherings of bacteria under the skin are easily picked up by fleas before the host dies and are transmitted to new hosts, spreading the disease and giving the bacteria new temporary homes before their rampage destroys them. Or, in the pneumonic form of the plague, the bacteria are simply spread to new hosts through the air.

This story of bacteria run amok turns out to be even more complex, for up to now we have only considered their effect on their human or animal host. They also affect the fleas of both rats and humans in such a way as to aid their own spread. The fleas are actually unusual hosts for *Yersinia* bacteria, only becoming important when the bacteria are prevented from spreading through the faeces and the soil.

When the fleas ingest large numbers of bacteria from their hosts they too become ill, and their illness helps to spread the disease. You will remember that the first scientists to work with rat fleas found that their guts were often clogged with masses of multiplying bacteria. As a result the fleas could not absorb moisture from their blood meals. They became progressively more and more thirsty, jumping from host to host in a desperate attempt to find moisture. They had been converted into living hypodermic needles, injecting the bacteria into the skins of their new hosts whenever they tried to quench their thirst.

Why should the bacteria be able to affect the fleas so dramatically? The fleas are not defenceless. Although they and other insects do not have the elaborate immune systems that are found in mammals and birds, they do have patrolling phagocytes that can destroy bacteria and other invaders. Indeed, the first phagocytes that were ever seen under the microscope belonged to water fleas, remote (but not too remote) relatives of rat and human fleas. Early in this century, the Russian scientist Elie Metchnikoff observed the phagocytes of these tiny crustacea engulfing bits of foreign matter. In theory, then, the rat or human fleas should be able to destroy the clots of bacteria in their guts, restoring them to normal working order.

However—and this is speculation—it may not be a coincidence that *Y. pestis* can multiply so readily in the bodies of fleas. Perhaps they can employ the same proteases that they use to damage human phagocytes against the phagocytes of fleas. This would make the fleas' phagocytes unable to engulf the invaders. It may be—although there is as yet no evidence—that the multiplication of bacteria in fleas as well as in humans and rats is aided by an inability to destroy the invaders.

There are also strong indications that the bacteria have been in their flea hosts many times before, and have reached a complex genetic adjustment with them. Although they must be able to make the fleas desperately hungry and thirsty, they cannot kill them too quickly, or they will not be carried to new mammalian hosts. This fine-tuning of their effects on the fleas is the result of a complex series of events.

Even before the bacteria multiply to large numbers in the fleas, they can immediately block their guts. Blood taken in by the fleas is rapidly clotted by a protein that is manufactured by the bacteria ingested at the same time. The fleas soon begin to starve and dehydrate. But before they can die, another protein begins to break down the newly-formed blood clots. The genes for both proteins are carried by a plasmid that is unique to *Y. pestis*, a plasmid that enables it to make the most out of its short existence in the infected fleas.

When Quan and his colleagues deliberately infected fleas with bacteria in which both of the genes had been destroyed, they died more rapidly than fleas that had been infected by intact *Y. pestis*. It seems that the blood-clotting proteins may not be as important as the protein that breaks down the clot once it forms. A little bit of breakdown of the clot of blood and bacteria in the gut of the flea may be enough to ensure that the flea will gain a little nourishment. At the same time, bits of the clot will break free and travel to the fleas' mouth parts—a kind of insect heartburn. All these elaborate events seem to be necessary because the bacteria cannot swim there on their own—you will recall that they have lost their ability to be motile. So *Y. pestis* has been aided in coping with the difficult situation that it must confront in the bodies of fleas by the acquisition of yet another plasmid, one that just happens to be around and just happens to be excellent at the task.

The fleas, of course, are nothing more than mobile hypo-dermic needles. Virtually any kind of flea can be invaded by the bacteria, if it happens to have fed on animals that have large numbers of bacteria in their blood. As a result, these sick bacteria can infect mice, rats, cats, perhaps farm animals, and of course humans. (It may have been more than just an unrea-soning fear of witchcraft that explains why so many cats were hunted down and killed during the Black Death, since these animals are highly susceptible to the plague.)

We now have many pieces of the puzzle. Rare as bubonic plague outbreaks are, they have still been shaped to a remark-able extent by evolution—even though it is a particularly crude and untidy sort of evolution. *Y. pestis* bacilli have acquired a number of mutations that block critical functions. At the same time, they have picked up plasmids that allow them to acquire other functions. These abilities protect them from the hosts' immune systems or allow them to survive in the fleas. Pro-vided that the plasmids are available in the bacterial environ-ment (and goodness knows what organisms they evolved in originally), it is presumably fairly easy for such bits and pieces to come together to make a nasty opportunist like *Y. pestis*—a kind of evolutionary Frankenstein's monster.

It is one of nature's supreme ironies that, during the unusual juxtaposition of circumstances that leads to an out-break of plague, all the major participants in the drama are sick. This includes the humans, the rats, the fleas, and the very bacteria themselves. And this may help to explain why, even in the filthy and squalid medieval world, severe outbreaks of plague were relatively rare. No ecological relationship in which all the interacting members are behaving abnormally is likely to persist for long.

Improved sanitation is the key to preventing plague outbreaks, even in situations where a few decades ago plague would have been a certainty. Parts of Hong Kong, where Alexandre Yersin cured the first cases of the plague in 1896, now have the highest population densities in the world. The Shamshuipo district of Kowloon has 165,000 people per square kilometre, and a single housing complex can contain 100,000 people. Yet plague in this clean, well-run city is now almost unknown.

Even though a few cases of plague, mostly from contact with wild rodents, appear every year in the US, we tend to think of the disease as being a thing of the past. These occasional cases, if they are diagnosed early enough, can now usually be controlled by antibiotics (though as we have seen, mortality even with the best medical care is still about fifteen per cent). And while the population of rats has certainly grown since medieval times (as have the rats themselves), we mostly keep them at arm's length—although they can still swarm over the steps of the New York Public Library at dusk, driving away hysterical tourists. But until recently we supposed that the unusual circumstances that engender plague had receded into history.

In fact, history may have caught up with us. Plague bacilli and their close relatives have certainly now escaped from their original foci in Africa and Asia, and have been carried to every continent. The sheer mass of our enteric bacteria, and the changing mix of bacteria in the soil and sewage that surround human population centres, particularly in the Third World, are something that has never been seen on the planet before. The niches available to these bacilli are more numerous than ever. Potential agents of the plague are everywhere in our food and in the soil.

from Secret Agents: The Menace of Emerging Infections

by Madeline Drexler

Food-borne pathogens make millions of Americans sick each year—and occasionally kill one of us. The problem is getting worse. The people fighting this problem include political activists as well as scientists.

n the autumn of 1996, Laurie Girand, a marketing consultant in Silicon Valley, came home from a Fiji vacation to find her three-year-old daughter Anna in constant stomach pain. "My tummy hurts. My tummy hurts," the usually resilient child kept saying. Within days, Anna was in the hospital, severely anemic, her red blood cells looking like shredded circles under the microscope. Doctors diagnosed her with hemolytic uremic syndrome, or HUS, a sometimes fatal complication of foodborne infection. The bacterium behind the disease, *E. coli* O157:H7, is usually linked to undercooked hamburgers—Girand vaguely remembered a huge Jack in the Box outbreak of a few years earlier. But her daughter hadn't gotten sick from eating hamburgers. Only as Anna lay in a hospital bed, ashen-faced, glassy-eyed, waiting for a blood transfusion, did Girand and her husband hear a news account that apple juice had been linked to an *E. coli* epidemic. Manufactured by Odwalla, Inc., its selling point was that it was unpasteurized, and presumably more wholesome. The apple juice had been a treat from Anna's grandmother while Girand and her husband were away. And though Girand didn't approve of apple juice—too many empty calories—for a long time she had been feeding her daughter Odwalla unpasteurized carrot juice. "I was under the seriously mistaken impression that feeding our daughter unpasteurized juice would be healthier for her," Girand says. "Odwalla's slogan at the time was: 'Drink it and thrive.' "

Though anemic for months, Anna recovered. But in Colorado, a child had died, while nearly 70 others, mostly children six and younger, had become severely ill in what was, until then, the country's biggest juice-associated outbreak. Catalyzed by the near-tragedy, Laurie Girand started giving speeches to parents and writing letters to government officials. But shocking as the Odwalla outbreak was, it was not sufficiently instructive. Three years later, in the nation's biggest juice outbreak, *Salmonella* in unpasteurized Sun Orchard orange juice struck nearly 500 victims and killed one. A few months later, the company had to recall another tainted lot. "I can't believe," Girand says, "since I am a marketing person, how badly I was fooled by industry marketing."

One of the most insistent marketing messages we hear, trumpeted by both industry and regulators, is that the United States has the safest food supply in the world. Yet according to the CDC's best calculations, each year 76 million Americans—nearly one in four, and that's a lowball estimate—become infected by what they eat. Most find themselves for a few days dolefully memorizing a pattern of bathroom floor tiles. About 325,000 land in the hospital. Two million suffer drawn-out, sometimes lifelong medical complications from unwittingly eating a contaminated morsel. More than 5,000—about 14 a day—die from indulging in what should be one of life's great pleasures. The "world's safest food supply" regularly doles out *E. coli* O157:H7 in hamburgers, *Salmonella* in alfalfa sprouts, *Listeria* in hot dogs, *Campylobacter* in Thanksgiving turkeys.

Change is what ushers new disease-causing organisms into our lives. And in the past few decades, there have been profound shifts in what we eat, where our food comes from, how it's made, and who makes it. Fifty years ago, grocery stores stocked about 200 items, 70 percent of which were grown, produced, or processed within a 100-mile radius of the store. Today, the average supermarket carries nearly 50,000 food items, some stores as many as 70,000. Agriculture and food manufacture have grown into global economies of scale, producing megaton quantities that, if contaminated, increase the potential for widespread epidemics. More fresh fruits and vegetables come from abroad, where sanitary standards may not be as high as in the United States. And our meals are increasingly cooked by people untrained in the techniques of safe food preparation.

This is not your grandparents' "food poisoning"—a now-quaint term that originated early in the twentieth century, when dramatic gastrointestinal distress was usually traced to toxins, especially staph toxins, that had grown on spoiled foods such as cream-filled pastries or chicken salads left out too long in summer heat. Literally cases of food "intoxication," these infections struck suddenly and fiercely, usually within two to six hours after the meal. When local health officials worked up these classic "point source outbreaks," they would inevitably find that a knot of victims had all eaten a single dish, and that cases sharply climbed and then plummeted as the well of exposed individuals dried up. Point source outbreaks haven't faded away; big-city health departments face dozens every year. In 1997, for instance, *Salmonella*-tainted hams from a church fundraising dinner in St. Mary's County, Maryland, sickened 700 people and killed an elderly woman. Today, however, the modest church picnic has given way to a giant food bazaar created by massive consolidation and global distribution. One contaminated tidbit—a shred of meat from an infected steer mixed with hundreds of other carcasses for hamburger, an iced box of tainted lettuce dripping down on the rest of an outbound lot, a soiled production line of cereal shipped coast-to-coast under 30 different brand names—spreads disease far and wide.

The pathogens in science's crosshairs have also changed—in part because improved technology permits scientists to see some for the first time, and in part because evolution has selected far more noxious creatures. Twenty years ago, today's most fearsome threats were overlooked or yet-to-be-discovered. *Campylobacter jejuni*, now known to be the most common bacterial agent in food, was considered a rare, opportunistic organism because lab workers didn't see it hiding among less fastidious bacteria growing in culture. A small, delicate, spiral-shaped microbe, it corkscrews its way into mucous membranes of the intestinal tract "with a speed that cannot be matched by other bacteria," according to one scientist's report. *Listeria monocytogenes,* the most deadly agent in our food supply, killing one in five victims it infects, wasn't even suspected of spreading through food. *E. coli* O157:H7, a potent threat to children and the aged, was identified only in

1982—and even then remained a medical curiosity until the infamous 1993 Jack in the Box hamburger outbreak. Norwalk virus, the top cause of foodborne illness in this country at 23 million cases a year, remained largely elusive until molecular tests revealed it in the 1990s. All of which suggests there are novel disease-causing agents still hiding incognito in our food. Even with modern diagnostic tools, in 81 percent of foodborne illnesses and 64 percent of deaths, doctors don't know what organisms to blame—in part because they don't know what organisms to look for.

To doctors and scientists, some of these bugs—particularly *E. coli* O157:H7—are scarier than anything seen before. "Foodborne pathogens are not purely a bit of nausea and vomiting and diarrhea," says David Acheson, an *E. coli* researcher at Tufts University School of Medicine. "They can kill a previously healthy person in the space of a week." Evolutionary biologists fear that our efforts to eliminate pathogens on the farm and in processing—by, for example, using disinfectant rinses—may paradoxically help select for more durable and virulent strains.

Meanwhile, more of us are more vulnerable to foodborne microbes. Individuals with impaired immunity—the very young, the very old, and people with cancer, organ transplants, diabetes, AIDS, and other conditions that weaken the body's defenses; all told, about a quarter of the population—are more apt to succumb to these infections. Men and women over 65, who in the next three decades will make up one-fifth of the population, produce less acid in their stomachs, eliminating the first line of defense against enteric pathogens; federal officials predict that the aging population could increase foodborne illness by 10 percent in the next decade. Americans are popping more prescription and over-the-counter antacids than ever, and in so doing, giving pathogens entree to the nether regions of our digestive system where they do the most damage.

Depending on the organism, the palette of symptoms associated with foodborne disease can include diarrhea, cramps, fever, nausea, and vomiting (the notable exception is *Listeria*, which can cause miscarriage, meningitis, and other nonabdominal problems). But that's just the beginning. In some people, researchers have discovered, the gastrointestinal distress that comes and goes with a foul meal may hang around in another form much longer. *Salmonella* can trigger reactive arthritis, an acute joint inflammation. *Campylobacter jejuni* may cause as many as 40 percent of cases of Guillain-Barré syndrome, a severe neurological disorder that can bring temporary paralysis and long-term nerve damage. Other complications include thyroid disease, inflammatory bowel disease, and, should someone survive the struggle against *E. coli* O157:H7, permanent kidney damage from hemolytic uremic syndrome. In these cases, contaminated food seems to provoke an uncontrolled autoimmune reaction. Up to 3 percent of foodborne disease victims—an enormous number, given the total caseload—may suffer lifelong physical problems.

Any depiction of emerging foodborne infections is necessarily panoramic, complex, and accompanied by more questions than answers. This discussion is no exception. As you will discover, debates about questions of farm management, government regulation, and individual versus institutional responsibility may elicit two—or three or four—diametrically opposed arguments that all seem persuasive. "Foodborne illness is more complex than people understand. The more I learn, the less I realize I ever knew," says Mike Osterholm, a former Minnesota state epidemiologist who has probably launched more successful food outbreak investigations than any other public health official in history. "The very nature of the ever-growing and complex food supply chain, and the desire of consumers to have many different kinds of foods available at a moment's notice, has allowed for a whole new spectrum of pathogens to arrive on the scene." What's more, says Osterholm, DNA fingerprinting has pulled back the covers from foodborne outbreaks, showing that "many of the old conclusions we had drawn about what was happening are not valid."

For those of us who don't think about it for a living, it's easy to underestimate the risk of falling ill from food, since the problem is largely invisible—hidden, one supposes, behind the bathroom door. CDC epidemiologists have factored in this cultural aversion by using numerical multipliers that translate the relatively few cases reported into a far higher and more accurate count of victims who never see a doctor. For instance, for every person known to suffer an infection caused by *Campylobacter* or *Salmonella* or *Cyclospora*, there are 38 who have eluded the net of public health officials; for every confirmed case of *E. coli* O157:H7, there are 13 to 27 doubled-over victims. Keep this in mind when you read news stories about foodborne epidemics. The scores of confirmed cases mentioned in wire service stories may actually represent hundreds or thousands of silent sufferers.

Foodborne infections are ubiquitous, sneaky, and regularly sold short. At the CDC, the foodborne and diarrheal diseases branch investigates more outbreaks than any other group in the agency. According to Paul Mead, a medical epidemiologist, "The paradox of foodborne illness is that, on a per meal basis, it's extremely rare. It's like getting hit by a meteor." But in the very act of eating, says Mead, "You're standing in a meteor shower three times a day from the time you're weaned until you die."

Secret Agent O157: The Evolution of a Killer

Every pathogen has a story, but the biography of *E. coli* O157:H7 is especially instructive because it shows how chance favors the prepared germ—and how we are giving certain disease-causing organisms more chances than a rigged roulette wheel. Though *E. coli* O157:H7 has turned up in unpasteurized apple cider in 1991, 1996, and nearly every year since the Odwalla outbreak, it is best known as the agent behind "hamburger disease." Hamburgers, in fact, are Rolls-Royce conveyances for O157. Think of your next Big Mac as the end product of a vast on-the-hoof assembly line. The story begins on hundreds of feedlots in different states and foreign countries. The animals are shuttled to slaughterhouses, where they become carcasses. The carcasses go to plants that separate meat from bone. The boning plants ship giant bins of meat to hamburger-making plants. The hamburger-making plants combine meat from many different bins to make raw hamburgers. At this point, your burger is more fluid than solid, because ground beef continually mixes and flows as it's made, its original ingredients indistinguishable. Grinding also multiplies surface area, so that the meat becomes a kind of soup or lab medium for bacteria. Finally, from the hamburger-making plants, these mongrel patties are frozen and sent to restaurants. A single patty may mingle the meat of a hundred different animals from four different countries. Or, looked at from another perspective, a single contaminated carcass shredded for hamburger can pollute eight tons of finished ground beef. Finding the source of contamination becomes impossibly daunting. (Making juice is also like making hamburgers: one bad apple can ruin a huge batch.) In the Jack in the Box outbreak, investigators found that the ground beef from the most likely supplier contained meat from 443 different cattle that had come from farms and auction in six states via five slaughterhouses. As the meat industry consolidates and the size of ground beef lots grows, a single carcass may have even more deadly potential. In 1997, Hudson Foods was forced to recall 25 million pounds of ground beef for this very reason: a small part of one day's contaminated beef lot was mistakenly mixed with the next day's, vastly spreading the risk.

E. coli O157:H7, the organism that this endless mixing amplifies, is a quiet tenant in the intestines of the 50 percent or so of feedlot cattle it infects, but a vicious hooligan in the human gut. In the bowel, *Escherichia coli*, rod-shaped bacteria first described by German pediatrician Theodore Escherich in 1885, perform a vital task by keeping disease-causing bacteria from taking over. For many decades, that knowledge obscured the fact that some forms of *E. coli* trigger violent disease. *E. coli* O157:H7 (the letters and numbers refer to immune system-provoking antigens on the body and on the whiplike flagella of the organism) was discovered in 1982, during an epidemic spread by undercooked patties from McDonald's restaurants in Oregon and Michigan. The outbreak wasn't highly publicized; even some scientists perceived O157 as more of an academic curiosity than a harbinger of bad things. Eleven years later, the Jack in the Box hamburger chain promoted its "Monster Burgers" with the tag line: "So good it's scary." These large, too-lightly-grilled patties killed four children and sickened more than 700 people—bringing the exotic-sounding bacterium out of the lab and into public consciousness. In fact, however, by the time of the Jack in the Box tragedy, 22 outbreaks of *E. coli* O157:H7, killing 35 people, had already been documented in the United States.

Suddenly, fast food hamburgers—a staple of American culture—were potentially lethal.

What makes *E. coli* O157:H7 so fearsome is the poison it churns out—the third most deadly bacterial toxin, after those causing tetanus and botulism. Known as a Shiga toxin, because it is virtually identical to the toxin produced by *Shigella dysenteriae* type 1, it is a major killer in developing nations. The distinctive symptoms of *E. coli* O157:H7 are bloody diarrhea and fierce abdominal cramps; many victims say it's the worst pain they ever suffered, comparing it to a hot poker searing their insides. Between 2 and 7 percent of patients—mostly young children and the elderly—develop hemolytic uremic syndrome, which can lead to death. HUS sets in when Shiga toxins ravage the cells lining the intestines. The bleeding that ensues permits the toxins to stream into the circulatory system, setting up a cascade of damage similar to that of rattlesnake venom. The toxins tear apart red blood cells and platelets, leaving the victim vulnerable to brain hemorrhaging and uncontrolled bleeding. Clots form in the bloodstream, blocking the tiny blood vessels around the kidneys, the middle layer of the heart, and the brain. As the kidneys give out, the body swells with excess waste fluids. Complications ripple through all major organ systems, leading to strokes, blindness, epilepsy, paralysis, and heart failure. Though doctors can manage HUS symptoms, and are working on new ways to stymie the toxin, they currently can offer no cure or even effective treatment.

For public health officials, the emergence of *E. coli* O157:H7 is an object lesson in how a new pathogen can lie low in the environment, biding its time until humankind changes a certain activity and in so doing rolls out a red carpet. Like other emerging pathogens, such as the AIDS virus, O157 had struck long before it caught the attention of public health officials. In 1955, a Swiss pediatrician in a dairy farm area first described HUS, which physicians today consider to be a gauge of *E. coli* O157:H7 infection. Over the ensuing years, the number of cases kept rising, suggesting that O157 was quietly spreading. In 1975, doctors took a stool sample from a middle-aged California woman with bloody diarrhea, cultured the apparently rare bacterium and sent it to the CDC, where it sat in storage until the McDonald's outbreak prompted researchers to scour their records for earlier evidence of the vicious organism. In other words, for nearly 30 years before the first bona fide epidemic, *E. coli* O157:H7 had turned up in scattered, sporadic cases of bloody diarrhea. It was out in the meat supply, but not in high enough concentrations to catch health officials' notice.

Where did *E. coli* O157:H7 come from in the first place? Scientists have pieced together a long, rather provocative history. Genetic lineages suggest that about 50,000 years ago, O157 and another closely related serotype—O55:H7, which causes infant diarrhea in developing nations—split off from the same mother cell. Since then, O157 has taken part in a series of biological mergers and acquisitions that left it as vigorous as one of today's giant pharmaceutical houses. Indeed, a 2001 study showed that O157, composed of more than 5,400 genes, picks up foreign DNA at a much faster rate than do other organisms. At some point, it acquired two deadly Shiga toxin genes after being infected by a bacteriophage, a tiny virus that insinuates its DNA into the chromosome of a bacterium. In the microbial world, phages are like squatters in Amsterdam, casually taking up residence in new bacteria, perhaps as a response to environmental stresses such as ultraviolet light or toxic chemicals. Bacteriophages are also the villains behind some of the most deadly human plagues; the genes coding for the cholera toxin, for instance, were borne on a phage. So what surrounding pressures compelled the phage carrying the Shiga toxin genes to light out for a new home in *E. coli*? In experiments on mice, Tufts University researcher David Acheson may have found the answer. When Acheson gave the animals low levels of antibiotics, the phage virus wildly replicated itself, and its magnified forces were more likely to infect other bacteria. Antibiotics also spurred the phage to pour out clouds of Shiga toxin. Acheson speculates that when farmers began the practice of feeding cattle small doses of antibiotics to spur growth, beginning in the 1950s—perhaps not coincidentally, when the first reports of sporadic HUS in children came out—they may have unleashed O157. More backing for this theory comes from epidemiological evidence. *E. coli* O157:H7 is a disease of affluent, developed nations—which also happen to be the ones that feed growth-promoting antibiotics to livestock.

What worries Acheson and other scientists is that the restless phages that manufacture Shiga toxin may jump to other disease-causing bacteria. Actually, they've already proven they're disposed to do this, having set up home in about 200 other strains of *E. coli*. One of these, *E. coli*. O111:H8, in 1999 caused a massive epidemic of nausea, vomiting, bloody diarrhea, and severe stomach cramps at a high school drill team camp in Texas, sickening dozens of the 750 teenage girls who attended. Though investigators never did find where the organism was hiding, they suspect it was either in the ice the girls used to soothe their parched throats during the drills or somewhere in the salad bar. Shiga toxin phages have also landed in *Enterobacter* and *Citrobacter*—other bacteria that stir up intestinal disease. To find out just how prevalent these mysterious strains of dangerous *E. coli* may be, Acheson analyzed ground beef samples from 12 supermarkets in Boston and Cincinnati. The results came as a shock. He found Shiga toxin in a quarter of the samples—toxin produced not by O157:H7, but by other kinds of *E. coli*. And this may not be the end of their roving, Acheson warns. "Suppose something like *Salmonella* developed the ability to produce Shiga toxins. That could be an extremely deadly pathogen." Not only is *Salmonella* common, but, more than *E. coli* O157, it has a talent for quickly invading the bloodstream, meaning it could speedily convey Shiga toxins throughout the body like tiny poison-tipped missiles. Even more problematic, the antibiotics normally used to treat *E. coli* O157:H7 infections may actually aggravate the illness, by kicking phages into overdrive and stepping up their production of toxins, leading to hemolytic uremic syndrome.

Along its evolutionary path, *E. coli* also became acid resistant, so impervious to a low pH environment that it can survive the incredibly sour bath in the human stomach. Grain-feeding cattle, which supplanted traditional hay feeding after World War II, may have made the bacteria more acid resilient. Because of this acid tolerance, as few as 10 organisms are enough to cause infection. Having acquired a mean set of toxin genes, acid resistance, and other virulence properties, all *E. coli* O157:H7 needed to become a truly fearsome threat was access. That it acquired by spreading in domesticated cattle and then entering the gears of modern industrial meat production, all within the past 2.5 years. Unfortunately, O157 may have left the door open behind it. Other strains of *E. coli*. "if tweaked in the right way" by phages and the mobile rings of DNA known as plasmids, could negotiate the same path, says Tom Whittam, a biologist at Pennsylvania State University who has studied O157 evolution.

Research is under way on vaccines that would prevent cattle

from carrying O157, and on feed additives—including competing intestinal bacteria—that would eliminate the pathogenic organism in livestock. Thoroughly cooking ground beef to a temperature of 160 degrees Fahrenheit is the proven method of killing *E. coli*. O157:H7. But in the United States, the organism retains a fighting chance because of the American love affair with rare burgers, which practically guarantees that one man's meat will be another man's poison. As a restaurant menu in suburban Dallas proudly informs its customers: "The Department of Health suggests MEDIUM-WELL for any ground beef product. Our burgers are cooked MEDIUM (PINK) unless you request otherwise."

Animal Farms

The *E. coli* O157:H7 saga shows how the denizens of an animal's GI tract find their way to our own digestive systems. This brings up a delicate point, rarely discussed in polite company, but one central to the rest of this chapter. Put simply, animal and human waste is the source of most foodborne illness. And what we eat usually becomes contaminated long before it reaches us—during processing, at the slaughterhouse, or right on the farm.

Of course, that's a resonant theme in public health. The sanitary revolution of the nineteenth century—the discovery that the diseases of squalor and overcrowding could be prevented with sewage removal and clean water—was occasioned by fear of cholera, typhoid fever, and other pestilential diseases. Before this transformative event, daily life was unimaginably filthy. "Thousands of tons of midden filth filled the receptacles, scores of tons lay strewn about where the receptacles would receive no more," observed an English medical officer in Leeds in 1866. "Hundreds of people, long unable to use the privy because of the rising heap, were depositing on the floors."

Which is precisely how the animals that become our food live today. And why, at the CDC, officials in the foodborne and diarrheal disease branch long for a sanitary revolution: clean piped water and sewage disposal and treatment—for animals. Like the nineteenth century innovations that controlled typhoid fever, animal sewage would be separated from the human food and water supply, and also from the *animal* food and water supply. "It's a paradigm shift," says the CDC's Fred Angulo. "Farmers don't consider themselves food handlers."

The site of modern meat production is akin to a walled medieval city, where waste is tossed out the window, sewage runs down the street, and feed and drinking water are routinely contaminated by fecal material. Each day, a feedlot steer deposits 50 pounds of manure, as the animals crowd atop dark mountains composed of their own feces. "Animals are living in medieval conditions and we're living in the twenty-first century," says Robert Tauxe, chief of the CDC's foodborne and diarrheal diseases branch. "Consumers have to be aware that even though they bought their food from a lovely modern deli bar or salad bar, it started out in the sixteen hundreds."

The feedlot is just the start of their fetid journey. At the head of the slaughterhouse line, a "knocker" wields a pistol-like device to drive a metal bolt into a steer's head. Other workers cut the animal's throat to drain blood, and use machines to sever the animal's limbs, tear off its hide, pull out its organs. More than 300 animals may pass through the line in an hour, each carcass weighing 650 to 800 pounds. At the slaughterhouse, writes journalist Eric Schlosser, "The hides are now removed by machine; but if a hide has not been adequately cleaned first, pieces of dirt and manure may fall from it onto the meat. Stomachs and intestines are still pulled out of cattle by hand; if the job is not performed carefully, the contents of the digestive system"—i.e., waste—"may spill everywhere."

A United States Department of Agriculture study published in 2000 found that 50 percent of feedlot cattle being fattened for slaughter during the summer months carried the *E. coli* O157:H7 bacterium in their intestines—a far higher figure than previous government estimates. Another study found that about 43 percent of the skinned carcasses tested positive before being eviscerated, suggesting that microbes were being spewed within the plant.

In early July 2000, the Excel Corporation—the nation's second-largest beef processor—allowed an Associated Press reporter to visit its huge Fort Morgan, Colorado, meat packing plant. Asked about the dangers of tainted meat reaching consumers, Excel's food safety director replied: "It's like a roll of the dice or a game of Russian roulette." Two weeks later, the face of three-year-old Brianna Kriefall, of South Milwaukee, appeared on front pages across the country. She had died from eating a slice of watermelon at a Sizzler restaurant. The watermelon had been sliced in the restaurant kitchen, on the same countertop where a meat grinder was used to convert steak trimmings—*E. coli*-contaminated steak trimmings—into hamburger. The trimmings came from sirloin meat packed in heavy vacuum-sealed bags. The bags had been shipped just a few days earlier from Excel's Fort Morgan plant.

Chicken farming is just as noxious. But before delving into that, a word about chickens: they're not all created equal. In the agribusiness world, there are two kinds of chickens—the broilers that give us meat, and the layers that give us eggs—and they are totally separate industries governed by different practices, riddled with different problems, and even centered in different parts of the country (the top broiler states are Georgia and Arkansas, while the top egg-producing locales are Ohio and California).

First, a look at broilers. In her book *Spoiled,* journalist Nicols Fox writes that "If chicken were tap water, the supply would be cut off." Oddly enough, the government doesn't have hard numbers on *Salmonella* and *Campylobacter* contamination rates, and what they do have is hardly appealing. A 1999 study from the USDA's Agricultural Research Service, for instance, found that 7 percent of chickens sampled at slaughterhouses had *Salmonella* and 30 percent had *Campylobacter*—but, as one scientist there admitted, those numbers are probably low. For many years, researchers assumed that clearing feces, rodents, and insects from the broiler houses where the birds live out their five to nine weeks would solve the problem. But new studies suggest that the source of chicken contamination may be more deep-rooted. The 9.5 billion young broilers that Americans eat each year are actually the fourth generation in a carefully husbanded line. Scientists now believe it's the three previous generations—the "breeders"—that regularly pass down infection. When he tested birds at the top of the pyramid—the great-grandparent breeder flocks—microbiologist Nelson Cox at the USDA's Russell Research Center found that 36 percent were positive for *Salmonella.* Cox suspects that these birds transmit pathogens to subsequent generations by contaminating their own eggs with feces that carry high levels of *Salmonella, Campylobacter, Listeria,* and *Clostridium perfringens.* Because the hen's body temperature is quite warm—between 104 and 107 degrees Fahrenheit—she usually lays her egg on a day in which the air is cooler than her body. That temperature gap forces bacteria on the porous surface of the egg to get sucked into the membrane underneath, where most organisms live contentedly while the fertile egg is incubating. When the chick pecks its way out, it eats the pathogens. "The largest contributor to contamination of a broiler flock," says Cox, "is the mother hen—the feces of the parent bird." That means the human disease on our end of the food chain won't end until farmers either clean up the three generations above, or scientists figure out how to snap the links of contamination. Vaccines may not be the answer, since they are only effective against diseases that make chickens sick—and both *Salmonella* and *Campylobacter* are benign commensals, living happily in the birds' intestinal tracts without causing harm. Another possibility, slaughtering the priceless great-grandparent breeder birds, would drastically raise chicken prices.

Now on to layers. Modern houses for egg production are avian megalopolises. In 1945 the typical henhouse sheltered 500 birds; today it can contain 80,000 to 175,000, with up to 20 houses in a single operation. (As in the livestock industry, this huge scale is a result of industry consolidation; in 1996 there were approximately 900 egg operations in the United States, compared to 10,000 in 1975.) Laying flocks stay in the same house for up to a year and a half, which means that detritus builds up. "You have a lot of everything," says Richard Cast, a microbiologist at the USDA's Southeast Poultry Research Laboratory. "A lot of birds, a lot of manure, a lot of moisture, a lot of dust. Everything that walked into that house—every two- and four- and six-legged creature—is a potential vector for moving it around."

What spreads in this tenement is *Salmonella enteritidis*, or SE, the villain behind most egg-related outbreaks. SE is a versatile bug, capable of infecting birds through two different routes. One is orally, since chickens eat feces. Another route—more troubling, because scientists haven't figured out how to interfere with it—ascends through the cloaca, the cavity in birds into which empties the products of both the intestinal and reproductive organs. SE is sucked up into the bird's reproductive tract and eventually into the ovaries. From there, it gets inside eggs even before the shell is laid down—indeed, most eggs become systemically contaminated with *Salmonella enteritidis* in this way. Just where SE came from, or why it spread so suddenly in the 1980s, remains a mystery. Found in 1 of every 20,000 eggs, SE makes French toast, Hollandaise sauce, and raw cookie dough risky culinary excursions.

Animal waste and its dangerous microbes aren't confined to the farm, of course. Manure—spread through fertilizer, irrigation water, insecticide solutions, dust, even wild birds and amphibians—gets on produce too. Typical is an outbreak that took place in 1998, when patrons of a Kentucky Fried Chicken restaurant in Indianapolis became ill with *E. coli* O157:H7. Zeroing in on KFC's cole slaw, investigators discovered that some of the cabbage came from fields supplying a Texas vegetable company—and that, during a severe drought, the fields were flooded with untreated water from the Rio Grande, where cattle had waded and relieved themselves in the irrigation canals. Similarly, at Disney World in Orlando, Florida, thousands of visitors from all over the country were believed to have been infected with *Salmonella* in 1995 after drinking unpasteurized orange juice at special "character breakfasts" at the park, in which costumed Disney characters mingle with the guests. The orange juice came from a small processing plant nearby—a plant where the walls and ceiling of the processing room had cracks and holes, and where frogs congregated near the equipment. Outside the plant, investigators found *Salmonella* in a toad, in tree frogs, in soil, and on unwashed oranges.

E. coli O157:H7 contaminates unpasteurized cider when fallen apples touch cattle or deer waste and are then mixed with other pieces of fruit. Numerous lettuce outbreaks have occurred after the heads were exposed to cattle manure. Organic foods are hardly immune to these pitfalls. In fact, microbiologists have found more bacterial contamination on organic than on conventionally grown produce, and no one is quite sure how much composting it takes to knock off pathogens in manure. That gap in knowledge has real-life consequences. In rural Maine in 1992, a woman who abided by a lacto-vegetarian diet, consisting almost exclusively of vegetables fertilized with manure from her cow and calf, developed *E. coli* O157:H7 when she failed to wash the vegetables well enough. Through improper handwashing, she passed the infection on to three neighborhood children, one of whom, a three-year-old boy, died of kidney failure.

Farm conditions create a wide-open channel down which emerging pathogens travel from food animals and produce to people, and the modern food industry has converted a two-lane country road into a 12-lane interstate. "Salmonellosis is rare in developing countries, where sanitation is poor and diarrheal diseases are endemic, but where food production and consumption are local," writes Martin Blaser, chairman of the department of medicine at New York University, in the *New England Journal of Medicine.* Blaser's dispiriting conclusion? "Salmonellosis—with the notable exception of typhoid fever—is a disease of civilization."

And outbreaks are not so much "point source" as pointillist. Changes in agriculture and food manufacture—vaster and fewer farms, slaughter plants, and processing facilities—have given pathogens a larger stage on which to strut. In this miraculous food economy of scale, when things go wrong, they go wrong in a big way. Mass-distributed items with spotty or low-level contamination are consumed by people living far from the source. This leads to a new, insidious kind of epidemic: one with low attack rates (less than 5 percent of the people who eat the contaminated food) but huge numbers of dispersed victims. Take the massive 1994 outbreak of *Salmonella enteritidis*. Usually, SE is linked to undercooked eggs or egg products. But Schwan's ice cream, made in Minnesota and delivered to homes in all 48 contiguous states, was made from premix that had been transported to the plant in tanker trailers—trailers that had previously carried unpasteurized liquid eggs. Though the insides of the tankers were supposed to be washed and sanitized after hauling eggs, drivers sometimes skipped that laborious step. Across the country, an estimated 224,000 ice cream aficionados—mostly kids—paid the price in the largest outbreak of salmonellosis ever recorded from a single food source.

The Path of Most Resistance

The antibiotics that food animals eat can also make you sick. Though the drugs are used to fatten livestock and protect them from disease, they have the paradoxical effect on humans of breeding mean, antibiotic-resistant infections. Here's how the process works: In an animal's gut, antibiotics foster the growth of bacteria such as *Salmonella, Campylobacter,* or *E. coli* that resist the antibiotics. If you eat undercooked meat from that animal, you swallow those antibiotic-resistant bacteria, and you may or may not get sick. By themselves, drug-resistant organisms in food don't necessarily trigger symptoms, because the bugs are held in check by other bacteria in the gut. But if you happen to be taking the antibiotic to which the organism is resistant—say, tetracycline—you can get very sick. That's because the drug clears out other benign bacteria in your intestines, opening the way for the very pathogen that resists the antibiotic to run rampant in your colon and sometimes beyond.

"The reason we're seeing an increase in antibiotic resistance in foodborne diseases is because of antibiotic use on the farm," says the CDC's Fred Angulo. In the United States, an estimated 70 percent of the antibiotics produced each year—nearly 25 million pounds, according to a 2001 report—goes to food animals, in low nontherapeutic doses. Farmers mix these antibiotics in animal feed for two reasons. One is to prevent disease. The other is to promote growth and boost the conversion efficiency of feed into flesh, though exactly how low-dose antibiotics accomplish this isn't clear. It may be that these drugs kill off not only disease-causing bacteria in the gut, but also the good bacteria that compete for nutrients. What's scary is the overlapping of farm and pharmacy. Of the 19 classes of antibiotics used in animals as growth promoters, seven are prescribed for people.

When foodborne pathogens turn antibiotic-resistant, they wreak all kinds of havoc. They are more virulent, and they afflict more people because it takes fewer organisms to cause infection. Patients with antibiotic-resistant infections stay in the hospital longer. The infections especially threaten children, the elderly, and people whose immune systems are weak, such as cancer or AIDS patients: all groups likely to take antibiotics. Foodborne infections that breach the intestinal tract and enter the rest of the body trigger bloodstream or nervous system infections—for which antibiotic treatment can be life-saving. When the pathogen resists the best drugs doctors can offer, death rates climb. Resistant foodborne infections also complicate treatment for other, unrelated infections.

For many years, farmers and regulators were resolutely skep-tical that antibiotics in animals could have downstream effects in people. It took a dramatic 1983 outbreak, in which 18 people in four Midwest states came down with a ferocious strain of antibiotic-resistant *Salmonella newport,* to erase the conven-tional wisdom. Just before becoming ill, most of the patients happened to have taken a form of penicillin for garden-variety infections: bronchitis, earaches, strep throat. So dramatic was the link between taking the antibiotic and coming down with salmonellosis—patients were 51 times more likely than those in the control group to have taken the drug—that public health officials first suspected the antibiotic itself was contami-nated. The truth was much more devious. When investigators gathered patients' food histories, they found that all had eaten ground beef shortly before falling ill. In each case, the hamburger meat had come from a South Dakota farm where beef cattle were fed "subtherapeutic" doses of antibiotics. On the adjacent farm, a dairy calf had died of *Salmonella newport.* Investigators conjectured that the dairy herd somehow trans-mitted the bacterium to the beef cattle which, being fed small doses of tetracycline antibiotics, went on to develop resistant strains of the organism. The infected beef cattle contami-nated at least 40,000 pounds of ground beef with antibiotic-resistant *Salmonella;* without a doubt, many more people ate it than came to health officials' attention.

Today, the link between antibiotic use on farms and human disease is richly documented. In Muslim countries, resistant foodborne bacteria in people are almost always identical to microbes found in poultry—not surprising, since pork is banned. In the Netherlands, vancomycin-resistant entero-cocci, or VRE—a looming problem in hospitals—are notice-ably absent from the intestines of strict vegetarians. Around the world, governments have been embroiled in the question of whether food animals should get the same antibiotics prescribed for people. This question is bound to loom larger, since many public health officials find antibiotic-resistant infections to be the most terrifying prospect on the horizon.

Mad Cows and Englishmen

Another insidious foodborne infection may be looming on the U.S. horizon. New variant Creuzfeldt-Jakob disease—the human form of mad cow disease—has proceeded narrowly and stealthily through a food chain whose links are masked by intensive food production and globalization. At this writing, more than 100 cases, invariably fatal, have been reported, mostly in Britain with a handful in Europe. What researchers don't know is whether these represent the waning aftermath of a narrowly averted public health disaster or the first rumbles of a terrible storm.

"Mad cow disease" is a term that had not even been coined in late 1984, when a veterinarian called to a farm in West Sussex, in southern England, found a dairy cow displaying "a variety of unusual clinical manifestations": panic, aggression, a staggering gait. By the spring of 1985, more cows came down with the mysterious malady, later named bovine spongiform encephalopathy, or BSE, the giveaway marker of which was brain tissue that resembled Swiss cheese. By the late 1980s, scientists began piecing together the puzzle. The epidemic likely began as a foodborne outbreak among livestock. In the early 1980s, cattle were fed remnants from sheep infected with scrapie, a brain-wasting disease (discarded animal parts are considered a cheap source of protein that increases milk production). In a further perversion of nature, the inedible parts of these infected cattle were themselves made into meat and bone meal for other cattle, a thrifty practice that not only permitted the recycled infectious agent to amplify but also to adapt to its new host. Changes in the rendering process also helped the agent survive. Before 1981, the carcasses of ruminants had been subject to high heat and organic solvents to remove fat and disarm disease-causing proteins, such as viruses. But that year, various economic factors persuaded manufacturers to turn down the heat and cut out the solvents, allowing the yet-to-be-discovered infectious agent to escape inactivation. Though hundreds of thousand of cows would eventually be diagnosed with BSE, and millions of animals destroyed as a precaution, the British government was stalwartly optimistic that the epidemic would stay put on the farm. As the Southwood Report noted in 1989, "It is most unlikely that BSE will have any implications for human health." By 1996, after a new variant of the neurological affliction Creutzfeldt-Jakob disease—featuring bizarre behavioral and personality changes, staggering, and dementia—appeared in startlingly young patients, the scientists changed their tune, to the horror of a carnivorous nation. "Beef is one of the great unifying symbols of our culture," lamented a *Guardian* editorial. "The Roast Beef of Old England is a fetish, a household god, which has suddenly been revealed as a Trojan horse for our destruction."

How much beef contaminated by prions—abnormally folded proteins—do humans have to consume to become infected? No one knows. And no one knows how long the incubation period is for new variant Creutzfeldt-Jakob disease, though judging from events in Britain it seems to be at least 10 to 15 years. No one knows how much BSE-infected beef was slaughtered for human consumption before the epidemiologic puzzle was pieced together—perhaps 750,000 animals, perhaps a million; the UN estimated that at the height of the mad cow epidemic, Britain dumped 500,000 tons of untrackable bovine byproducts on Western Europe and other nations. No one knows whether mad cow prions have infected people through blood or organ donations, contaminated surgical instruments, or consumer products and drugs that contain bovine material. The upshot of all this uncertainty is that no one knows where we are on the epidemiologic curve: at the end or the beginning of an outbreak? So murky is the science, Oxford University's esteemed epidemiologist Roy Anderson calculated that human cases could conceivably range between 63 and 136,000, while a British government study put the high-end figure at 250,000.

Will the human variant of mad cow disease turn up in the United States? "The odds are that sooner or later we will see a case here," says CDC director Jeffrey Koplan, "whether it's an imported one, whether it's home grown, whatever. None of us should be surprised if we have a case in the next week or the next ten years." As of the fall of 2001, no cases have been reported. To prevent the spread of BSE to American farms, the U.S. government in 1989 banned the importation of live cows and sheep. Since then, it has erected regulatory fences to screen out other bovine products and has upgraded surveillance for brain-riddling spongiform diseases in domestic animals and humans. The American Red Cross has tightened its blood donation rules for people who have been to Europe. Critics say these measures aren't enough—that, to borrow from W. C. Fields, the United States has failed to "take the bull by the tail and face the situation." The U.S. still imports bio-medical products, for instance, that contain materials made from ruminants in countries harboring mad cow disease. In 2001, the Food and Drug Administration reported that companies were using ingredients from BSE countries to make nine widely used vaccines, including those for polio, diphtheria, and tetanus. The FDA has also failed to regulate dietary supplements such as those claimed to stimulate energy, sexual vitality, and memory—all of which can contain nervous system, organ, and glandular tissue from cattle. And the surveillance net for potentially infected cattle in the United States has big holes, while inspection of feed manufacturers and rendering companies is lax. Meanwhile, some scientists worry that spongiform disease could strike Americans, not through the consumption of beef, but of hunted wild animals such as deer and elk, which are succumbing to another prior-related epidemic, chronic wasting disease.

In echoes of the mad cow crisis, another agricultural infection struck Britain in 2001—foot and mouth disease, one of the most contagious of all animal diseases. How did the culpable agent—in the same family as the common cold virus—get there? Likely from contaminated meat smuggled into Britain from countries where the disease is rife. The British army admitted supplying untreated waste food to a pig farm in Northumberland, where the virus incubated and then wafted over air currents to a flock of sheep. By the time the disease was identified days later, the virus had spread all over the country through markets and dealers. The government response was swift and shocking. Bonfires of livestock carcasses shot flames into the night sky—one writer described the giant pyres as "archaic precautions." Europe and the United States, long protected against the infection, went on red alert, disinfecting the shoes of hundreds of thousands of arriving airline passengers from the British Isles—another reminder that the world is not just a global village, but a global pathosphere.

from Mad Cow U.S.A.: Could the Nightmare Happen Here?

by Sheldon Rampton and John Stauber

The story of Kuru, an illness discovered among the Fore Highlanders of Papua New Guinea during the 1950s, continues to inform contemporary debates over Mad Cow disease. One key issue: Does Mad Cow pose a serious threat to humans?

The chain of events that culminated in Carleton Gajdusek's scientific adventure began in the spring of 1955, in the fledgling South Pacific island nation of Papua New Guinea. Dr. Vincent Zigas, a young Lithuanian physician, had attended the birth of a child and felt obliged to attend the christening party hosted by its parents, members of the Australian upper class who still ruled the island in the years prior to its formal independence. Personally, Zigas had come to detest the Australians' social gatherings, where "ice tinkled in the glasses, beer foamed, champagne spouted, and . . . erotic puppetry . . . was in abundant evidence." To him, their affairs seemed like cheap imitations of the European

culture he had left behind. In his memoirs describing the circumstances that brought him together with Gajdusek, Zigas
disparaged the Australian elite as a "shabby gentility" who
"live in self-imposed seclusion, succumbing to frustration,
neurosis, and the inability to enjoy living." He preferred the
company of other doctors, and of New Guinea's Highlander
natives, whose lives by comparison seemed vital and
authentic.

Tall, fair-haired and emotionally sensitive (some people
thought he resembled the actor Danny Kaye), Zigas had
arrived on the island with his own set of Western biases—
"blinded and made halt of mind," as he put it, "by the cruel
doctrine of racial prejudice." He had been told that the Highlanders were savage warriors and cannibals. As he came to
know them personally, however, he began to admire the
region's "inhabitants so separated and durable, its rituals so
essential and so graceful, that being here feels like purifica-
tion." At night he would listen to "the melody of New
Guinea's waters . . . a tune rising from every rock, root and
rapids . . . rivers and cascades. . . . Then on still nights when
the campfire is low and the moon amid Aurora Australis has
climbed above the rimrocks, one needs to sit quietly and listen
for a distant beat of drums and the wailing cry of bamboo
flutes. . . . Then you may hear it—a vast undulatory harmony;
the score inscribed on a thousand hills and mountains, its
notes like the life and death of humanity. . . . There I was
among martial people no one knew: this people, unscarred by
civilization, capable of inhabiting a natural realm without disturbing the harmony of its life."

Zigas found the Highlanders remarkably friendly and
charmingly free from the inhibitions that afflicted the Euro-
peans. Their customary greeting was considerably more

intimate than a handshake: a standing embrace in which both men and women handled each other's genitals. "It appeared that they were in need of continual exposure to the possessiveness that characterized their relationship by direct physical contact with other people," Zigas observed. "Even in the villages, among people who saw one another every day, hands were continually reaching out to caress a thigh, arms, and searching mouths hung over a child's lips or nuzzled a baby's penis."

The sensuality of the indigenous culture seemed to appeal to some of the European settlers, who took advantage of the opportunity to indulge in behaviors that would not be allowed in "civilized" society. On one occasion a Highlander showed Zigas an abandoned hut where a white man had lived some years previously. The man had been tolerated, even though he was not well liked. "He did no harm," the villager explained, "but this man did not make love to women—he liked small boys."

Another white man—like Zigas, a physician from Lithuania—found happiness in his reputation among the natives as a peculiar kind of faith healer: "His respective enjoyments were focused on gastronomy, tippling, and, as he called it, 'roasted coffee beans'—the fawn-colored maiden's bosom on the topless brown supple body with long, firm nipples. . . . During his Sunday promenade in the local market there would be a number of pubescent girls, either in the company of elders or alone in groups, showering him with demonstrative affection and solicitously proffering their young virgin breasts at the first cast of his touch. The natives were convinced that his 'magic touch' would enrich the supply of milk after marriage." Zigas considered the man a friend and colleague, and insisted that "his fondness for caressing the firm young breast was more for the pleasure of being 'privileged' rather than from any carnal intent. His every 'magic touch' was accompanied by a soft chant in a language alien to the native, which they regarded as a beneficial spell."

The Australians gathered at the christening party, by contrast, struck Zigas as a bunch of boring, sexually frustrated bigots. Distraction came in the form of an argument among several of the men gathering around the host's well-stocked bar. For the first time, Zigas noticed a young Australian patrol officer. Fortified by several glasses of rum, the officer was vigorously challenging other members of the group as they mocked the character and merits of their Highlander servants.

"They don't really want a job, they don't want to work, any of them, lazy bastards; no loyalty, no responsibility," argued one of the drunken Australians.

"For two dollars and fifty cents a month you would be lazy too," countered the patrol officer, whose name was John McArthur. The others replied that native labor wasn't even worth two-fifty a *year*. McArthur maintained his lonely defense of the natives, and Zigas found himself taking a liking to the young man. After the argument ended, the two struck up a personal conversation.

McArthur, it turned out, was stationed in the North Fore (pronounced FOR-ae) region of the Highlands, a remote outpost still considered "uncontrolled" by the colonial administration. Although his job was to pacify the natives, he had taken a personal interest in the region and its people. Turning to the topic of health, McArthur asked if Zigas had seen his patrol report describing a form of local sorcery called "kuru," a word that meant chill, trembling or laughter. Zigas replied that the report had not reached his desk, drawing a stream of profane commentary from McArthur. He had been trying for two years to interest the colonial authorities in kuru, which was killing large numbers of Fore tribespeople, but no one in authority seemed to "give a bloody damn." Zigas said he'd be interested in taking a look, and three months later a native guide arrived at his hospital, with directions leading to a rendezvous in the Fore region that McArthur described as "mountains fretted with evil spell."

The Kuru Curse

It was a two-day hike to the village where McArthur was waiting. On the first day of the journey, Zigas saw his first kuru victim, a middle-aged woman sitting incapacitated in her dilapidated hut. "She looked odd, not ill, rather emaciated, looking up with blank eyes and a mask-like expression. There was an occasional fine tremor of her head and trunk, as if she were shivering from cold, though the day was very warm."

The Highlanders believed powerfully in magic spells and taboos. Their superstitions were so strong that Zigas had seen a man collapse and die simply from the psychosomatic impact of the suggestion that he had violated a taboo. Beginning with the assumption that kuru sorcery was either psychosomatic or treatable, Zigas had brought medicines that he hoped would enable him to work his own brand of counter-magic. "The sorcerer has put a bad spirit inside the woman," he told the natives who gathered to watch him work. "I am going to burn this spirit so that it comes out of her and leaves her." To make his magic convincing, he rubbed her legs and stomach with warming liniment. When he commanded her to walk, however, she just looked back at him, unable to rise. "I took her by the arms and lifted her; she sank limply back to the ground," he recalled. "In an even sterner tone I let out: 'Stand up!' The woman struggled feebly as if to rise, then, exhausted, started to tremble more violently, making a kind of foolish laughter, akin to a titter. I lifted her again; again she sank back. Only now I realized I was helpless. . . . The audience looked at me triumphantly and cackled, and I suddenly felt as naked as a conjurer whose white rabbit had burrowed too far up his sleeve and fallen down his trouser leg."

By the time he reached McArthur's village, Zigas had concluded that there was more to kuru than native superstition. McArthur led him to other cases of the disease in various stages of its progression: a young boy, staggering clumsily as he walked, showing the first symptom of impaired coordination; another boy, further advanced, "a limp figure grossly emaciated to little more than skin and protruding bone, the shivering skeleton of a boy, looking up at me with blank crossed eyes. On both his hips were large bed-sores, and when I tried to apply a dressing to protect them against blowflies his tremor became more pronounced and from his cracked lips came a moan-like sound. He could not utter a single word." McArthur pointed out another boy, stumbling along a path, his facial expression rigid as though frozen. According to McArthur, the boy had been perfectly fine a month before. Now he was barely able to speak and remain upright. "He stood, erect on a wide base, holding his hands together in an attempt to control the involuntary tremors and maintain his equilibrium," Zigas wrote. "As if he sensed, in a very slow motion, some threat from behind, he gradually turned his head to one side. With his outstretched arms, he uttered a single rasping inarticulated shriek of laughter. He couldn't keep his balance any longer—I caught him before he fell."

Zigas saw more cases of kuru in the women's huts. Middle-aged and elderly women were succumbing, along with adolescents and children. All of them showed similar signs of trembling, awkward movements and progressive paralysis, combined with the frozen, mask-like smiles and occasional spasms of uncontrollable, humorless laughter that were the basis for the name "kuru." Zigas was transfixed by the sight of a young girl who "got up, though very awkwardly, and bracing herself with a stick, studied me. With the corner of her little mouth lifted, a slight tremor of her slender body, and with the shadow of a timid smile, she looked forlorn. She could not yet be eleven." He witnessed the grotesque mourning of a middle-aged woman as she cleaned the body of her small son, who had died hours previously: "With one hand she was wiping off brown porridge-like feces from the boy's puny buttocks with a handful of grass. Each soiled grassy wad was tossed to the pig waiting eagerly for the flings. Her other hand was fondling the boy's penis and she was talking to him. There was no response from the still figure. . . . Interrupting her action, she busily tried to chase two wretched dogs away from the boy's stiff body. One beast had managed to lap up quite a bit of the gray-yellow maggot-filled slough from a huge bedsore on the boy's hip. The other beast was obstinately trying to follow suit, but was driven away by a kick."

Zigas became obsessed with finding a cure for kuru. He scoured books for information on diseases of the cental nervous system, and made additional trips into Fore territory, collecting information about the disease and its symptoms. He sought out colleagues for their advice, but found that they showed little interest in kuru and knew even less than he did about what might be causing it. He took advantage of rare visits to New Guinea by medical experts from England and the Netherlands, who theorized that the symptoms he was seeing might be related to malaria, measles, pneumonia, encephalitis, meningitis, Parkinson's Disorder, brain tumors or tuberculosis. The most famous visitor to hear his harangue was Sir Macfarlane Burnet, the "pope of Australian virology," who was soon to receive the Nobel Prize for his research into the body's reactions to skin grafting and organ transplants. Zigas passionately expounded on kuru while Burnet "pretended to look adequately interested, nodding and smiling whenever he guessed it to be appropriate. . . . I felt he must look upon me as a freak, obviously unbalanced. Perhaps, I thought, my description of kuru was delivered with too much gusto, giving an impression to this austere figure that my discovery was just a new obsession. The days of his visit frittered away, leaving me in doubt about his promised cooperation in the investigation."

Early in 1957, however, letters arrived giving the green light for kuru research, with the assistance of facilities at Burnet's laboratory in Melbourne. An anthropologist visited and interviewed a number of Fore clansmen about their customs and their experiences with the disease. In February a letter came from Burnet stating that he had agreed to send a scientist to undertake an epidemiological investigation, although Burnet worried about "the possible dangers from hostile native reaction" and cautioned that he "should not be justified in consenting to the project" if the natives turned against it.

"Atom Bomb" Gajdusek

Carleton Gajdusek was not the scientist that Burnet was planning to send. His arrival, on March 13, came unannounced and uninvited. Gajdusek simply showed up at the hospital and began asking questions. "At first glance he looked like a hippie, though shorn of beard and long hair," Zigas said. "He wore much-worn shorts, an unbuttoned brownish-plaid shirt revealing a dirty T-shirt, and tattered sneakers. He was tall and lean, and one of those people whose age was hard to guess, looking boyish with a soot-black crewcut unevenly trimmed, as if done by himself. He was just plain shabby. He was a well-built man with a remarkably shaped head, curiously piercing eyes, and ears that stood out from his head. It gave him the surprised, alert air of someone taking in all aspects of new subjects with thirst." Gajdusek said he had worked in Melbourne with Macfarlane Burnet, whom he referred to as "Sir Mac." He had heard about Zigas and his work with kuru from Roy Scragg, the acting director of New Guinea's Public Health Department. This introduction struck Zigas as odd. Why hadn't Sir Mac himself told Gajdusek about kuru?

In any case, Gajdusek was finally showing the type of interest in the disease that Zigas thought it deserved. "I was machine-gunned by his numerous questions. I had barely answered one when another would be asked. . . . My suggestion that he accompany us the following day to Okapa and my assurance that he would be in a position to observe several dozen kuru victims of different sex, age, and phases of the disease was met with shining, eager eyes full of enthusiasm."

In fact, Macfarlane Burnet *did* have a reason for declining to tell Gajdusek about kuru. At age 33, Gajdusek had already earned a reputation both for his genius and for his eccentric personality, and Sir Mac considered him something of a loose cannon. "His personality . . . is almost legendary among my colleagues in the U.S.," Burnet would later write. "Enders told me that Gajdusek was very bright but you never knew when he would leave off work for a week to study Hegel or a month to go off to work with Hopi Indians. Smadel at Washington said the only way to handle him was to kick him in the tail, hard. Somebody else told me he was fine, but there just wasn't anything human about him. . . . My own summing up was that he had an intelligence quotient up in the 180s and the emotional immaturity of a fifteen-year-old. He is quite manically energetic when his enthusiasm is roused and can inspire enthusiasm in his technical assistants. He is completely self-centered, thick-skinned, and inconsiderate, but equally won't let danger, physical difficulty, or other people's feelings interfere in the least with what he wants to do. He apparently has no interest in women but an almost obsessional interest in children, none whatever in clothes and cleanliness; and he can live cheerfully in a slum or a grass hut."

Gajdusek's scholarly accomplishments included studies in physics and mathematics before entering Harvard Medical School at age nineteen, where he studied pediatrics, neurology and biophysics. Among his professors, his brilliance and explosive passions had won him the nickname, "Atom Bomb Gajdusek." Since then he had traveled to all corners of the globe, working with some of the world's leading scientists on laboratory and field research into rabies, plague, hemorrhagic fevers, arborvirus infections, scurvy and other epidemiological problems in exotic and isolated populations. He had studied problems of survival on life rafts during World War II and developed techniques for purifying blood products. During the Korean War, he had helped study an epidemic of hemorrhagic fever among the troops. Those studies were followed by medical and anthropological explorations in Iran, Afghanistan and the Amazon jungles of Bolivia, and then a two-year stint studying hepatitis and autoimmunity at Burnet's institute in Australia.

Since his days at Harvard, Gajdusek had been especially fascinated with diseases affecting children. During medical school, he had virtually lived at Boston Children's Hospital, where he was famous for his devotion to young patients, often maintaining round-the-clock vigils at the bedsides of stricken children. After finishing his work with Burnet, he was planning to combine his passion for children with his passion for exotic travels by developing a research project called the "Program for the Study of Child Growth and Development and Disease Patterns in Primitive Cultures." He believed that studying pre-industrial societies could provide valuable insights into human health problems. While based in Australia, Gajdusek had made medical expeditions to Australian aboriginal communities with the Royal Flying Doctor Service, and in 1956 a medical survey of several remote populations in New Guinea and New Britain. In keeping with his desire to study some "primitive cultures," he had arranged to join Mac Burnet's son, Ian, on a New Guinea expedition to previously unvisited groups and to spend several months on pediatric studies with Stone Age peoples.

Other than this brief tour, though, the Australians had no intention of letting their eccentric American guest run amok and unchaperoned among the Highlanders. They were dismayed to discover how quickly he was capable of developing his own agenda. One night's talk with Dr. Zigas was enough to convince Gajdusek that the Fore were suffering from a new, lethal neurological disease—exactly the type of scientific challenge he was looking for. He immediately abandoned his plans to travel with Ian Burnet and joined Zigas on a trek into Fore territory. After seeing the ravages of kuru firsthand, he became completely obsessed with the disease. Within a week he had drafted a letter to Joe Smadel, his former superior at the Walter Reed Army Medical Center, providing detailed and graphic descriptions of the kuru cases he had witnessed.

"I am in one of the most remote, recently opened regions of New Guinea," Gajdusek wrote, "in the center of tribal groups of cannibals only contacted in the last ten years and controlled for five years—still spearing each other as of a few days ago, and only a few weeks ago cooking and feeding the children the body of a kuru case, the disease I am studying. This is a sorcery-induced disease, according to the local people; and that it has been the major disease problem of the region, as well as a social problem for the past five years, is certain. It is so astonishing an illness that clinical description can only be read with skepticism; and I was highly skeptical until two days ago, when I arrived and began to see the cases on every side. Classical advancing 'parkinsonism' involving every age—found overwhelmingly in females although many boys and a few men also have had it—is a mighty strange syndrome. To see whole groups of well-nourished healthy young adults dancing about, with athetoid tremors which look far more hysterical than organic, is a real sight. But to see them, however, regularly progress to neurological degeneration in three to six months (usually three) and to death is another matter and cannot be shrugged off."

The Australians, meanwhile, were not pleased. Suddenly they felt that *they* had first claim on any investigations into the disease. Gajdusek received a cordial but blunt letter from Sir Mac, thanking him for his "extremely interesting" reports and "invaluable" help, and asking when he intended leaving "Australian New Guinea" so that kuru research could become an "Australian affair."

In reply, Gajdusek dashed off a lengthy letter providing more details about the cases he had seen. "I should like to remain in Australian New Guinea until I have exhausted what little I can contribute to this kuru problem on the spot," he wrote. "At the moment, I consider myself the most qualified pediatrician—both clinical and investigative—in the Territory.

. . . I doubt that there is anyone around or likely to soon be around who can complete these studies any better than I. I therefore consider it a duty both to kuru patients and to my intellectual curiosity to stick to it for a month or longer, as the matter works out."

As for Sir Mac's suggestion that he had invaded the territory of other researchers, Gajdusek diplomatically alluded to the complete absence of any other actual researchers on the scene. "Here on kuru research," he stated, "we could immediately use a dozen workers—epidemiologists, microbiologists, and pathologists; two dozen would not hurt or exhaust the problem, and the quicker they arrive, the better. . . . The problem of medical investigation is an open field, and one that to me has always been noncompetitive."

In a letter some months later to Joe Smadel, Gajdusek expressed himself more frankly: "Zigas and I are now preparing a paper for submission to the U.S. journals. . . . We both see clearly that unless we work out and publish our preliminary and very extensive studies, Zigas will be cheated out of anything by administrative super-structure. Secondly, I suspect a good deal of jealousy by the Australian sources shortly, as the word crops out. The fact is, that besides Zigas and myself, no other medical man in the world has investigated or seen the disease, excepting for a few administrative M.D.'s who saw some cases for a few hours, when Zigas brought them out of the region to 'civilization.' " In short, Gajdusek said, Sir Mac's "interests are here, but no one is doing a thing."

Come hell or high water, Gajdusek planned to stay. "I have the 'real thing' in my hands," he told Smadel. "I tell you Joe, this is no wild goose chase, but a really big thing. . . . I stake my entire medical reputation on the matter." He was prepared, if necessary, to support the research out of his own pocket, figuring that "on my own I can hold out for one or two months and still have enough to get home via Europe." He was hoping, however, that Smadel could come up with some money to buy axes, beads, tobacco and other items that the natives would take in trade so Gajdusek and Zigas could "purchase bodies (along with autopsy permission) and food for our patients."

By this time, the Australians were livid. As far as they were concerned, Gajdusek was a sneaky interloper, a medical pirate who had used the pretext of a brief visit to New Guinea as an excuse to intrude where he had not been invited. Roy Scragg, New Guinea's recently-appointed Director of Public Health, sent a bluntly worded radiogram stating that the Australians would be sending a doctor of their own soon to look into the matter. Scragg reminded Gajdusek that he had not received authorization to undertake research among the Fore, and advised him "on ethical grounds" to "discontinue your investigations."

Impossible, Gajdusek shot back in a hastily-scribbled reply: "Intensive investigation uninterruptible. Will remain at work with patients to whom we are responsible."

The next letter came from Scragg's superior, Dr. John Gunther, who expressed amazement "that you had the discourtesy not to call upon me or make some contact with me while you were in Port Moresby. . . . Without sponsorship by Sir Macfarlane Burnet or his Institute, you have come to this Territory and are working in a field that we had proposed for Sir Macfarlane. . . . Whilst I agree that there may be scope for more and more research within this area, I believe it was grossly unethical for you to enter the area, as you have done, without the approval of either Sir Macfarlane, Dr. Scragg, or myself."

The Australians could fume and sputter all they liked. As a practical matter, they knew it would be difficult to absolutely

force Gajdusek to leave. Simply *finding* him could be a challenge as he moved about in the eastern Highlands of New
Guinea, which comprised several thousand square miles of
largely uncharted, mountainous terrain inhabited by warring
tribes of cannibals. And Gajdusek was moving around a *lot.*
Over the course of the next eight months, he performed one
of the most remarkable feats ever undertaken in medicine, a
two-thousand-mile marathon trek by foot through Fore territory. Since geographic maps of the territory did not exist, Gajdusek drew up maps himself along the way, as well as
recording native customs in the process of drawing a detailed
clinical and epidemiological profile of kuru. He was also
rapidly teaching himself to communicate in the eleven native
languages spoken by the groups afflicted with the disease.
(Among his other talents, Gajdusek was a brilliant linguist
who would eventually boast of speaking a dozen languages.)

Zigas, who accompanied Gajdusek, found this odyssey "the
most trying experience in my seven years in the mountainous
jungles." During a single six-day sojourn, for example, "the
climb of about 7,000 feet was such that we had to ascend
hand over hand. Once attaining the ridge, we then had to
descend to 3,000 feet, and then climb another ridge for about
6,000 feet; like a yoyo, straight up and down for long, strenuous hours. There we encountered the major environmental
hazard—the swampy sago country. Here we all suffered badly
from leeches, which were extremely numerous and aggressive.
Every member of our party also developed bleeding legs and
feet each day from the trek. Another hazard was afforded by
wild bees. . . . Mosquitoes were also a problem. . . . The final
hazard was the long, razor-sharp elephant grass. Try as we did
to avoid contact, when we lightly brushed against it the sharp
edges would cause deep cuts."

During these travels, Zigas was amazed by Gajdusek's strength and endurance. "Upon our arrival in a village after the most strenuous 'thrills,' soaked to the skin, numbed and short-winded, Jack and I would have to rest for a while. Carleton, however, would immediately commence to interview the villagers and collect blood specimens. There was a smack of fanaticism in the way he collected blood from every willing person, including infants, regardless of sex or age."

Gajdusek's remarkable charisma with children helped him recruit a "cargo line"—an entourage of boys, some as young as five or ten, who volunteered to help carry supplies and who served as interpreters of the native languages. They enabled Gajdusek to cross streams and ravines by constructing suspension bridges of vine or by balancing tree trunks on rocky outcrops. Without their assistance, he would have been helpless. With them, he achieved miracles. He came to see himself as their "Pied Piper," enticing the children to follow him with "the sincerest notes in my repertoire. All else is but exercise for these tunes, and all work is but practice for the pipes."

In the absence of a proper laboratory, Gajdusek set up makeshift facilities at first in the one-room home of Patrol Officer Jack Baker. They used the dining table to examine patients and perform autopsies. Unwashed plates and bottles of rum from dinner sat on the table alongside a typewriter, a microscope, and enamel wash basins containing the human brains that Gajdusek was extracting from kuru victims. Later the natives built a separate house for Gajdusek, along with a field laboratory. They were simple, thatched-roof structures with bamboo mat floors, lacking running water and electricity, but Gajdusek and Zigas managed to obtain laboratory reagents and essential equipment that they used to carry out a host of tests: blood counts, hemoglobin determinations, urine tests, and assays of brain and spinal fluids.

After tempers cooled, the Australians began to supply valuable laboratory backup at Macfarlane Burnet's Hall Institute. Although Sir Mac said he was "still considerably irked at Gajdusek's actions," he admitted that "there is little doubt that he has the technical competence to do a first-rate job. . . . I have a sort of exasperated affection for Gajdusek and a great admiration of his drive, courage, and capacity for hard work. Also, there is probably no one else anywhere with the combination of linguistic ability, anthropological interest, and medical training who could have tackled this problem so well."

In the space of five months, Gajdusek identified 750 people suffering from kuru, 50 of whom had died since his arrival. The disease was responsible for half of all deaths occurring among the Fore. A clear pattern was emerging, confirming his early observation that kuru tended primarily to afflict children and women. Through numerous interviews, Gajdusek concluded that the disease was a relatively new phenomenon. It had emerged some decades before first European contact, which had been made by German Lutheran missionaries just before World War II. In the space of a few decades, it had grown from a rare problem into a devastating plague. It was killing so many women that it was jeopardizing the ability of the Fore to reproduce themselves. Extinction of the tribe was beginning to seem like a real possibility.

For therapy, Gajdusek tried every medicine he could secure: antibiotics, antimalarials, antifungal drugs, aspirin, vitamins; anticonvulsives, detoxifiers, tranquilizers, drugs against roundworms, parasites and multiple sclerosis. On the theory that male hormones might account for the low rate of incidence in men, he tried injections of testosterone. He tested

Fore food and water for toxic substances and found nothing. He treated them with nutritional supplements, to no avail. His patients suffered with stoicism as he loaded them with painful shots of everything from crude liver extract to cortisone to antibiotics. None of these treatments showed any ability whatsoever to halt or even slow the inevitable fatal course of the disease.

Efforts to identify the cause of kuru were equally frustrating. Gajdusek took samples of blood, urine and feces, as well as culture swabs for fungi, bacteria and viruses. If patients agreed he would also perform lumbar punctures to examine their cerebro-spinal fluid. He scoured the native landscape in search of unusual plants, spiders, fleas or mites that might carry some previously unknown neurotoxin. He carefully sifted epidemiological data in hopes of finding some factor common to all the victims. The disease was occurring in clusters of people, suggesting that it was probably infectious. But the classic symptoms of infection never showed—no fevers, sweats or changes in white blood cells or in cerebrospinal fluid. He sent back tissue samples to labs in Melbourne, Port Moresby and the National Institutes of Health (NIH) in the United States. Clinical tests in those labs found no antibodies that could be linked to the disease. He arranged for small laboratory animal inoculations using ground-up autopsy tissue samples from kuru victims and injecting them into mice and other test animals, but the animals all stayed healthy.

The Fore, meanwhile, had developed their own theories about the disease. They believed that sorcerers cast their spells by stealing items intimately associated with their intended victims—their excrement or leftover scraps of food—binding it up in a "magic bundle" with special pieces of bark, twigs and leaves, and burying it to the accompaniment of a chanted curse.

Periodically the sorcerer would return to the spot and beat the bundle with a stick, causing the victim's symptoms to intensify.

The Fore punished suspected sorcerers with a ritual revenge called "tukabu"—brutal, murderous beatings, bashing in heads and crushing genitals with stones and wooden clubs. As the number of kuru cases rose, so did the level of desperation among the Fore, until ritual murders were causing as many deaths as the disease. "With the disease progressing relentlessly to speedy complete helplessness and death before our eyes, the Fore nation in turmoil because of it, and with ritual murders and savage killings in reprisal for kuru sorcery comprising the major administrative problems in the region at the moment, we certainly feel we should be doing more for our patients—even if these trials are based on the most remote chances of benefit," Gajdusek wrote. "Therapeutically, we are licked. Sorcery seems as good an explanation for kuru as any we can offer them."

Gajdusek was certain that victims' brains held the key to understanding the disease. Whenever possible, he performed autopsies in which he extracted the brains, preserving them in formalin for later laboratory examination. For lack of proper equipment, he performed his first autopsy using a carving knife, working at 2:00 a.m. by lantern light in a native hut surrounded by a howling storm. Until then, the natives had been friendly and cooperative as he poked and prodded and stuck them with needles. It was another thing entirely, however, to watch him cut open someone's skull and plop the brain into a smelly jar of chemicals. Other victims' survivors were reluctant to let him remove tissue from their family members, and some of the Fore suspected that he was taking the brains so other people could eat them. He advised his colleagues back at the National Institutes of Health to treat each brain they received as though it would be their last. By August, 1955, his relationship with the Fore had begun to deteriorate, and some families were turning angry. It was difficult to stay calm when surrounded by angry cannibals, but Gajdusek and Zigas struggled on. "It looks as though further autopsy materials may be unobtainable," Gajdusek wrote in a November letter to Joe Smadel. "The natives have given up on our medicine; they know damn well it does not work, and I am fighting verbal battles in Fore, bribing, cajoling, begging, pleading, and bargaining for every opportunity to see a patient, and strenuously working tongue muscles for hours, for every day we get a patient to stay in the hospital, accept therapeutic trials, etc., etc."

By December, Gajdusek was preparing to leave New Guinea, discouraged by the absence of visible progress toward identifying the cause of the disease. As he packed, another spat erupted with the Australians, who thought they should be entitled to retain possession of his field notes. Wearily, Gajdusek pointed out that not only did they belong to him, but it would be impossible for anyone else to decipher his handwriting.

Spongy Brains

At the National Institutes of Health (NIH) in Washington, neuropathologist Igor Klatzo was assigned to examine the sixteen kuru brains that Gajdusek had managed to obtain. Klatzo was dismayed at the condition of some of the brains, which Gajdusek had removed without proper tools. Twelve of the brains, however, were in remarkably good condition. Klatzo and his technician photographed them, impregnated them with wax, and pared them into microscopically thin slices which were placed on slides and stained. Under the microscope, Klatzo saw for the first time the visible evidence that something unusual had happened. The brains were riddled with gaping holes and strange plaques—flower-shaped waxy buildups of a protein called amyloid. Kuru brains had holes where neurons used to be, accompanied by enlarged astrocytes, the star-shaped cells that attach themselves to blood vessels inside the brain. Klatzo had never seen anything like it before.

"Whatever the problem was, it didn't look to me as though it was caused by toxicity, or by heredity, or by infection," Klatzo recalled. "I was forced to think very hard about what the condition did resemble, and suddenly, something clicked." He remembered an obscure neurological disease that he had heard about back in his days as a medical student in Germany. It was so obscure that he had to search the German medical literature to find any reference to it—Creutzfeldt-Jakob Disease, a condition so rare that only 20 cases had ever been reported. Microscopic examinations of the brains of CJD victims had shown similar signs—enlarged astrocytes, holes, and amyloid plaques.

Klatzo's insight led to another in the spring of 1959, when a museum in London hosted an exhibition based on Gajdusek's kuru research. By chance, one of the visitors to the exhibit was William Hadlow, a young American veterinarian working on scrapie research at Bill Gordon's research laboratory in Compton. Looking at Klatzo's microphotographs of kuru brain sections, Hadlow was struck by their similarity to the spongy holes he had observed for years in the brains of sheep afflicted with scrapie. As he read Klatzo's pathology report and case studies of kuru, he was struck by other parallels: similar behavioral changes; the absence of antibodies or other response from the immune system; the inability to isolate a causal agent; and, of course, the unbeatable nature of the disease on its irreversible trajectory toward death. Hadlow became the first person to theorize that kuru might be a human version of scrapie.

In the absence of other explanations, the scientists studying kuru were moving steadily toward the opinion that it was a genetic disease transmitted by inheritance. This explanation was hard to reconcile with the rapid way the disease had emerged and multiplied within the Fore population, but researchers had failed in every experimental attempt to induce the illness by infecting test animals. Based on his background with scrapie research, Hadlow quickly realized that there was a flaw in their methodology. They were testing for kuru on the assumption that it was a normal virus or bacteria—the type of condition that doctors refer to as an "acute infection." Acute infections show symptoms within days or weeks after exposure. Accordingly, Gajdusek's team had only observed their test animals for a few weeks after inoculation. But what if kuru was caused by a *subacute* infection, a "slow virus" like scrapie? With an infection that slow, nothing *could* happen within the time frame of Gajdusek's experiments.

Hadlow began corresponding with Gajdusek and published a letter detailing his theory in the British medical journal, *The Lancet*. In late 1959, he toured the United States, talking to U.S. sheep farmers about methods for controlling scrapie. Gajdusek showed up at his first lecture and began pressing him for more information. After learning of Iceland's experience with scrapie, Gajdusek traveled there to study their theories on slow viruses. Following their model, he persuaded Joe Smadel to let him launch a new series of tests—expensive experiments, using monkeys and chimpanzees as test animals. It was important to test on primates because of their similarity to humans and because they had a sufficient life-span to allow long-term observation. To oversee the experiments, Gajdusek selected Dr. Clarence Joseph Gibbs, Jr., a career scientist whose administrative competence was the perfect counterpart to Gajdusek's stormy genius. At first, Gibbs didn't want the job. "Goddamn it," Smadel told him, "you're going to Gajdusek. You are going to give stability to an otherwise unstable program."

While Gajdusek continued his travels to the South Seas and other exotic locales, Gibbs held down the fort at the National Institutes of Health. He oversaw the creation of the Patuxent Wildlife Center, a research lab occupying 5,000 acres of secluded park in the Maryland countryside. Caretakers were hired, and Gibbs purchased a colony of 54 chimpanzees, squirrel, macaque and other monkeys. In August of 1963, scientists began their attempt to kill these animals by injecting them intracerebrally with ground-up brains of human kuru victims. They were lively, likeable animals, and the researchers gave them human names—Daisy, Hermann, George, Georgette.

In New Guinea, meanwhile, a husband-and-wife team of anthropologists, Shirley Lindenbaum and Robert Glasse, carried out further investigations among the Fore. Their sponsor was Dr. John Bennett, a specialist in mathematical genetics who was convinced that kuru was caused by the presence of a single, dominant gene. In previous encounters, Zigas had come to perceive Bennett as one of the conspirators in the Australian intrigues against Gajdusek. Zigas even hated Bennett's handshake, which "was like a wet cloth, cold and clammy. I dropped it as one would a burning coal. He looked to me more like a garden gnome than an academician." Worse, Bennett had offered to make Zigas "director of kuru research," on condition that he disassociate himself from "Gajdusek and his collaborators." Zigas considered this offer "the most blatant piece of bribery I had ever seen. His ill-mannered address and offensive overture stunned me. I felt stricken by emotional dysphoria at the thought of selling out one's friend."

On the basis of his genetic theory, Bennett was proposing a "eugenic" solution to the kuru problem, placing the Fore under strict quarantine and prohibiting migration of tribal leaders from their own ethnic areas. The policy was supported by Roy Scragg, the director of public health for New Guinea who had clashed previously with Gajdusek. Zigas became embroiled in a heated argument when Scragg ordered him to "submit a written statement that no accommodation was available for Gajdusek" as a "pretext for the postponement of Carleton's return." Zigas protested, but Scragg "simply smirked. And the faster I advanced arguments against his policy relating to Carleton and eugenics, the more he smirked. As it dawned on me that I was in fact struggling for the right to proper research, I became more vocal. . . . An exchange developed with charges and countercharges made on both sides. Scragg had finally said that now as in the past I had acted in a cowardly way toward 'controlling Gajdusek.' I contained my anger with difficulty. He dared to judge and accuse me of cowardice. Why and how was I to 'control' Gajdusek, the genuine researcher? My impulse was to charge Scragg, choke him, blind him."

Lindenbaum and Glasse, however, proved to be the genuine article—careful researchers, respectful of the Fore, and adept at forging relationships with the natives. After nine months in the field, they had amassed genealogical and chronological data that thoroughly exploded Bennett's genetic theories. As recently as fifty years previously, the Fore said, kuru had not existed at all. It first appeared in the north Fore territory around the turn of the century, and since then had spread southward. It had spread so rapidly in living memory that there was no way a genetic model could explain it. Bennett accepted their report with polite disappointment and encouraged them to continue their research.

The Cannibal Connection

The team's next breakthrough was inspired by a suggestion from R.W. Hornabrook, an epidemiologist from New Zealand. Hornabrook had also clashed with Zigas and Gajdusek, but his advice to Lindenbaum and Glasse provided precisely the focus they needed. "Go and find out," he said, "what it is that the adult women and children of both sexes in the Fore tribe are doing that the adult men are *not* doing."

Lindenbaum had formed a close relationship with a number of Fore women and began to interrogate them more closely. Gradually, the anthropologists realized that there were important differences in the way men and women practiced cannibalism. The practice of eating dead relatives was not an ancient tradition but a newly introduced custom, practiced first around the turn of the century by a group of elder women. Over the years the practice had caught on, especially among women. Partly this was because women had less access to other food sources than Fore men.

The Highlanders in general showed a social pattern marked by constant warfare and severe sexual discrimination. They cultivated food in vegetable gardens, and kept pigs which were a constant source of friction between neighbors who quarreled over whose pig belonged to whom, and who was responsible for the destruction of whose garden. They had no formal way of resolving their disputes. Instead, they engaged in perpetual, intermittent clan warfare based on continually shifting alliances among neighbors. Their leaders were called "Big Men," and their authority stemmed in large measure from their fearless leadership in acts of aggression against rival groups. During battles, which were fought up close and personal, they would verbally abuse their opponents with insults similar to the ones you might expect to hear among feuding boys on a school playground: "You are weak like babies, we are strong like wild pigs." "We make you eat woman's vulva." "We make you eat our shit and drink our piss."

Big Men would also broker marriage arrangements, in which the groom's kin would purchase the bride through payment of pigs or other valuables. The rules against marriage within a clan meant that women were often sent to marry members of neighboring, warring tribes, and the fact that your sister was likely to someday marry your enemy contributed to attitudes of suspicion and discrimination against women. In some of the Highlander societies, men learned to shun female companionship from an early age. Adolescent males and young men went into periodic seclusion to free themselves from the polluting aspects of female contact. They especially feared contact with menstruating women, believing that it could sicken a man, cause vomiting, turn his blood black, corrupt his vital juices, wrinkle his skin, dull his wits and eventually lead to a slow decline and death.

Outside of marriage, men and women lived largely separate lives. Boys beyond eight or ten years lived in separate houses with the men, who hunted wild animals and kept the meat for themselves. Women raised pigs, but the men ate the better meat, leaving the entrails for women and children, who supplemented their diet with vegetables, frogs, insects or rats. They were also responsible for preparing bodies for burial, and although eating of the dead was a rite of respect, love and mourning, simple hunger also seemed to play a role. Older widows even began attending funerals of people to whom they were only distantly related, joining in the mourning rituals so they could catch a bite of the deceased afterward. Men rarely joined in the feast, and when they did, they ate the good parts, leaving the women with the brains and other internal organs.

With these facts established, Gajdusek and Gibbs had a theory capable of explaining how kuru had originated and spread. In 1965, Gibbs attended a meeting on scrapie in France and explained the hypothesis: Creutzfeldt-Jakob Disease, which was similar to kuru, appeared to occur "spontaneously" at very low rates of incidence in the human population. No one knew what caused these cases, but they seemed to occur everywhere in the world. Normally, these spontaneous cases would die without infecting anyone else. Among the Fore, however, the unique context of ritual cannibalism had given the disease an opportunity to multiply and develop into an epidemic.

Of course, Gibbs admitted, all of this was hypothetical, simply a theory. The experiments with monkeys had been initiated almost two years previously, and so far they had shown no signs of illness. Without sick monkeys, there was no direct evidence that the disease could be transmitted infectiously. Moral considerations precluded the possibility of attempting experimental transmission directly on humans. If the monkey experiments failed, Gajdusek and Gibbs would have no way of testing the theory further.

Upon conclusion of the conference, Gibbs flew back home from France. He had barely walked in his front door when a phone call came from the Patuxent Wildlife Center. Something odd was happening with Georgette, one of the chimpanzees.

Gibbs didn't bother to unpack. He drove straight to the laboratory to see for himself.

• • •

Georgette was indeed shaking with kuru tremors, and she wasn't alone. Daisy was also showing signs. Both of their faces had taken on the frozen, blank expression that Zigas and Gajdusek had noted as one of the classic symptoms. The similarities to kuru were so striking that at first Gibbs could barely believe what he was seeing.

Over the next several weeks, Gibbs watched as Georgette and Daisy deteriorated. Then Hermann fell sick, and then George. Gajdusek was in Australia, but he made his manic presence felt by phone, issuing a stream of directives for autopsies and examinations. Georgette's brain was flown to England for examination by Dr. Elizabeth Beck, a neuropathologist. Her report confirmed that Georgette's brain showed the same type of microscopic lesions as in brains affected by kuru. Autopsies of the other animals showed identical results. Under the microscope, the brains were so full of holes that they looked like Swiss cheese. The results provided dramatic, unambiguous proof that kuru could be transmitted as an infectious disease.

How the Wise Men Brought Malaria to Africa

by Robert S. Desowitz

This 27-year-old essay from Natural History *illustrates how efforts to improve living conditions in Africa altered the ecosystem, leading to outbreaks of malaria.*

Once upon a time (but not too long ago) there lived a tribe deep within the Dark Continent. These people tilled the soil to raise crops of roots and grains, for they had little meat to lend them strength. Illness often befell them, but even so, in this dry land they were not overly troubled with the fever sickness brought by the mosquito. Now in the Northern World there was a powerful republic that had compassion on these people and sent their Wise Men to relieve the mean burden of their lives. The Wise Men said, "Let them farm fish," and taught the people to make ponds and to husband a fish called tilapia.

The people learned well, and within a short time they had

dug 10,000 pits and ponds. The fish flourished, but soon the people could not provide the constant labors required to feed the fish and keep the ponds free of weeds. The fish became smaller and fewer, and into these ponds and pits came the fever mosquitoes, which bred and multiplied prodigiously. The people then sickened and the children died from the fever that the medicine men from the cities called malaria. The Wise Men from the North departed, thinking how unfortunate it was that these people could not profit from their teachings. The people of the village thought it strange that Wise Men should be sent them to instruct in the ways of growing mosquitoes.

At about the same time, from 1957 to 1961, that this ecological misadventure was taking place in Kenya (for it was no fable), on the other side of the world the impoverished villagers of the Demerara River estuary in Guyana were enacting their own calamity. Striving to improve their lot by converting from subsistence farming of maize and cassava to cash-producing rice, they cleared the region for rice fields, displacing the livestock that formerly abounded in the villages. Mechanization on the roads and fields also progressed, bringing a further diminution in the numbers of domestic animals, particularly of cattle and draft oxen.

The major potential carrier of malaria in the region was the mosquito *Anopheles aquasalis,* but since subsistence agriculture created few suitable water collections for breeding, the mosquitoes were present in only modest density. The wet rice fields, however, provided an ideal larval habitat and the vector population increased rapidly. Even so, all would have been well had there been no alteration in the livestock since the genetically programmed behavior of *A. aquasalis* directs them to prefer blood meals from domestic animals rather than humans. With the disappearance of their normal food supply, however, the hungry mosquitoes turned their attention to people. Intense mosquito-man contact now enhanced malaria transmission to epidemic proportions. And so the combination of rice and tractors contrived to bring malaria to the people of the Demerara River estuary.

These two stories of ecological disaster are not isolated phenomena. In the endemic regions of the tropics, many human activities create and multiply the breeding habitats of malaria-bearing mosquitoes. Thus, in their very attempts to break from the bondage of poverty, food shortage, and ill health, third world peoples too often sow the seeds of disaster in the form of malaria.

Malaria of humans is caused by four species of a protozoan parasite of the genus *Plasmodium*—*P. falciparum, P. vivax, P. malariae,* and *P. ovale.* While all four species of parasites can produce debilitating illness, only *P. falciparum* is sufficiently virulent to cause death. The complicated life cycle is, in the main, the same for all species. Two hosts are required: man and a mosquito of the genus *Anopheles.* Infection in man begins with the bite of the mosquito, which injects sporozoites, microscopic threadlike forms, into the human host. The sporozoites enter liver tissue, where they divide asexually to form daughter cells. A single sporozoite may give rise to as many as 30,000 daughter cells. After a sojourn in the liver that may last from several weeks to months or even years, depending on the species and strain of parasite, the cells are released from the liver and enter the circulation, where they invade red blood cells.

Within the red blood cells the parasite grows, the nucleus divides, and in a manner analogous to the liver phase, ten to sixteen daughter cells are produced. The red cell finally bursts, freeing the daughter cells to invade new red blood cells. Since the cycle is synchronous, it causes periodically recurrent episodes of chills and fever—hallmarks of malaria infections.

Several days after the onset of the blood phase, new forms appear within the red blood cells. These sexual stages, the male and female gametocytes, undergo no further change until ingested by the feeding mosquito. A marvelously adaptive process has evolved in which the gametocytes are mature and infective to the mosquito for only a short period of the day. This period of infectivity occurs at night, matching the time that most anopheline carriers take their blood meal.

In the mosquito stomach the gametocytes are transformed into male and female gametes and fertilization occurs. The fertilized female gamete penetrates the mosquito stomach wall, coming to rest on the exterior surface where it forms a cystlike body, the oocyst. Within this cyst intense cytoplasrnic reorganization and nuclear division take place, and as many as 10,000 sporozoites form. The formation of the oocyst takes seven to fourteen days, depending on temperature and other factors. Upon maturation it bursts, releasing the sporozoites, which invade the salivary glands. The mosquito can now infect a human when next it feeds.

The anopheline mosquito is the critical link in perpetuating the malaria parasite, and the nature of man-mosquito contact greatly influences the level of endemism. An important factor in this relationship is the life cycle of the mosquito to interaction with its environment. Each anopheline species has characteristic biological and behavioral traits that determine its interaction with man and other hosts. Thus, the selection for breeding water, host upon which to feed, and resting behavior are genetically controlled characteristics, which may or may not place a particular anopheline mosquito in proximity to man. In many regions of the tropics, human activities, particularly those associated with agriculture, alter the environment, producing suitable breeding sites and increasing the likelihood of human contact with malarial mosquitoes.

Of all the agricultural practices that alter the natural tropical ecosystem, rice culture is one of the most important in creating optimal conditions for malaria transmission. Rice farming requires large, open areas of water, also the preferred habitat of many of the most efficient anopheline carriers of malaria. These conditions are especially evident in new rice fields, where the young plants are placed well apart. Also, the generation time of the mosquito is accelerated in the sun-elevated temperature of the exposed water, and breeding is prolific. In addition, a relatively large body of standing water increases the humidity of the surrounding biosphere, and the higher humidity prolongs the mosquito's life. The longer a mosquito lives, the more people it bites during its lifetime.

A vicious series of events may develop beginning with the intense man-vector contact. Because rice culture is seasonal, peak densities of mosquitoes generally occur for relatively short periods. The limited transmission period prevents the development of a protective immunity. When farmers are incapacitated by malaria during the planting season, crop production suffers, leading to economic loss and food shortage.

The ecological changes described above have been excellently documented in a study carried out on Kenya's Kano Plain rice development scheme. Prior to establishment of the rice plots, the Kano Plain landscape was characterized by villages of scattered huts, maize farms interspersed with seasonal swamps and water holes in which *Pistia* plants grew. In this unmodified environment, 99 percent of the mosquito population were *Mansonia*, a non-vector of malaria, while only 1 percent were *Anopheles gambiae*. After the land was modified for rice fanning, 65 percent of the mosquitoes were *A. gambiae* and 28 percent *Mansonia* (the other 7 percent were another variety). Similar alterations in mosquito populations following the introduction of rice fanning have occurred in such diverse areas of the world as Venezuela, Tanzania, India, Syria, and Morocco, where until 1949 the French colonial government had, for health reasons, banned rice growing.

In the tropical world the ecosystem undergoing the most rapid and extensive alteration for human purposes is the forest. These alterations have frequently resulted in an intensification of malaria, often out of all proportion to the small degree of disturbance created.

Within the intact tropical rain forest there are relatively few species of mosquitoes that transmit human malaria. Not only are there few permanent or semipermanent water collections but also the main anopheline carriers prefer sunlit breeding sites and avoid shaded conditions. But breeding conditions abound in the exposed water collections created when the forest is cleared by the farmer digging his plot of ground, by tractors and other machines used for lumbering, and by the rutted roads used to service the new settlements.

Conversely, on at least one occasion, the creation of forests has also led to problems. When the cacao industry was begun in Trinidad, a man-made forest of immortelle trees was planted to provide the shade required by cacao plants. Certain South and Central American anophelines, showing the remarkable specialization a mosquito species may have, breed exclusively in water contained in the bromeliad epiphytes of the forest gallery. When bromeliads colonized the high immortelle trees, *A. bellator* proliferated, carrying malaria to the plantation workers and their families.

In an attempt to solve their problems—overcrowded cities, land shortage, and the need for establishing a market economy—political and technical authorities in the developing countries have opened new lands to agricultural development. Such projects commonly begin with the clearing of the jungle, followed by resettlement of transmigrants and cultivation of cash crops such as cotton, tobacco, rice, and corn. But all too frequently, the ecological alterations brought about by deforestation, creation of irrigation systems, and other human activities enhance the vector population. More often than not, settlers brought into the area have had little exposure to malaria and have not acquired sufficient immunity to protect them from severe attacks. For example, within eight months of leaving nonmalarious urban centers of Java for an agricultural project in south Sulawesi, 32 percent of the settlers were stricken with malaria and the enterprise nearly collapsed.

The ability to protect the settlers by chemical control of the anopheline carrier has often been negated by prior use of agricultural insecticides such as DDT. Spraying crops to protect against the ravages of destructive insects and spraying for the control of anopheline vectors involve different and generally incompatible techniques. Where insecticide has been broadcast for crop protection, the anopheline population contracts sub-lethal doses that eventually render it physiologically or behaviorally resistant. Thus, by the time antimalaria measures are instituted, the avenue of mosquito control by chemical means has been closed.

Cost accounting of the economics of ecological alteration is difficult, particularly when the influence of a single factor, malaria, is traced through a complicated, interacting mosaic. One excellent exercise in ecological-economic sleuthing was carried out by the Pan American Health Organization after new lands had been opened for agricultural development in Paraguay. In the first year of the scheme, malaria seriously afflicted the settlers and the impact of the disease reduced the over-all production of cash crops—tobacco, cotton, and corn—by 36 percent. Worker efficiency, particularly during the harvest, which coincided with the height of the malaria season, was reduced by as much as 33 percent. Debilitated by malaria, the farmers devoted their limited energy to their cash crops, abandoning for subsistence all but the easily cultivated, but starchy, manioc. As a result, deterioration of their nutritional status was added to the burden of malaria.

In subsequent years there was reduced expansion of farms in the malaria-struck region. Tragically, the Paraguayan government and its advisers were aware of the health hazards, but having expended a large amount of capital on land development, it had too little left in the kitty to secure its "beachhead" by providing the infrastructure of health, education, and other social services. The Paraguayan experience has been repeated throughout the tropics.

In addition to agricultural development, third world governments have expanded electrical power resources in their attempts to promote economic development. But along with the kilowatts, rice, and fish, these giant hydroelectric and water impoundment schemes also produced malaria. The seepages and canals have provided optimal breeding habitats for malaria mosquitoes in such geographically diverse projects as the Aswan Dam in Egypt, the Kariba project in Zambia, the Lower Seyhan project in Turkey, and early in its history, the TVA scheme in the United States. On occasion, the dams and man-made lakes were not in themselves responsible for ecological change leading to intensified malaria transmission but, rather, set in motion a train of events that led to the situation. Construction of the Kalimawe Dam in Tanzania, for example, extended cultivation far beyond the original plots. This made it necessary to graze cattle, the preferred host of the local *A. gambiae*, farther from the villages. When the cows were no longer kept near houses at night, the peridomestic mosquitoes were diverted to man, and malaria transmission was intensified.

Ecological alterations have been caused not only by man's struggles toward progress but also by his conflicts; throughout the course of history the environment has been a casualty of war. This ecological havoc has often created conditions conducive to malaria transmission in both temperate and tropical regions, and epidemics of malignant malaria have victimized military personnel and civilians.

During World War II, for example, the bloody fighting near Cassino, Italy, destroyed dikes containing the rivers. Anopheline mosquitoes bred profusely in the flooded areas and bomb craters. Malaria, possibly introduced by foreign troops, occurred in its most violent form, with some villages totally infected and suffering a mortality rate of 10 percent. But it was in the Vietnam conflict that a new and devastating tactical strategy was applied—the ecosystem became a deliberate target of massive destruction. The use of aircraft-spread herbicides for the defoliation of forests and destruction of crops introduced a new dimension to the horror of war. Scientists throughout the world were alarmed, and a number of studies were conducted to determine the consequences of defoliation.

One such study, that of the congressionally funded National Academy of Sciences committee, included an investigation of epidemiological-ecological interactions in the defoliated mangrove forest south of Saigon, a region known as the Rung Sat. This area, repeatedly sprayed with herbicide, had become a desolate, barren wasteland denuded of virtually every living tree. Studying an intact mangrove forest as a control, the NAS medical ecologists did not detect any breeding sites of anopheline mosquitoes. Other mosquitoes were abundant but the Southeast Asian mangrove ecosystem was not the kind of real estate suitable for anophelines. In the Rung Sat, however, the mosquito population consisted largely of *A. sinensis* and *A. lesteri*. Malaria was endemic throughout the region.

Again, rice seems to have been the final ecological culprit. As people were deprived of their main livelihood from woodcutting, they turned to rice culture in the less saline areas of the dead mangrove. The rice fields provided ideal breeding sites for the two anopheline specks.

In Vietnam the main foci of malaria are found in the montane forests, the vectors being *A. macutatus,* breeding in exposed hillside streams, and *A. balabacensis,* living in sunlit standing collections of water. Removal of the forest's shade cover created new breeding sites for these mosquitoes. At the time of the NAS study in Vietnam the temperature of the war was too hot to permit on the ground study, but when the study group flew over the deforested mountain areas, they saw a landscape typically colonized by these two efficient vectors. Notably, American soldiers fighting in the Vietnam highland forests were severely afflicted by malaria, with the attack rate in some units as high as 53 cases per 1,000 troops per day.

Paradoxically and cruelly, in the absence of an effective control program, a community's welfare and stability often depend on continuous, intense exposure to malaria. Under these conditions, as in the agricultural villages of Africa and Southeast Asia, malaria accounts for high infant mortality;

some 40 percent or more of the children under the age of five may die of the infection. Those who survive, however, develop a protective immunity, and adults, the productive segment of the community, remain relatively free of the pernicious clinical manifestations of the infection. Usually, the high infant mortality is compensated by a high birthrate, and so a population equilibrium is achieved in which the workers are sufficiently healthy to provide the community's food requirements.

The relatively slow acquisition of functional immunity to malaria and its concomitant cost in infant life have led to several disasters of good intent and have presented new moral dilemmas for discomfited public health workers. The Western and Western-trained health professionals have held, by tradition and education, the philosophy of the importance of individual human life and the right of every member of the community to good health. The heroic efforts begun in the mid-1950s to realize global eradication of malaria were rooted in this moral premise. But where these control programs were successful in the developing tropical countries, population numbers increased rapidly, while technical-agricultural resources to accommodate the burgeoning community lagged sadly behind. Following a successful control scheme in Guyana, infant mortality was reduced to one-third its former rate; in one study group, a sugar plantation village, the population rose from the precontrol level of 66,000 in 1957 to 110,000 in 1966. Some students of public health, as well as health officials, are now beginning to question the wisdom of instituting such measures as malaria control unless they are accompanied by effective population control programs or by expansion of resources to feed, clothe, educate, and house the increased population.

The disasters of good intent are related to malaria's tendency to return several years after a successful mosquito control program. During this period the mosquito populations have once again returned to former density, and the human population's collective immunity has waned. Wherever it recurs under these circumstances, malaria is explosive and clinically severe.

It is doubtful whether progress for the peoples of the developing world, as we define progress, can be achieved unless malaria and other diseases draining their intellectual and physical energies can be brought under control. Yet the enterprises of progress contribute, with monotonous regularity, to the deterioration of health. What is now required is a holistic approach. Engineers, agronomists, epidemiologists, economists, ecologists, demographers, cultural anthropologists, and political leaders must all contribute to the planning, execution, and evaluation processes. In this way, malaria and many other diseases can be reduced to a manageable state if not actually eradicated. Human needs demand it; human intelligence and ingenuity must be turned to achieving a degree of progress, rather than disaster, for the peoples of the third world.

Death of a Continent
by Brian O'Reilly

The financial consequences of AIDS in Africa will play an enormous role in the increasingly bleak outlook for the continent and its inhabitants. This story originally appeared in the November 13, 2000 issue of Fortune.

At a trade show in Botswana, one of the most prosperous countries in Africa, a well-dressed crowd gathers to celebrate. The party, hosted by the De Beers-Botswana diamond monopoly, has attracted the nation's best and brightest: Miss Botswana Universe, business leaders, government ministers. They sip chardonnay and chatter with the aplomb of Manhattan socialites. In conversation, a television anchor calmly dismisses the extent of the AIDS epidemic in Botswana and disputes whether HIV even causes AIDS. Amid the good cheer, a jarring thought intrudes: Half the people in the room will probably be dead in five years.

The HIV/AIDS epidemic moving through Africa is unlike any plague the world has ever seen. It is bigger: More than 25 million Africans have already contracted the virus that will kill them within a decade; millions more will die in decades to come. It is crueler: Most epidemics decimate a population with frightening but merciful swiftness. This one travels in slow motion, hiding in its victims for years before they die slowly and painfully—but spreading all the while. And it is wreaking economic devastation in ways that epidemics rarely do, by attacking not the weak, the young, and the elderly, like most plagues, but killing off the most productive people in Africa: the well educated, the prosperous, the powerful, the parents of young children.

Although AIDS will claim many more victims than the medieval Black Death, which killed 20 million, Africa is in denial about the disease. Whole governments are struck dumb, unwilling to acknowledge the cause and extent of AIDS, and paralyzed by a lack of resources to fight it. The disease is strangely silent, almost underground. You don't see emaciated victims on city sidewalks in Botswana, South Africa, or Zambia. The people who return to their villages to die don't tell their families why they are sick. Wives don't admit that their husbands died of AIDS, and vice versa. Nurses at a small, tidy hospital near the gold mines west of Johannesburg say they have treated just 38 cases of AIDS among the 26,000 miners—even though miners have one of the highest HIV infection rates of any group in South Africa.

"Africa will never be the same," says Clem Sunter, an executive director of Anglo American, South Africa's gold and diamond mining colossus. "We don't know yet what the social and economic consequences will be, but AIDS will define the shape and structure of society in Africa. It is the biggest thing, bar none." Yet in South Africa, says Sunter, the silence on the subject is so great that "you can hear that proverbial pin drop."

AIDS lurks in rank back alleys and in plushly carpeted bedrooms; in thousands of grass-hut villages, where parents sell their last cow to raise money for a dying son or daughter; in hundreds of corporate boardrooms, like the one where eight of 12 top executives are HIV positive; in national parliaments, like Malawi's, where more than a dozen ministers have died; in the armies of Angola and Congo, where, according to the CIA, half the soldiers are HIV positive; in Lusaka, the capital of Zambia, where a TV ad promotes FUNERALS FOR YOUNG AND OLD!; in Uganda, where coffins with see-through portholes are pulled along the streets behind bicycles.

The statistics are stupefying. Africa, with just 11% of the world's population, is home to almost 75% of the people with AIDS. In Botswana, a Texas-sized country that borders South Africa, a United Nations report says 35% of men and women between 15 and 50 are HIV positive; if the infection continues to spread at its current rate, a 15-year-old Botswanan boy will have an 85% chance of dying of AIDS. South Africa, with by far the largest economy in Africa, has more HIV-positive people than any country in the world—about four million. (Except where noted, the statistics in this story are from the United Nations or the U.S. Agency for International Development—USAID).

Ironically, apartheid shielded South Africa from the epidemic. For years the country was isolated politically and economically by a global boycott protesting its treatment of blacks. When apartheid ended in 1991, South Africa's borders became more porous, trade with its neighbors resumed, and HIV exploded. Barely 1% of the country's adult population was infected ten years ago, vs. nearly 20% today. The economic boom that came with the end of apartheid is now in serious jeopardy. Other African countries, already among the world's poorest, are seeing AIDS devour modest gains in life expectancy and economic growth.

Not all of the continent is suffering. The disease is rare north of the Sahara, where less than 1% of the population is HIV positive. In Africa's western bulge, around Senegal and Liberia, only about 3% are infected. More conservative sexual practices in the mostly Muslim northern countries and a less contagious form of HIV in western Africa may explain the lower rates.

By contrast, in a broad swath south and east of Lake Victoria, the rates are hideously high. The measure of devastation is not revealed in coarse economic statistics like GNP. The vast majority of Africans are subsistence farmers whose output doesn't even appear on macroeconomic radar. The GNP of countries with valuable natural resources isn't much affected by AIDS either. Botswana, with about two million people, has only 6,000 diamond workers. Nigeria, with 121 million residents, employs just 10,000 in the petroleum business. Because there are enough healthy workers to quickly replace those who fall ill, diamond and oil production don't slow down. Lack of rain or shifting prices of key commodities produce more dramatic shifts in economic activity than AIDS.

GNP statistics don't just fail to measure Africa's misery— they are beside the point. Although it sounds callous to say so, the world would hardly notice if Africa's entire economy disappeared overnight. Nigeria might be the exception; it provides 18% of the U.S.'s oil. Still, the combined economic output of the 45 sub-Saharan African countries, including South Africa, is about the same as Argentina's. Many African countries, despite populations of eight or ten million, produce about the same amount of goods and services as an American town of 60,000 people. What little manufacturing there is—Africa accounts for a fraction of 1% of the world's manufactured goods—is mostly for local consumption. AIDS in Africa, in other words, won't make a blip in your retirement portfolio.

Where it should be making a very large dent but mostly isn't—because the developed world is inured to suffering in Africa—is in our collective conscience. AIDS is genocide by Mother Nature, and it is killing a continent. For millions of families, the devastation is immeasurable. Because HIV attacks the immune system, a victim typically develops a series of debilitating diseases before dying. A farmer's ability to work is diminished, of course, but so is the entire family's, as his wife, children, and relatives spend more time caring for him and less time tending crops. A study by a farmers union in Zimbabwe reported that maize production dropped 61% after the death of a breadwinner. Cotton and vegetable production fell by half. Families that grow more lucrative but labor-intensive crops to sell to cooperatives or along the roadside often must revert to subsistence farming when the male adults become sick.

Funeral expenses are large because the many friends and relatives obliged to attend must be fed. But the economic damage doesn't end with the funeral. Families desperate for a cure sell their most valuable assets to pay for treatment. The cattle go first, then the plow or the bicycle used to carry crops to market. "I know the family is on the brink of ruin when the bike or the plow get sold," says Jill Donahue, an American working to make small-scale credit available in Zambia. Even healthy farmers can be haunted by AIDS when their children move to cities to seek more opportunities, contract the virus, then return to their parents' village for care. "In Botswana, we go home to die," says Prisca Tembo, an AIDS prevention worker in the capital city of Gaborone.

In the course of impoverishing itself, a family frequently enriches people with virtually no modern medical skills. Traditional healers treat 70% of AIDS cases in Botswana. They charge $10 to $20 per visit to patients whose yearly income might be $500. For that they offer prayers and burn incense, or suggest that a victim cure his AIDS by having sex with a virgin. "If you want to get rich, come to Botswana as a traditional healer," says Karen Sorensen, a Lutheran missionary.

Benjamin Raletatsi runs an AIDS education center on the outskirts of Maun, a town of 35,000 in northern Botswana largely devoted to tourists viewing wildlife at the nearby Okavango Delta. Painted a cheery red, the center is near the riverbank, perhaps 500 dusty yards from the center of town, so visitors can come and go discreetly. Raletatsi says he urges AIDS victims returning to their villages to tell their families the disease is incurable though he admits that most parents would ignore the disclosure. Robert Clay, a USAID health official who specializes in fighting AIDS in Zambia, saw this firsthand when a woman in his office got sick. "Her parents did everything to save her, even flew her to Harare [in Zimbabwe] for treatment," says Clay. "Her mother told me, 'I've already lost four sons to AIDS. I'm not going to lose my daughter.' " The daughter died too.

Every family with AIDS is miserable, but each family is miserable in its own way. Take, for example, a woman married to a prosperous man who dies of AIDS. Even if she manages to avoid catching the disease from her husband, she is subjected to family rituals that condemn her to poverty and make her vulnerable to the virus. The dead husband's brothers often claim his property—his home, his savings, his life insurance, even death benefits from his employer. Although some countries have outlawed property grabs, tribal customs can be too strong for widows to resist. A widow must be "cleansed" by her husband's brothers to avoid becoming an outcast. "Cleanse" is a cruel word, for it means having sex with the husband's brothers to wash away his spirit. The brothers may refuse to perform the cleansing until the widow hands over all her property.

Sometimes a widow is assigned to a brother and cared for as a spare wife, but not always. One of the saddest scenes in Africa is the women sitting by the roadside in Lusaka, pounding rocks with a hammer. They collect the rocks from a nearby field, then break them into coarse gravel. If they are fortunate, a contractor may come by and buy the gravel for a few cents, to mix with cement. Many of the women appear to be starving.

In families with young children, AIDS causes its own special problems and heartbreak. First, the father dies. A year or two later, the mother dies, having caught the virus from her spouse. They leave a handful of orphans who, maybe, can move in with grandparents. But the grandparents have often spent their savings on their dying son or daughter. At a time when they were counting on their children to support them in their old age, they instead have grandchildren to feed. Many such families face starvation. Even orphans taken in by relatives who can feed them have bleak futures. Zimbabwean orphans are half as likely to finish school as other children, mainly because their foster parents can't afford the minuscule school fees.

Africa's orphan problem is immense. The United Nations estimates that there are 13 million. David B. Dunn, the U.S.

ambassador to Zambia, says that more than 25% of Zambia's children are orphans. The number is rising fast in the slums of South Africa. Driving through the rutted, narrow streets of Alexandra, a township on the outskirts of Johannesburg, health worker Linda Twala points out small hovels. "Six children in there. No parents. Four children in that one." Some youngsters eke out a living making trinkets to sell by the roadside, but often the girls become prostitutes, catching and spreading HIV, and the boys become petty criminals.

As a pediatrician in Zambia, Mutinta Nyumbu watched as AIDS invaded her country more than a decade ago. Now it has invaded her home. "I got a call yesterday from my cousin that another cousin had just had an AIDS-related stroke. He has eight children. I am already caring for my three sisters and their children. All their husbands have died of AIDS. How can I care for eight of my cousin's children? I just learned about this yesterday. I can't stop thinking about it." Other workers at her Lusaka health center have similar problems. "I've lost 20 relatives to AIDS," says Andrew Mlewa. "Now it's hitting my dad. He divorced my mom and married another woman. She died, her kids died. I have to drive eight hours to see him."

Certain sexual practices have hastened the spread of AIDS. African men often demand "dry sex," claiming that a dry vagina is more pleasurable. The women are forced to use herbs and other means to dry themselves, but dry sex results in vaginal tears and abrasions that increase the rate of HIV transmission. Most men in eastern and southern Africa are uncircumcised, which seems to make them more vulnerable to HIV. Africans also have high rates of untreated syphilis, gonorrhea, and other sexually transmitted diseases, increasing by 20-fold their chances of catching HIV.

Condom use is rare; a Zambian survey found that only 6%

of people reported using a condom in their last encounter with a spouse or live-in partner. Nils Gade, head of the Society for Family Health, a nonprofit organization in Zambia that distributes condoms, says Africans know, intellectually, that unprotected sex leads to AIDS. "If you quiz them on it, 95% of their answers are correct," says Gade. "But their behaviors don't change. It's like talking to teenagers about smoking. They know it kills, but they do it anyway." Gade says attitudes are changing, but slowly. "Ten years ago when our workers went into bars and tried to distribute condoms, they got thrown out. People would say there was no such thing as AIDS. Now they know."

Many men take young girls as partners, assuming they are less likely to have the virus than older, more sexually active women. Other men believe they will cure their own HIV by having sex with 100 virgins; they claim the virus is passed on to the girls. A survey of 1,600 children in Lusaka found that 25% of 10-year-old girls in poor sections of town had had sex, and 60% of 16-year-old girls. In countries where sex with young girls is most prevalent—Zambia, Botswana, Zimbabwe—overall rates of HIV are far higher.

Well-educated, well-paid men are at particularly high risk for AIDS. They can afford to give clothes and a cell phone to a girlfriend in exchange for sex, to pay a prostitute, or to set up a mistress in an apartment. Men in authority can often demand sex from powerless underlings. The AIDS rate among schoolteachers, who are mostly male, is astoundingly high. About 85% of the teachers who died during the past few years in the Central African Republic were HIV positive. The reasons aren't entirely clear, but it appears that many demand sex from the children or their mothers in lieu of fees. Because women tend to be less educated than men and much less likely to have a job, it doesn't take much wealth to buy or barter for sex. A South African truck driver making $400 a month is rich to local women who don't earn that much in a year. Men from Mozambique and Tanzania leave their families to work in South African mines. Bored, lonely, and well paid, they spend their money on prostitutes.

Educated women appear to be just as much at risk as their male counterparts. They, too, are mobile and can travel and party in ways poor rural women cannot. "This is a very materialistic society," says a black American woman who has worked in Johannesburg for many years. "Two men I know were told by their girlfriends that their cars weren't good enough, that if the men didn't get new cars, they would leave." In Zambia, educated women past their teens are three times more likely to contract HIV than uneducated ones.

No society can afford to lose its best and brightest, least of all African countries that have yet to recover from a century of colonialism that excluded virtually all blacks from higher education and managerial positions. When Rwanda won independence from Belgium in 1962, it had one African high school graduate. Congo had five black college graduates at independence. Many African countries pursued Soviet-style socialism for decades after independence, with disastrous economic results, but schools, at least, began to improve. When some governments finally began privatizing utilities, mines, and factories in the 1980s, a new generation of managers began mastering the intricacies and terrors of capitalism. After decades of economic decline, the growth rate in southern Africa nudged up to 4.5% a year in the early 1990s.

Now the homegrown managerial talent Africa so desperately needs is being decimated. The prevalence of HIV among skilled and highly skilled workers in South Africa is predicted to peak at 23% and 13%, respectively, in five years. That is below the rate for miners, 29% of whom are expected to be HIV positive by 2005. Like all epidemics, AIDS in Africa will eventually run its course. Unlike measles or smallpox, HIV is relatively hard to catch. As fewer people engage in risky sexual behaviors, the infection rate will stabilize and eventually decline.

Until that happens, the impact on companies will be considerable. Kristina Quattek, an economist in Johannesburg for the British brokerage ING Barings, says that while just 9% of people in South Africa's finance and insurance industries are estimated to have AIDS, "99% of them are skilled or highly skilled." In city after city, executives tell of hiring two or three trainees for each new managerial job in anticipation of attrition from AIDS. In Zambia, corporate expatriates who come for a year or two to train executives find their plans to return home thwarted. "We've had people set to leave, then they discover that the people they trained are dying of AIDS," says Margaret Mwanakatwe, who until recently ran the Zambia Investment Center in Lusaka and is now head of the Barclays Bank there. "Sometimes they stay, but sometimes the government won't extend their visas because it wants Zambian citizens to fill those jobs. So the expat leaves, and the company struggles."

A large, foreign-owned copper-products company in Zambia offered to provide life insurance for its dozen or so senior managers. None would take the HIV test the insurance company required, says a company consultant. The foreign owners have increased their investment, but they will probably have to bring in expatriates to run the plant. "That's not something we wanted to do," says the consultant. "We wanted to hire and train local people."

Roseanna Price, president of Mars International, an HMO-like firm in Zambia, studied the potential impact of AIDS on several Zambian industries for a doctoral thesis. She says the electric-power sector is likely to get clobbered. Eight of 12 top executives at one power company are HIV positive, she learned. The crews that maintain power lines and equipment are also becoming less efficient, as skilled workers take time off to attend funerals or get sick and die themselves.

Other observers in Zambia say AIDS has diminished rail-road track crews—the last thing a landlocked country, already hampered by the high cost of getting goods to markets, can afford. A large Lusaka bank is ailing because so many of its loan officers have become ill. "The bank does all the right things," says Price. "It offers all kinds of benefits and treatment. It knows sick people are walking around the office, but it doesn't know how to get them to treatment." The employees, afraid that co-workers will learn of their illness, won't visit the bank's HIV centers.

It is difficult to calculate the full damage AIDS will wreak on Africa's formal economies, because companies themselves don't have a good grasp of the problem. Lisa Cook, deputy director of the Center for International Development at Harvard, says the center did a survey of 2,000 companies in 20 African countries and got wildly inconsistent answers. "It was hard for companies to even know how to answer. AIDS masquerades as so many different diseases. Their workers leave, and no one knows exactly why." Many companies apparently don't want to know what lies ahead. "People are burying their heads," says Gillian Nur Samuels, who led a study for Metropolitan Life, an independent South African insurance company. "Most companies feel it won't impact them. They are trying to ignore it."

It seems almost forgivable—sometimes—that people avert their eyes from such crushing problems. Even if no other

African caught HIV again—which is inconceivable—the plague would continue to kill for a decade or more. In the absence of treatment to stop or delay the onset of symptoms, that's how long it takes for a victim's immune system to be destroyed and for AIDS to begin. The infection rate in many countries is continuing to rise; 3.7 million more Africans became infected last year, 22% more than in 1995.

Kristina Quattek, the Barings economist in Johannesburg, was near tears as she talked about what might have been in South Africa. "There were such great prospects for investment and trade after apartheid ended," she says. "Mandela was President, and we were avoiding overt racial tension. The country had everything going for it. We had a well-developed financial section, and the government was doing all the right things on macroeconomics and trade. We hoped that foreign investment would flow. That hasn't happened. It seems so unfair."

The governments of some of the countries most affected by AIDS have been alarmingly inert, even counterproductive, in attacking the problem. By far the worst offender is Thabo Mbeki, President of South Africa. He claims to have personally investigated the disease and doubts that HIV leads to AIDS. He questions whether AZT, one of the most useful medicines in slowing the progress of HIV, really works. (Nelson Mandela spoke out only once about the disease while he was President.) Partly as a result of Mbeki's foolishness, South Africa refuses to give AZT to pregnant women close to term—even though it greatly reduces the spread of HIV to newborns. Dr. Colin Eisenstein, medical director at Anglo Gold, the nation's biggest gold-mining company, is furious. "If there were a foreign army camped out on our border that we knew was going to kill 25 million people, we'd do something about it," he says.

In other African countries, civil servants work to educate people about AIDS, but top leaders are invisible, rarely speaking out in public and failing to convey a sense of urgency. Only in Uganda, perhaps the hardest-hit country in the world, has the President, Yoweri Musevini, led the charge. The prevalence of HIV in Uganda has actually declined over the past 20 years, from 15% to 8%. Miss Botswana Universe, Mpule Kwelagobe, is crusading against AIDS in her country. In Zambia, where government workers, foreign charitable organizations, and groups like the U.S. Agency for International Development have worked hard, there are signs of progress. In areas of Lusaka, the HIV rate among 15- to 19-year-olds has dropped sharply. Robert Clay, the USAID employee, says it's not clear whether rates will stay down as the youngsters become more sexually active, "but it's a beginning."

Perhaps the safest place to be in southern Africa is at a large, foreign-owned company. After Ford flew in officials from the Centers for Disease Control and Prevention to educate local executives, its plant in Pretoria, South Africa, shut down operations and assembled everyone on the factory floor for a day of seminars, a speech from the local CEO, and dramas on AIDS. John Strydom, Ford's medical director in Pretoria, installed condom dispensers and plastered walls with laminated posters proclaiming Ford's obligations to HIV-positive workers. He has brought in employees' wives to teach them about prevention and is now planning to invite their teenage children. Strydom, a burly Scot with a thick brogue, says he is hopeful that the HIV rate among Ford's workers will stay below the national average. Most live with their families and walk to work, which may enable them to avoid the temptations that befall so many itinerant Africans. He admits, though, that he doesn't know what's in store. "We just hired 300 new workers. What percent of them are HIV positive? How many will be dead in two or five years? I just don't know."

AIDS in Africa presents the rest of the world with a complicated, maddening dilemma. How do compassionate people even begin to help? Whom should they help first? The terminally ill suffering from painful AIDS-related infections? Orphans who face a life of Dickensian bleakness? Healthy people who need to be educated about how to avoid contracting the virus in the first place? Or should the U.S. and other rich countries allocate money to provide the expensive medicines, widely available in the West, that can delay the onset of symptoms for years?

Here's another question: Would any of it make a difference? The billions of dollars wealthy nations have spent on roads and dams and malaria eradication haven't changed the lot of the average African. If African men refuse to use condoms and continue to view women as nothing more than sexual objects, how much sympathy do they deserve? Or are they just as insensitive as men everywhere—and unlucky enough to have been born in a place where 100 variables have conspired to make AIDS so ruinous?

No large-scale solution to AIDS in Africa is possible until the continent's leaders acknowledge their plague and cheap medicine becomes widely available to fight it. In the meantime, there are some things ordinary people can do. Persuade your church to bankroll a village orphanage. Help young girls buy school uniforms and books so that they can attend class. Contribute to an organization that sends medical supplies to nursing stations. Travel to Africa; it needs the tourist dollars. After you've oohed and aahed at the wild animals, visit a U.S. embassy to ask which private and government agencies deserve help.

No matter what well-intentioned people do, the suffering in Africa will linger for decades. AIDS will not come close to killing everyone there, of course, but it is certain to prove more devastating than any epidemic in history. It's as mind-boggling as it is heart-wrenching that as the developed world races over the Internet into the third millennium, Africa is falling ever deeper into poverty and death from a pestilence right out of the Old Testament.

from This Wild Darkness
by Harold Brodkey

The American writer Harold Brodkey was diagnosed with
AIDS in 1993. He kept a journal of his illness. Brodkey
died on January 26, 1996.

October 25, 1995: It is my birthday. And for the first time in my adult life, it matters to me that the age I have reached is a specific number. I am sixty-five years old, but it is not so much that I am sixty-five as the idea of birth and near old age and now death. I do not know at what rate of speed I am moving toward my death. The doctors cannot tell me—the only hard medical fact with AIDS is death. The hard social fact is the suffering. One approaches the end of consciousness—or the end of consciousness approaches one—and strange alterations of the self occur: a hope of cure, a half-belief in treatments that could extend life. (By a year, two years? Three years is so vast a time, one thinks of life as being extended indefinitely if one can hope to live three more years.) The less luck one has, the stronger is one's new conviction in one's luck. This while the doctors back away. They have nothing more to offer. They conserve their energies and the hospital's medical resources, but what it feels like is being locked out of the house when I was six years old. The experience is closer to the early angrier descriptions of AIDS than I had expected it would be for me or others after all these years.

I am sleeping without a detritus of dreams or symbols now, without images, not lions or tigers, not flowers or light, not Jesus or Moses—but a few memories, chiefly of childhood, perhaps because of the night sweats, which I have all day long sometimes. I am rolling down the grassy hill behind the house in Alton. It is twilight. Dark shapes flit in the air—bats, I say now, like a schoolchild answering a question in class. And the birdsong! The pre-DDT birdsong: I had no idea I missed it so harshly. Sing! Chitter! A train travels on the tracks below the cliff, below the limestone bluff. Chug-a-chug, chuff-chuff. The grown-ups sit in those heavy wooden lawn chairs of the 1930s: so still, so handsome. And I, a pudgy child who will not use words yet, this soon after his mother's death, in high-sided shoes and white socks, I am shouting, yelling, in my own sort of birdsong, yelling and grumbling as I roll; stones and pebbles bite into my ribs. I am magnifying my size with the sound I make. Faster and faster I go, then either my father stops me or I curl up against a tree trunk, I'm not sure which.

The change in momentum changed everything, how the light darkened and had a name, like dusk; how the trees and faces emerged and could be named. I remember feeling large from the adventure but small as well, factually small. And because I was in my own mind no one thing, large or small or boy or son of this household, I remember the dreamlikeness of being no one, of being lifted and of being of no important weight. The smells, the grass, my father's shirt—they were more important than I was. I was no one and nothing, about to be devoured by sleep.

I take 300 milligrams of AZT and 300 milligrams of 3TC daily, and my T-cell count is over 100 again. This might be delusive, but I am grateful. I inhale pentamidine about every three weeks. I take between fifteen and twenty pills a day. The cost is astronomical, and so are the fees of the lawyers even when they shave them out of friendship. Tina Brown of *The New Yorker* and Deborah Karl said from the start they would protect us. I don't know if you can understand what such warriors' support means when you are helpless. Kindness always conveys a great deal of meaning about the universe, but perhaps it matters more, shines more brightly, in relation to this disease than to any other at the moment. I think it is because this disease makes an even greater mockery of everything one was before—mentally and physically, socially and erotically, emotionally and politically.

I wish someone would find a cure. I really don't want to die this way. (And I would like to feel my death had some meaning and was not an accident and that it belonged to me and not to those who talk about it.) But at the same time I have to confess that I haven't a great deal to complain about. I often want to go along the street, chanting *Save me, save me, save me,* but I do not do that, partly because almost every act of charity and compassion brings me some meaning and ease. My grandson Harper said, *Are you sick?* And I said, *Yes,* and then he changed the subject. When the visit ended, he made a point of telling me that he liked me quite a lot. I like him quite a lot. He was going off with his other grandfather to

Kenya and South Africa for a few weeks. I told him to whisper my name to the grass when he was in Africa, and he very unsolemnly repeated my words and said he would do it.

Today I cannot find anything in my life to be proud of—love or courage or acts of generosity. Or my writing. My life has been mostly error. Error and crap. It seems to have been a load of crap to have been alive. Everything in language goes dead, in a morbid Rockettes march.

I have not been able to work for six weeks, but when I could I was working on a memoir piece about Frank O'Hara, who introduced me to the work of Pollock and Rothko. Today I was thinking about my first sight of a drip Pollock: the paint hardly dry, and the madness and vitality, the quivering beauty, the shock, the immense, immense, freshness.

I remember Chartres in 1949 before the stained glass was restored. No one I had spoken to and nothing I'd read had prepared me for the delicacy of the colors, the pale blue, a sky blue really, and the yellow. The transcendent theater of the nave while the light outside changed moment to moment—clouds blowing over—and the colors brightening or darkening in revolving whorls inside the long, slanted beams of lady-light. I had never been *inside* a work of genius before.

I have started to die again. I made a recovery with new pills, but then collapsed. I am what is called a disconnector: some measurements of my condition are favorable and others are not, but they move in ways unrelated to one another when they should move conjointly.

I sometimes see in the mirror the strange rearrangement of an adopted child's face in preparation for entering his new household.

I find operatic arias to be very moving now—showy and subtly coarse, technically elaborate, lengthy, embarrassingly detailed and impolitic, un-American, and beyond the hemming and hawing of dialogue.

My dreams are mostly of vacations again and have a still-sweet quality; they even comment on the sweetness of the air and light in the strange, new place where I am a tourist. It is a maybe cheapened version of paradise. The dreams usually end in a gentle drowning, and then I wake.

I ought to have dinner. I haven't eaten or taken my pills— just a little suicide. I mostly live because of Ellen, although I might put on a show if any of the grandchildren were in the apartment. It is unbelievably strange to live when things are *over*, when things are done with. Poor Kundera. It is the unbearable lightness of not-being. What do you suppose an embrace of mine would be worth now?

In New York one lives in the moment rather more than Socrates advised, so that at a party or alone in your room it will always be difficult to guess at the long-term worth of anything. When I first started coming to New York, I was in college at Harvard. This was six years after the end of the Second World War. New York didn't glitter then. There were no reflecting glass buildings but, rather, stone buildings that looked stiff-sided and had smallish windows that caught sun rays and glinted at twilight: rows of corseted, sequined buildings. Driving through the streets in a convertible owned by a school friend's very rich mother, one was presented with a series of towering perspectives leaping up and fleeing backward like some very high stone-and-brick wake from the passage of one's head. Advertising flowed past, billboards and neon and window signs: an invitation to the end of loneliness. New York was raunchy with words. It was menacing and lovely, the foursquare perspectives trailing down the fat avenues, which were transformed in the dimming blue light of the dissolving workday. Overwhelming beauty and carelessness, the city then—one of the wonders of the world.

New York was the capital of American sexuality, the one place in America where you could get laid with some degree of sophistication, and so Peggy Guggenheim and André Breton had come here during the war, whereas Thomas Mann, who was shy, and Igor Stravinsky, who was pious, had gone to Los Angeles, which is the best place for voyeurs. I was always crazy about New York, dependent on it, scared of it—well, it *is* dangerous—but beyond that there was the pressure of being young and of not yet having done work you really liked, trademark work, breakthrough work. The trouble with the city's invitation was that you were aware you might not be able to manage: you might drown, you might fall off the train, whatever metaphor you preferred, before you did anything interesting. You would have wasted your life. One worked hard or not at all, and tried to withstand the constant demolishing judgment. One watched people scavenge for phrases in other people's talk—that hunt for ideas which is, sometimes, like picking up dead birds. One witnessed the reverse of glamour—that everyone is jealous. It is not a joke, the great clang New York. It is the sound of brassy people at the party, at all parties, pimping and doing favors and threatening and making gassy public statements and being modest and blackmailing and having dinner and going on later. (It was said you could get anyone to be disliked in New York merely by praising that person to someone nervous and competitive.) Literary talk in New York often announced itself as the best talk in America. People would say, "Harold, you are hearing

the best in America tonight." It would be a cutthroat monologue, disposable with in passing, practiced with a certain
carelessness in regard to honesty. But then truth was not the
issue, as it almost never is in New York.

Learning to write: I remember the sheer seriousness of the
first acquisition of some sort of public ability, learning
something; learning also the fragility of mental acquisition,
the despair as this new thing slipped from my mental grasp.
You become rigid in your attempt to hold the acquisition; if it
stays, or more exactly, if it recurs, others join to it. Perhaps you
build your daily life around this oddity. You don't let it go
when people talk to you or when fucking or when people
tease your deepest attention. *You are a cold person*, people say
of this trait.

I am an addict of language, of storytelling and of jour-
nalism. I read, not frenziedly anymore, but constantly. I long
to love other people's words, other people for their words,
their ideas. I do dearly love conversation as a self-conscious,
slightly or greatly social climber's art. I love to talk, and I
prefer it by a large amount if nothing depends on the talk, not
money or sex or invitations—just the talk, like experiments in
pure science, or as a funny mix of chemical and electrical
investigation that has to be immediately comprehensible—
and immediately comprehended—and in which no one can
dominate, and dexterity really is all.

Telephoning is a wonderful waste of mind, the vocal do-
jiggers, all of it lost as soon as said. And behold the little faxes.
The little faxes devour the tender gripes.

As someone who is ill, I feel I have only dubious rights to
interrupt anyone else's life, and I try to control access to my
own time. I do not like to watch people wrestle with the fact
of who I am and with my death and what it means to them,

but if one is open about having the disease, such reactions and intrusions are inevitable. I did not really expect to live this long. I do not think I am reasonable, but I do not care if I am reasonable or not.

I have tried some of the new drugs. There is an as-yet-untried one called saquinavir and to get it I entered a lottery for patients with very low T-cell counts, a salvage drawing, I think it's called. I won a lottery once before, in the fourth grade. This time it appears there will be a delay: a special hospital board has been set up to review the lottery and the allotment of the drug—I think it is mostly to prevent doctors from being trapped by sympathy. Or self-importance. There is a rumor that the drug, a protease inhibitor, besides being the weakest of the PI's, is difficult to manufacture. There may well be a shortage and a delay, which means we could all die before we try it anyway.

For me, neurotic (if that word still has meaning) or not, illness had never been a useful reality, never a landscape (or kingdom) of increased sensitivity or heightened storytelling. I remember thinking a year or so ago that if my strength went it would not be possible to think, to write. I have no gift for sickness. And I am not graceful in my dependence.

I did apologize to Ellen once. I said I was sorry, really sorry, to do this to her, to be so much work, and after a rather long pause, she said, "Harold, you were always this much work. All that is different is that I give you meals in bed and I cry when you are in pain. But you were always work."

And I am still writing, as you see. I am practicing making entries in my journal, recording my passage into nonexistence. This identity, this mind, this particular cast of speech, is nearly over.

Late Fall 1995

I am at the end of the list of AIDS drugs to take. I wake frightened now; it is a strange form of fright—geometric, limited, final.

Being ill like this combines shock—*this time I will die*—with a pain and agony that are unfamiliar, that wrench me out of myself. It is like visiting one's funeral, like visiting loss in its purest and most monumental form, this wild darkness, which is not only unknown but which one cannot enter as oneself. Now one belongs entirely to nature, to time: identity was a game. It isn't cruel what happens next, it is merely a form of being caught. Memory, so complete and clear or so evasive, has to be ended, has to be put aside, as if one were leaving a chapel and bringing the prayer to an end in one's head. It is death that goes down to the center of the earth, the great burial church the earth is, and then to the curved ends of the universe, as light is said to do.

Call it the pit, the melodramatic pit: the bottomless danger in the world is bottomed with blood and the end of consciousness. Yet I don't wake angry or angrily prepared to fight or to accuse. (Somehow I was always short of rage. I had a ferocity and will but without rage. I often thought men stank of rage; it is why I preferred women, and homosexuals.) I awake with a not entirely sickened knowledge that I am merely young again and in a funny way at peace, an observer who is aware of time's chariot, aware that the last metamorphosis has occurred.

I am in an adolescence in reverse, as mysterious as the first, except that this time I feel it as a decay of the odds that I might live for a while, that I can sleep it off. And as an alteration of language: I can't say *I will see you this summer*. I can't live without pain, and the strength I draw on throughout the day is

Ellen's. At times I cannot entirely believe I ever was alive, that I ever was another self, and wrote—and loved or failed to love. I do not really understand this erasure. Oh, I can comprehend a shutting down, a great power replacing me with someone else (and with silence), but this inability to have an identity in the face of death—I don't believe I ever saw this written about in all the death scenes I have read or in all the descriptions of old age. It is curious how my life has tumbled to this point, how my memories no longer apply to the body in which my words are formed.

Perhaps you could say I did very little with my life, but the *douceur*, if that is the word, Tallyrand's word, was overwhelming. Painful and light-struck and wonderful.

I have thousands of opinions still—but that is down from millions—and, as always, I know nothing.

I don't know if the darkness is growing inward or if I am dissolving, softly exploding outward, into constituent bits in other existences: micro-existence. I am sensible of the velocity of the moments, and entering the part of my head alert to the motion of the world I am aware that life was never perfect, never absolute. This bestows contentment, even a fearlessness. Separation, detachment, death. I look upon another's insistence on the merits of his or her life—duties, intellect, accomplishment—and see that most of it is nonsense. And me, hell, I am a genius or I am a fraud, or—as I really think—I am possessed by voices and events from the earliest edge of memory and have never existed except as an Illinois front yard where these things play themselves out over and over again until I die.

It bothers me that I won't live to see the end of the century, because, when I was young, in St. Louis, I remember saying to Marilyn, my sister by adoption, that that was how long I wanted to live: seventy years. And then to see the celebration.

I remember the real light in the room; I say real because it is not dream light. Marilyn is very pretty, with a bit of self-display, and chubby, and she does not ever want to be old like Gramma. If she is alive, she would be in her seventies now; perhaps I would not recognize her on the street.

I asked everyone—I was six or seven years old—I mean everyone, the children at school, the teachers, women in the cafeteria, the parents of other children: How long do you want to live? I suppose the secret to the question was: What do you enjoy? Do you enjoy living? Would you try to go on living under any circumstances?

To the end of the century, I said when I was asked. Well, I won't make it.

True stories, autobiographical stories, like some novels, begin long ago, before the acts in the account, before the birth of some of the people in the tale. So an autobiography about death should include, in my case, an account of European Jewry and of Russian and Jewish events—pogroms and flights and murders and the revolution that drove my mother to come here. (A family like mine, of rabbis, trailing across forty centuries, is a web of copulations involving half the world and its genetic traces, such that I, wandering in the paragraphs of myself, come upon shadows on Nuremburg, Hamburg, St. Petersburg.) So, too, I should write an invocation to America, to Illinois, to *corners* of the world, and to immigration, to nomadism, to women's pride, to lecheries, and, in some cases, to cautions. I should do a riff on the issues of social class as they combine with passionate belief and self definition, a cadenza about those people who insist categorically that they, not society, not fixed notions, will define who they are. My life, my work, my feelings, my death reside with them.

My own shadows, the light of New York, sometimes become too much now; I pull the shades. I have been drawing spaceships for my grandsons.

I feel very well, and for a week now, as part of some mysterious cycle, I have felt very happy. Also, today, for no particular reason, I am enormously conceited about my writing. Everyone is more interested in my death. I cannot be bothered with my death except as it concerns my books. When I write it out like this, it is a pose, but inside me, it is very real, very firm, this state, very firm for a while. Actually, all my states are now very precarious, just as if I were dancing except that the motion is that of time, or of my time, and it is this time that might stumble and fall, might seem to—that is what I mean by precarious.

The world still seems far away. And I hear each moment whisper as it slides along. And yet I am happy—even overexcited, quite foolish. But *happy*. It seems very strange to think one could enjoy one's death. Ellen has begun to laugh at this phenomenon. We know we are absurd, but what can we do? We are happy.

Me, my literary reputation is mostly abroad, but I am *anchored* here in New York. I can't think of any other place I'd rather die than here. I would like to do it in bed, looking out my window. The exasperation, discomfort, sheer physical and mental danger here are more interesting to me than the comfort anywhere else. I lie nested at the window, from which I can see midtown and its changing parade of towers and lights; birds flying past cast shadows on me, my face, my chest.

I can't change the past, and I don't think I would. I don't expect to be understood. I like what I've written, the stories and two novels. If I had to give up what I've written in order to be clear of this disease, I wouldn't do it.

• • •

One may be tired of the world—tired of the prayer-makers, the poem makers, whose rituals are distracting and human and pleasant but worse than irritating because they have no reality—while reality itself remains very dear. One wants glimpses of the real. God is an immensity, while this disease, this death, which is in me, this small, tightly defined pedestrian event, is merely real, without miracle—or instruction. I am standing on an unmoored raft, a punt moving on the flexing, flowing face of a river. It is precarious. The unknowing, the taut balance, the jolts and the instability spread in widening ripples through all my thoughts. Peace? There was never any in the world. But in the pliable water, under the sky, unmoored, I am traveling now and hearing myself laugh, at first with nerves and then with genuine amazement. It is all around me.

from Level 4: Virus Hunters of the CDC
by Joseph B. McCormick and Susan Fisher-Hoch with Leslie Alan Horvitz

> *Husband-and-wife team Joseph McCormick and Susan Fisher-Hoch, formerly of the Centers for Disease Control, have spent years tracking the hemorrhagic viral diseases, which include the likes of Ebola. Joe begins the narrative in this selection, which describes an outbreak of the Lassa virus in Chicago.*

It was late in the afternoon, January 13, 1989, and Azikiwe was sitting in his Chicago office, reviewing a blueprint. The phone rang. It was his wife, Veronica. It was unusual for her to call at work, particularly at this hour, when the children would already be home from school. With six boisterous kids, Veronica was kept very busy. It was clear from the sound of her voice that she was upset.

"Azikiwe," she said in her lilting West African English, "it's your mother. Valerie called to say that she suddenly took ill and died."

The blood seemed to drain from his head. Was he hearing her right? His mother hadn't been ill. There had been no warning, nothing. Azikiwe had just been thinking about bringing his parents over for a visit. They had never seen the United States. What a pity that his children barely remembered their grandmother. The oldest boys, Ogbejele and Oyakhi, had a vague recollection of the old lady, but the other four children were just too young.

Realizing he could not afford to surrender to his grief, he picked up the phone and called his boss to explain that he would need some time off. Then he booked a seat on a flight leaving for Lagos, Nigeria, via New York, the next afternoon. He dreaded this trip, and not just because of all the emotions that it was certain to stir up inside him. Even under optimal conditions, the trek was a hassle. He detested the airport at Lagos, one of the most corrupt and inefficient in the world, and then he would have to endure a long journey over treacherous two-lane roads with crazy traffic and police road blocks all the way. But he steeled himself and left.

The journey proved every bit as excruciating as he'd imagined it would be. At least he emerged from Lagos airport with all his baggage. He was bringing gifts for his family, and he had pretty much resigned himself to seeing them disappear. They had not. But then he had to face a six-hour bus ride to Benin City, from which it would be another two hours, again by bus, to Ekpoma, near his native village. In theory, the bus was spacious and air-conditioned. But it was so packed that people were sitting four abreast in rows intended for three. Other passengers were standing in the aisles. Of course, the air-conditioning didn't work. The bus driver drove like a man possessed. Swerving incessantly to avoid smashing into oncoming vehicles, he kept his foot on the gas almost the whole way. The ride was so jarring that several passengers actually fell ill, but with the stoicism bred of the struggle to survive in rural Africa, no one complained.

The routine police road blocks made for an additional nuisance. Money had to change hands before the bus would be allowed to continue on its way. Azikiwe felt like a man blessed just to be off the bus in one piece when he reached Benin City. He made the final leg of the journey in a smaller Nissan bus filled with women returning home from market. There was hardly room for them, let alone for the produce they carried: woven banana-leaf cages of chickens and ducks, sacks of fermenting cassava flour, and tins and bottles of pungent, deep orange palm oil. Many of the women carried dozing babies, which they strapped on their backs in colorful cloth swaddles. Only babies could have slept through all the noise. Noise was part of the experience of travel in rural Africa. Everyone was always talking and gesticulating, trying to make themselves understood over the rumble of the motor and the squealing of frightened animals.

When Azikiwe finally alighted in Ekpoma, he had to shake out his limbs and recover his equilibrium. He was exhausted, but he was unexpectedly exhilarated to be close to home. As he began to search for someone to take him to his village, Ishan, he realized that Ekpoma had grown since his last visit. It seemed curiously unfamiliar, even though he had been there a thousand times. For several minutes, he failed to recognize anyone. He was quite disoriented, a bit uneasy, even frightened. After wandering around for a while, he finally spotted an old friend who agreed to give him a lift on his motorbike. They left his bags in a secure place. One of his brothers would drive back and fetch them.

Arriving at his parents' house, he was overwhelmed by conflicting emotions. Instinctively, he looked for his mother.

Then it sank in: he would never see her again. But he had the consolation of the rest of his family. How wonderful it was to be among them once more. After exchanging greetings with everyone, they all moved into the *bafa,* the traditional thatched pavilion, with open sides to catch the cool breezes, used for family or village gatherings. He found himself gazing at his father. He looked a different man, Azikiwe thought. How much he had aged in the four years since he had last seen him.

When Azikiwe woke, it was the small hours of the morning. He was still on Chicago time. He sat up in bed, alarmed. Something was wrong. Then he realized what it was: the silence. The village was dead quiet. No cars, no engines, no clock ticking, no dogs barking, nothing. He got up from his woven-mat bed and slipped outside, stepping across several sleeping forms. It was still dark. The African night sky was wondrous, clear, and filled with stars that shone so brightly he couldn't believe it was the same sky that he was used to seeing above Illinois. The night air was not so heavy as that of the day, and it even brushed cool against his skin.

He sat down on a low stool near the *bafa* and reflected. He thought about his family and childhood friends. About how most of his educated friends had followed his example by abandoning the life of a subsistence farmer for work in the big cities. Probably none of his friends had been as financially successful as he'd been. But in his disquiet, he thought: to have cut himself off from his roots like this—had it been worth it?

He had never wanted for food or for shelter as a boy. He'd had plenty of adventures while he was growing up. So what was it that drove him away? Boredom? Desire for a better life? He certainly led a comfortable existence in the States, he worked for a top engineering firm, he had all he wanted . . .

but even so, he felt uneasy, as if he had left undone something important and undefined.

The next day, Tuesday, was consumed in preparations for his mother's funeral and the period of mourning that would follow. As the head of the family, Azikiwe also had to see to it that important funeral rituals were carried out. This meant that he had to get in touch with village elders, wise men, drummers, and a juju man (the local shaman, magic man, and traditional healer). Without them, the rituals could not be properly performed, and without these rituals, there would be no way to ensure his mother the smooth transit to the next world that was Azikiwe's responsibility to provide. Of course, all the elders and the juju man would have to be adequately compensated for their contributions. Then Azikiwe would also have to see to it that enough food was stocked away, because the mourning period would last for several days, and many relatives who lived far away would have to be put up for the duration.

The funeral next day required the participation of all members of the family, including the children. Throughout the proceedings, the body remained under the watchful eye of the juju man, who was there to guarantee that the spirits permitted the proceedings to go ahead without a hitch. In Africa, it didn't matter which particular religious faith you believed in; no one ever questioned the existence of the spirit world. It was as much a reality as the things you could touch, the scents of the frangipani, and the whistle of the wind in your ears. In this sense, Azikiwe was truly African in his ability to remain a committed Christian, while simultaneously honoring the power of the spirit world.

The formalities took most of the day. It wasn't until late in the evening that Azikiwe at last had the opportunity to ask his family about his mother's final illness. Surprisingly, no one seemed anxious to talk about it. His sister was rather vague, and his uncles equally unforthcoming. Even his father seemed uncertain. Azikiwe couldn't quite figure out why he in particular was being so reticent. What was the problem? After all, his mother was an old lady—in the demographic context of rural Nigeria, at any rate—and her death couldn't have come as a total shock.

Azikiwe spent the next few days with his family in the expectation that he would leave before the end of the month. But just five days after the funeral, his father started to complain about feeling cold. He said that his back was sore and that he had a headache. Azikiwe went to the local village dispenser to obtain some medication. He was given chloroquine, a drug widely used at the time for treating malaria. Given the prevalence of malaria, it was the therapy of first choice for almost every fever in much of Africa and was doled out much as aspirin is in the West. His father took the chloroquine, but didn't get any better. He began to complain of a severe sore throat and nausea. Soon he was unable to eat, or even to swallow very well. His fever soared. Azikiwe noticed something else even more disturbing. His family begin to recoil in fear from the old man.

It was only then that his sister told him that his father appeared to be suffering from the same illness that had struck down his mother.

The terror that his father's illness provoked wasn't restricted to members of his family. His neighbors were responding the same way. The silence that Azikiwe felt deep in the night had taken on a new meaning. He now heard rumors of juju at work. No one spoke openly. If you said too much, it would touch you next.

While it was true that Azikiwe had grown up here and had absorbed the village culture, he was also a Western-trained engineer. He had been trained to think like a scientist—and, to some extent, like an American. Certainly, he didn't look on disease as a curse. But now he was torn between two worlds, one based on science and rationality, the other on the unknown or the spiritual realm, with all its rituals. In the world in which Azikiwe had come of age, the juju man was master; it was he who was responsible for maintaining order and harmony. Every phenomenon could be explained by juju. If your animals died, it must be juju, and it was necessary to find out who had cast the spell and stop him.

Was Azikiwe's father under a spell?

Apparently, his mother hadn't been the only one who died recently from this strange illness. People, they said, were getting sore throats and dying all up and down the street. No one had any explanation. Why would you die of a sore throat? Nor did anyone know what to do about it. In spite of all his Western training, Azikiwe, too, could see where juju might be the only way to account for what was happening. How else to explain this strange illness? For as long as Azikiwe could remember, there had been stories about the presence of witches in the village. Some people even claimed to know who they were. It was possible—just possible—thought Azikiwe, that there really was a witch at work.

Meanwhile, his father continued to deteriorate. He no longer talked, but only lay in his bed, mute in his agony. Perhaps, Azikiwe thought, this was his father's response to the loss of his wife. Maybe he only wanted to join her in death.

On January 28, his father died.

Azikiwe now had to remain in order to see to his father's burial, but immediately after the second funeral, he left

Nigeria; his job and family responsibilities in America demanded his return. With a heart that beat in pain and a mind full of confusion, he made the preparations for his departure.

Azikiwe was greeted by Veronica at Chicago's O'Hare Airport when he returned on February 1. It was a tearful reunion. He'd lost both his parents in a manner completely incomprehensible to him. Neither the religious support he'd gained from his church nor the spiritual upbringing he'd had as a child offered a satisfactory explanation or consolation. The world of spirits and spells receded, but the sense of loss remained as sharp as ever.

Things hadn't been easy for Veronica while Azikiwe was gone, either. She and two of their children had been bedridden with the flu. Indeed, half of the community had been struck by this epidemic, which was still going on. But maybe things would be better now. After a restless sleep, Azikiwe got up the next morning and reported back to work.

A couple of weeks later in Atlanta, I was preparing an EPI 1, the document that offers a brief description of any epidemiological investigation the CDC has agreed to undertake. It is drawn up upon notification of an outbreak, prior to sending a team into the field. A brief factual account of the situation, the EPI 1 indicates why the investigation is being launched and what it hopes to achieve. The document also includes the names of those involved in any aspect of the outbreak. The EPI 1 for February 15, 1989 reads as follows:

> On February 15, 1989, Joseph B. McCormick,
> M.D., Chief, Special Pathogens Branch, Division of

Viral Diseases, Center for Infectious Diseases, Centers for Disease Control, received a telephone call from Robert Chase, M.D., an infectious disease practitioner in Winfield, Illinois, about a case of suspected Lassa fever in a forty-three-year-old Nigerian-born man who had recently returned from a trip to his hometown of Ishan, Nigeria. Upon review of the patients history, physical findings, and laboratory results, Lassa fever was considered to be highly likely.

Azikiwe had no sooner returned to work than he began to feel feverish. It was now February 3. He reasoned that he was so fatigued and emotionally drained that it was no wonder he felt unwell. Or maybe he'd contracted the same flu Veronica and the children had come down with the week before. His mind was on what had happened in Nigeria. He decided to leave the office early and go home. Yes, he thought, it was probably the flu.

But something nagged at him.

His children and wife had been ill with fever for two or three days, but then they had started to improve. Azikiwe's illness was different. His fever mounted as the days went by, accompanied by an excruciating headache. Aspirin barely touched it. He also began to have a sore throat; he was lucky if he could swallow a spoonful of soup. His children would join him in the evening, since he was unable even to sit at the table, and would try to encourage him to take some food. Sitting at his bedside, they even shared food from his plate.

Veronica and the older children were not unmindful of what had transpired in Nigeria and were naturally worried. A few days later, on February 7, Azikiwe began to complain of an intolerable pain behind his eyes. His fever was still high. Veronica decided that enough was enough: he needed to see a doctor. Bundling him into the car, Veronica drove him to the HMO clinic. The doctor who examined him found that he had swollen tonsils and lymph glands; and some degree of abdominal tenderness. His white blood count was low, but this was thought to be a symptom compatible with influenza. So Azikiwe went home with a diagnosis of flu and a prescription for acetaminophen, which was supposed to alleviate his fever.

On the morning of the eighth, Azikiwe summoned the energy to return to work and somehow managed to make it through the day. But the next day he again left early, after putting in only an hour or so at his desk. As much as he might have wanted this to be the flu, he knew in his heart that this was something worse. Much worse.

He went back to the HMO clinic. In addition to the fever and a painful throat, he told the doctor that he had a bitter taste in his mouth. At no time, during this visit or the earlier one, did Azikiwe mention what had gone on in Nigeria. Nor did the doctor ever ask him whether he'd recently been abroad. Besides, they were in the middle of a flu epidemic; why worry about zebras when herds of horses were thundering through the clinics? Still, Azikiwe's illness was something of a puzzle, since it had persisted for much longer than the flu usually does, and it had become much more severe than would ordinarily be expected in an otherwise healthy forty-three-year-old man.

On the occasion of this visit, the doctor did observe something that he hadn't noticed before. Azikiwe appeared to have pus in his throat. This time, the doctor diagnosed a strep throat, even though the strep screen was negative. Azikiwe was given penicillin and sent home.

He became much worse. On February 12 he developed

bloody diarrhea. Then he began to complain of severe pain in his ribs and back. Veronica noted that he was coughing up thick sputum. She could no longer even get him to drink water, because his throat was so painful. She did not know what to do next.

When Veronica brought him back to the same clinic, he was running a fever of 103°F, which had been present for nine days straight. His systolic blood pressure was low, just over 100, he had marked swelling in the neck, and still more pus on his tonsils. His abdomen was just as tender as before. Veronica made certain to mention to the doctor that he had blood in his stool. Although she was panicked, she tried to bear in mind what Azikiwe had told her. American doctors weren't like they were in Nigeria; they knew what they were doing, so she shouldn't think that they would fail to find the cause of his illness. Now, after these three visits to the HMO, she wasn't so sure.

But once again, neither she nor Azikiwe thought to say anything about the deaths of his parents the previous month. The physician diagnosed strep pharyngitis and hemorrhoids. He continued to treat Azikiwe with penicillin.

A blood test was done to check on a number of things, including the level of his liver enzymes. Remarkably, although his enzymes proved to be sky-high, no one seemed to take note of this. Now Azikiwe was manifesting every symptom necessary to establish a diagnosis of Lassa fever. It was no longer tenable to diagnose his condition as strep throat or even a complicated flu.

Desperate, Veronica took him to another clinic. Not that it did any good. The ear, nose, and throat specialist who saw him diagnosed tonsillitis and doubled the dose of antibiotics. Still, no one asked him about travel.

Again the couple returned home. Completely distraught, Veronica sat by her husband's bedside, wiping his brow, looking after his every need. At least she wasn't alone. The minister at their church was a great support; so were several members of the congregation, who came over to help prepare the meals and look after the children. To Veronica, it must have made more sense to turn to the church and to God, since Azikiwe had now been to four different doctors without seeing any improvement in his condition.

Azikiwe began to slip into a fitful sleep punctuated by periods of incoherent rambling, mostly in his native language. His wife tried to speak to him, but he seemed not to hear her. She collapsed in tears, no longer able to contain her grief.

On the night of February 14, Veronica took her husband to the emergency room of the DuPage County Hospital. The physician who saw Azikiwe in the ER didn't know what to make of this patient. Here was a man who had had high fever for nearly two weeks, who had lost fifteen pounds, according to his wife, and who was obviously confused and very sick. His sore throat had failed to respond to various antibiotics, and now, in addition to bloody diarrhea, he was also suffering from severe nose bleeds.

In spite of Azikiwe's incoherence, the physician could see that he didn't have either jaundice or hepatitis, both of which can cause hallucinations and dementia. By now, it was late at night. The physician admitted the patient, put in an IV to try to restore fluids, and ordered some tests to be run immediately. When the results came back a few hours later, the physician was puzzled and surprised by the level of the liver enzymes. Ordinarily, such a high level might have indicated hepatitis. Yet it was already clear that the patient wasn't jaundiced. Early the next morning, another physician, Robert

Chase, the infectious-disease consultant of DuPage Hospital, came to see the patient. He was the first one to think of asking Veronica about whether Azikiwe had been traveling any time recently. It didn't take him long to establish that Azikiwe had recently been in Nigeria. He immediately realized that he needed outside help and called CDC.

It was a Thursday, and I was sitting in my office working on a paper when Dr. Chase came on the line and began to describe his patient's symptoms.

"Is there anything that can do this sort of thing in Nigeria?" he asked.

"Absolutely," I replied. "Lassa fever. This sounds like a classical case."

After fourteen days of agony for Azikiwe, at least an answer was in sight. But I recognized that the prognosis was not a good one. I told Dr. Chase that Azikiwe was well beyond the stage in his illness when ribavirin, the drug that had proven so successful with Lassa in West Africa, might reasonably be expected to save his life. But, I said, there was still a chance: provide him with all the life-support care possible and hope that it might pull him through the acute crisis of his infection. It might also give the ribavirin time to work against the virus. In West Africa, a patient this far advanced would die—no question about it. But no patients in West Africa ever had the support offered by a modern intensive care unit. It might just work.

"Is it safe for us to intubate him and put in a Swan-Ganz catheter?" he asked.

We had updated and published our recommendations for handling such cases in the United States just a year before, basing them on our experience with Lassa patients in Sierra Leone as well as other published data on hemorrhagic fevers.

This case presented us with our first opportunity to apply our new guidelines. I assured him that he could safely go ahead and intubate and catheterize the patient. I provided him with detailed instructions about how to proceed with Azikiwe's care without endangering the staff. Although it might be too late, Dr. Chase agreed that he would obtain intravenous ribavirin and begin administering it to the patient as soon as he had it in his hands.

I told him that he wouldn't have to deal with the situation alone. I assured him that I would be there later that day with a team from CDC. I put the phone down and dialed the manufacturers of ribavirin. They promised they would get the drug to Chicago as fast as humanly possible. Sue was in Senegal, so I called Cuca Perez, the technician who worked with her.

"Put the lab together, Cuca," I said. "We leave this afternoon."

We needed five hours to put together our mobile laboratory, arrange transportation to the airport, rush home for a bag of clothes, and make the necessary arrangements with the DuPage County Health Department before we could leave for the airport. There were several issues at stake. We had a rip-roaring case of Lassa fever right in a Chicago suburb. A lot of people were going to be interested, and most of them would want to know whether we were at risk of seeing more cases. In one respect, though, we were lucky. With the AIDS epidemic, a heightened awareness had developed among the medical community that was almost totally absent a few years previously. Most physicians and other healthcare workers knew about the risks of infection from blood-borne viruses and excretions. When it came to treating patients, attitudes and practices had changed dramatically. People now automatically put on gloves whenever they handled blood and secretions, and they were taking far greater care to avoid needle-stick injury. Their caution extended even to those patients not diagnosed with AIDS, for the sensible reason that no one could be absolutely certain, without a reliable test, that the person might not be positive for HIV. It was quite possible, I reasoned, that doctors at the hospital, as well as those who'd first examined Azikiwe at the HMO clinic, had escaped contracting Lassa themselves because they'd followed these standard precautionary measures.

Just as Azikiwe's physicians were getting ready to put him on life support, he began to develop a problem often seen in cases of severe Lassa fever: Adult Respiratory Distress Syndrome (ARDS). This is what Jenny Sanders had had in Sierra Leone. Simply put, Azikiwe couldn't get enough oxygen to his blood because his lungs weren't allowing enough of it to pass into his circulatory system. Viral hemorrhagic fevers like Lassa cause extensive damage to the capillary bed, the tiny network of blood vessels that supplies oxygen to all the organs and the tissues. This is particularly true in the lungs, because the blood vessels become leaky and fill up with fluid. It's almost as if the individual is being held under water. To assist his breathing, Azikiwe was placed on a respirator. At the same time, a Swan-Ganz catheter was inserted in order to monitor and manage his failing heart. The willingness of the anesthesiologist to intubate Azikiwe and put him on life support, including a respirator, all on the basis of a recommendation from a physician he had never seen, was a testament to the confidence invested in those of us who worked at CDC.

The measures I had proposed, though, weren't enough. Azikiwe had been on life support for no more than two or three hours before he went into cardiac arrest and died. The ribavirin had not yet even arrived from California.

• • •

Just as I was leaving my office to go to the airport with our team, Dr. Chase called to tell me of Azikiwe's death. This changed our mission. A team was no longer necessary, so Cuca repacked the mobile laboratory. We wouldn't need it unless we had a second case. If more cases did occur, we would be prepared for them. Undoubtedly, several people had been exposed, so further cases were certainly possible. I took with me only one person, a young medical officer named Gary Holmes. The trip to Chicago was to be Gary's first experience with hemorrhagic fever—and a rather dramatic introduction it was, too.

Our objective was to set up a system of surveillance for secondary cases. Then there was another question to deal with.

"What should we do with the body?" Dr. Chase asked me over the phone.

I recommended that he arrange for a postmortem liver biopsy and blood specimen analysis to be done, so that we could be certain of the diagnosis. I also told him to ensure that whoever handled the body wore the appropriate barrier protection of gloves and gown, and at all costs avoided accidents with sharp instruments. I further suggested that the body be embalmed, since cremation was unlikely to be culturally acceptable. Though embalming was likely to kill any residual virus, I still had some anxieties. While whatever happened to the body afterwards was up to the family, I did have one suggestion to offer: at the funeral, they should make do without an open casket.

Once in Chicago, Gary and I talked to anyone who had been involved in the case. Little by little, we began to piece together Azikiwe's story. It became apparent that something might be happening in Nigeria, but we would have to get to that later. Right now, our priority was to ensure that we identified everyone who had been in contact and determine the degree of contact for each one. Anyone who had come into close contact with Azikiwe was put under surveillance for three weeks, time enough for the virus to make itself known if it were present. We decided that the only people with a high risk of infection were his wife and children. So his family was given oral ribavirin.

Two days later, we were in Azikiwe's home talking to his family when Veronica received a phone call from Azikiwe's sister Valerie in Nigeria. She had already been notified about Azikiwe's death. But this wasn't what she'd called about. Since Azikiwe had left Nigeria, other members of the family had been stricken with the same ailment. Another sister, who was twenty-eight, and an eight-year-old cousin had become ill, too. While both of them had recovered, Azikiwe's thirty-six year-old brother, a physician himself, was stricken. He had died almost at the same time as Azikiwe had in Chicago. Valerie told Veronica that the family was making efforts to contact other relatives who'd attended the funeral to discover whether any of them had also fallen ill. But it wasn't easy. Some of them lived far away, and it would take time to get in touch with them. It was a nightmare of suffering for the family.

It seemed to me that we had to get much more information about what was happening. We needed someone on the ground in Nigeria who was an experienced professional. Luckily, I knew our man: Oyewale Tomori, better known as Wale. Wale had worked with us at CDC and was now a professor of virology at the University of Ibadan in Nigeria. Given the unreliability of the Nigerian phone system, I counted it as a minor miracle to get through to him without delay. When I related Azikiwe's story to him, he promised to get out to Ekpoma right away to see whether he could find out what was going on. This was the start of a complex investigation for which we had practically no precedent. The next part of the story belongs to Sue.

Joe and I emerged into the unrivaled chaos of Lagos airport, bleary eyed after twenty-four hours on the go. In all our years of travel, we'd never seen an airport that displayed such total anarchy. In the midst of our confusion, we began to realize that we were being met by two competing parties. One was a representative of our CDC colleagues working in Lagos, and the other was composed of two Nigerians. We had no idea who they were, but they certainly knew who we were, and insistently tried to corral us.

They had tickets for us, they said, adding that we must fly at once to Enugu.

Why Enugu? We weren't sure, but we knew that the reason we had finally received a formal government invitation to come to Nigeria was because of a physician with connections in high places who was based at the Medical School of Anambra State, in Enugu. Otherwise we might never have got into the country. In the six weeks that had passed since Azikiwe's death, we'd been trying to get to Nigeria to find out where he'd become infected—so far, to no avail. So we were obviously grateful to the man who had expedited the process. Whether the two fellows who met us now had any connection with the physician in question was impossible to determine.

"By the way," one of the Nigerians said, "where is the ribavirin?"

Ribavirin, it soon became clear, was an obsession for these gentlemen. They loomed over us while we slumped down on the edge of the nonfunctioning baggage belt, trying to gather our wits. They wouldn't take no for an answer.

"You have to come with us," they asserted.

Then, before we could reply, they repeated, "Where is the ribavirin? Where is the ribavirin?"

They wanted ribavirin. Now. If we wouldn't go with them at once to Enugu, then why didn't we just give them the ribavirin? Where was the ribavirin?

I suppose that we should have expected such a bizarre welcome to Nigeria, after the events of the previous two days. We'd been besieged by phone calls. Calls from Nigerians in high places in the United States, calls from friends of Nigerian friends or relatives of somebody important—whoever. We lost track. One thing was certain: someone in Nigeria was scared of Lassa fever.

And about time, we thought to ourselves.

We had been in touch with Wale Tomori. He confirmed our worst fears: he was finding case after case of Lassa fever. There were rumors of many deaths. So we knew that there was an outbreak of Lassa, maybe more than one, but we weren't sure exactly where. Although we'd brought ribavirin with us, we weren't about to give it to our Nigerian welcoming committee. For one thing, we had no idea what was going on, much less who these people were. For another, use of the drug for Lassa was not FDA approved, and we were authorized to distribute it only as part of an experimental protocol. So we slipped away from the two men, accompanied by our CDC colleagues, promising them that we would bring ribavirin to Enugu tomorrow.

The words "Ribavirin, ribavirin, please give us the ribavirin," were still reverberating in my ears long after I left the airport.

Before anything could be done about investigating the

outbreak, though, we first needed to sit down and discuss the situation with representatives of the Nigerian government. Dealing with the government here is a chastening experience. Nowhere else in the world have we found negotiations to be quite so convoluted. We made the rounds at the Ministry of Health, going from one office to the next. Either one of two things happened: the person we were supposed to see wouldn't be there, or else he would be there and insisted on giving us a lecture about how we were to go about our business. Once he was done, he would remember to add that actually, come to think of it, he wasn't the one we should be speaking to at all; the person we wanted was in another department, but first, of course, we would have to make an appointment. We soon realized that an appointment was no guarantee that anyone would show up.

Occasionally, we'd find some official who would assure us of his cooperation, expounding with such eloquence that I doubted he could be trusted.

Of course, nothing would come of it. We waited, but nothing happened. There were many excuses, but the people giving them to us seldom bothered to make them plausible. It soon became clear that no matter what anyone said, there was only thing they were really talking about: money.

A government official promised to provide us with a vehicle and cover some of the field expenses. We didn't believe him, but, then, I supposed, anything was possible.

Eventually, we decided to leave Lagos for the interior and see what was happening for ourselves. But first, we were interested in finding out whether anyone else Azikiwe had come into contact with—either his friends or his family—was infected. The answer was to be found in the laboratory of the chief virologist of Lagos, whose name was Nasidi. Wale had found the family after our phone call, and had obtained information and some blood samples from them. He'd then taken the samples to Lagos and delivered them into the hands of Nasidi, who also happened to be a good friend of his. Nasidi had received his training in the Soviet Union. When he returned home, he not only had a medical degree, but a Russian wife as well. Although he was a practicing Muslim, he took a pragmatic approach to both religion and life. And he had a very sharp sense of humor. What he didn't have were any reagents to test Wale's samples, so he had to wait until our arrival to process them.

In spite of our jet lag, we unpacked the reagents and performed the tests. We all stood around in anticipation as we waited to read the slides. It was Nasidi who examined them first. We stood beside him, and noted down the results against his list of Azikiwe's family members and friends. Then, wordlessly, Nasidi stood up and allowed Joe to have a look. No one had read more Lassa tests than Joe. Nasidi started jumping around in obvious delight.

"That's it!" he cried. "All the positives are from those who gave Wale a history of Lassa-like disease."

It was the correlation that pleased him, not the plight of the victims. "Then that must have been just about everyone you took a sample from," Joe said, glancing up at me, "because almost everyone here is positive."

The next day, with Nasidi in tow, we were on the road again, bound for Ibadan, a distance of about two hours. There we were hoping to find Wale, so we could hear his account of the outbreak in person. In the back of our truck we carried a liquid nitrogen container for any samples we could gather, as well as gloves and materials to bleed people. That was all. Though Nasidi had a long string of promises of government support, I very much doubted that we'd ever see any tangible evidence of it.

At least we had the use of a vehicle with diplomatic plates, lent to us by John Nelson, the director of the Child Survival Program. In fact, we were entirely dependent on him for in-country support. Without him and the assistance of the U.S. Embassy, we wouldn't have got very far at all. Once again, the U.S. State Department proved to be highly effective. The police had a bad habit of erecting roadblocks at periodic intervals, stopping traffic so that they could extort money: Since they were well-armed, no one was about to protest too strongly. But they were sufficiently impressed by our diplomatic plates to wave us through without subjecting us to harassment.

When we arrived in Ibadan, we immediately went to look for Wale. We found him in great shape. He said that he was doing a lot better than Nigeria was.

"The country is going to ruin," he said. "A beautiful country, a rich country, and the people who are running it are killing everything."

Tribalism was rampant, corruption a way of life, the oil wealth was disappearing, presumably into secret bank accounts in Switzerland and the Cayman Islands, and all over the world Nigerians were acquiring a sordid reputation as drug couriers and con artists. Not a happy state of affairs.

In the days when he worked with us at CDC, Wale had made himself famous by singing riotously while wearing his space suit. His songs were spirited, but there were times when some of us would have preferred to have gone about our business in silence. The technology of the lab didn't allow for this, however, since we were all connected by air hoses. Whether we liked it or not, Wale's Nigerian tunes were piped into everyone's ears.

Wale kept us in suspense about our real destination as he filled us in about his first visit to Ekpoma, near Ishan, where Azikiwe's parents had lived.

"As soon as I heard from Joe about the engineer dying in Chicago, I thought I would go and see what was going on in Ekpoma," he said. "When I got there, I found devastation. Both parents were dead, so were many of his relatives. It was awful. So I found as many family members as I could and took blood samples. It seems that they all became infected about the time of the funerals, probably at the funeral itself. The outbreak there now seems to be over. Some of the dead man's relatives fled in terror to Port Harcourt on the south coast. So I think we will have to go there, too, to find out what happened to them, but we have to go to Enugu first."

Enugu. It was the same place that the Nigerians at the airport wanted to take us. Why Enugu? we wanted to know.

"I'm afraid," Wale said, "that the Lassa epidemic has spread."

How could he be so sure? we asked.

While he was investigating the situation in the village, Wale went on, he happened to attend a meeting at the University at Enugu, in adjacent Anambra State. The subject was HIV. While AIDS hadn't made a significant impact on Nigeria yet, there was good reason to assume that it soon would. Cases of AIDS had already turned up, some in Anambra State itself. In fact, a physician at the meeting informed Wale that there were two AIDS patients in the local hospital. Wale was told that, if he wished, he could take a look at them.

The two patients—a man, Dr. Ikeji, and a woman, Dr. Anamba—were desperately ill with high fevers, and they were in shock and bleeding. Wale was told that they were both surgeons who had worked in the same hospital. Wale is trained as a veterinarian, but he looked at the dying surgeons carefully and reached his conclusion.

"There was little I could do," he said. "They were beyond hope. But there was something else I knew at once. What they had wasn't AIDS. No way was it AIDS. It looked like Lassa to me."

So he proceeded to inform the staff that they were mistaken about their diagnosis and that they needed to take all possible precautions to avoid becoming infected themselves. Then he drew some blood samples from the two patients, got back in his car, and headed straight for Lagos.

"The samples were sitting on the floor of the car. I didn't want to have an accident and then have them fall off the seat and break open, so that's why I put them on the floor. I had two full vials of Lassa fever with me, and I kept looking at them, scared stiff that they might break as they rolled about."

We later isolated one hundred million particles of Lassa virus per milliliter from those samples. It was among the highest virus concentrations we have ever seen in human blood.

Wale now revealed that we were expected in Enugu. Not only that, but authorities there had even gone so far as to arrange a conference for us. Well, I thought, now I can understand what the two were doing at the airport.

We decided that first we would go to Enugu and try to track down the source of infection of the Lassa victims there. Then we would return to Ekpoma, the closest city to Azikiwe's village.

When we arrived at Enugu hospital, we learned that the two surgeons Wale had seen were now dead. We were greeted by Professor Nwokolo. He was the physician who'd cared for them in a private clinic before they were admitted to the hospital. He was now a very worried man. In fact, everyone who worked at the hospital was very worried. They were all convinced that, at any moment, they were going to come down with Lassa and die. As we began to talk to Professor Nwokolo, it dawned on me that this was the man with connections in high places, this was the man who'd obtained our invitation to the country, this was the man who'd sent two emissaries to the airport for the ribavirin.

He wanted it for himself.

We talked to everyone we could, taking careful histories and blood samples. We then hastened to explain to them that the incubation period for Lassa was almost over and that if they were going to get the infection, they would have already fallen sick. We were able to conclude that Enugu Hospital had no further cases of Lassa fever. We were all relieved—until we heard about the third dead surgeon.

Where had he come from? From the south, we were told, in Ibo territory, Imo State. The two surgeons had come from another part of the same state. Were there any samples of his blood? No. But some people knew the names of the hospitals where he and the other surgeons worked. It was complicated, but we collected as much information as we could and headed south for Imo.

Our next stop was Owerri, Imo State's capital. There we met with the state Minister of Health. In Africa, you cannot go into a government office and simply ask questions. Elaborate greetings are essential and certain formalities must be adhered to. Great ceremony was attached to these encounters, especially since we were a joint Ministry of Health/CDC team. And no ceremony in Ibo country can take place without cola nuts.

Cola nuts contain great dollops of caffeine, which explains why, in times gone by, messengers and travelers could sustain themselves with them, and little else, over long distances.

More importantly, cola nuts are the currency of hospitality. The Ibo people revere the cola nut. It is the object of special presentation ceremonies, which have to be performed in order to ensure friendly relations. People will even talk to the cola nut, which they invest with great powers. However, only men can take part in these cola nut rituals; women don't get to eat them—or talk to them. This was no loss to me.

So it was only after the cola nuts had been duly addressed, appreciated, and consumed—by the men—that we could finally get around to asking the minister whether he was aware of any cases of Lassa. Yes, he said, he knew of the physician named Ezirike who had died in Enugu. He came from a semi-urban area called Aboh Mbaise, located just outside of Owerri. The death of this third physician was shrouded in mystery and rumor, however. Depending on whom you believed, he was either a victim of a business conspiracy—poisoned by rivals who ran a competing hospital a mile away—or else he was a victim of witchcraft. Whatever the explanation, you couldn't prevail on taxi drivers to take you there. They'd put their feet to the gas pedal and floor it until they were well out of sight of the village where the hospital was located. When we reached it on our own, the hospital was deserted.

Though the hospital was new, it was tiny and miserable. Two dark rooms served as the wards, holding about twelve beds in all. The operating theater was nothing more than a small concrete room. There was no equipment. I had little difficulty imagining what it must have looked like just two or three weeks before. A few patients in iron beds. A few young girls as nurses. Very little in the way of drugs and equipment, and no sense of safety or good medical practice. Surgery would be performed in primitive conditions. Nothing moved except the flies and the mosquitoes, and the lizards chasing them over the walls and into the light fixtures.

As we sat outside on a bench under the eaves, Ezirike's widow emerged from a nearby house. She was sullen and angry, and she refused to talk. But the dead surgeon's father soon put in an appearance, and then one of his brothers. They proved more communicative. Their stories were embellished with further dark hints of juju, chicanery, and intrigue. They had no doubt that their family was being targeted by nefarious elements.

While Joe and Nasidi began to explore the surrounding village to see what evidence they could find of a Lassa fever outbreak, Wale and I returned to the hospital to go through the contents of the physician's tiny office. As hot and humid as it was outside, it was worse inside, so we propped open the door for some air. The office was infested with mosquitoes, making it a magnificent breeding ground for malaria. I resigned myself to being eaten alive. We went to look for the charts to find out the names of the patients whom the physician had been treating. There were no charts. No outpatient records, no inpatient records, no operating records. Nothing. Only one set of papers existed for each patient: the drug charts. We started to go through them. Each chart we looked at turned out to be a detailed list of every drug each patient had received. It was only when we came to the end of each chart that we understood the reason why only the drug charts had been maintained so meticulously while no other records had been kept at all. These charts were not medical documents, but financial papers. The more drugs a patient was given, the more the hospital could charge him.

Nonetheless, there was information to be learned from these records. We decided to use them to reconstruct a clinical picture of each patient. We had the dates of admission and discharge, and the dates of death. Ezirike had only four or five antibiotics available to him. It was clear that he went by a set regimen. A patient with a fever received a certain set of drugs. If the fever persisted, Ezirike switched over to a second set of antibiotics and, for good measure, added chloroquine on the off chance the patient might have malaria. If a patient vomited, he'd give him an antiemetic; if he experienced any pain, he'd give him an analgesic. Despite his limited stock, he administered drugs in amazing numbers and combinations. He would prescribe up to six injected drugs and as many oral ones, including vitamins and other substances of marginal benefit to his patients. It was a good way to make money.

Finally, we discovered that the patients were being given iron and blood transfusions. That gave us pause. Did that mean that they had started to bleed? Then we found that the patients were being given anticonvulsants. Lassa patients have seizures in the final stages, and anticonvulsants control seizures. And if all else failed, Ezirike would give steroids in a desperate and futile attempt to bring back their blood pressures as they went into shock and died.

Sometimes we'd turn up a note in the margins that confirmed our assumptions that we were dealing with Lassa, such as "bleeding per rectum," or simply, "convulsions." We felt as though we were translating a Rosetta Stone, deciphering one ancient script in order to interpret another. In most cases, the notes would trail off, and the bill would be tallied up.

We found some notes about those who had not paid. Apparently payment was left up to the patients' families. The patients themselves were dead.

For two days, we sat in the little room, our legs munched by mosquitoes, studying these charts. By the time we'd finished, we were able to piece together the terrible story of this little hospital.

Seventeen patients had died of an acute febrile illness with shock, convulsions, and bleeding. Many had had terrible sore throats. We were able to trace the infections as they spread from patient to patient. There was one week in February (about the time Azikiwe had died in Chicago), when several patients had died within hours of one other. It was at this point that the handwriting in the charts had changed. It wasn't a nurse who was keeping track of the drugs anymore, it was Ezirike himself. We imagined that he must have been frantic to save his patients, resorting to whatever medications he had left at his disposal, trying anything in any combination to see whether it would have any effect.

But nothing worked; nothing was ever going to work. He couldn't save his patients, and in the end, he couldn't even save himself.

We traced the story even farther back, to January, when Ezirike's nephew, a student about nineteen years old at Enugu University, had come home for a few days. This was the same town we had just visited, the same town where Ezirike had gone to die. Apparently the nephew had been afflicted with a sickle-cell crisis, which comes from a condition called sickle-cell anemia, a commonly inherited disease in West Africa. The name of the disease is derived from the shape of the patient's red blood cells. Normally, these cells have the appearance of little round red-brimmed hats under the microscope. In sickle-cell anemia, they take the form of a sickle, or a crescent moon. The boy was admitted to his uncle's little hospital. Like every other patient, he'd received lots of injections. Unlike most other patients, he quickly got better.

About a week after being discharged, however, he developed a fever and a severe sore throat. He was readmitted—and given a great many more injections. So were the other patients, regardless of what was wrong with them. All the evidence indicated that syringes and possibly even IV drips were shared. They were, after all, expensive.

This time, the boy got worse. His chart—dry and technical as it was, cluttered with the names of antibiotics, dosage levels, and sums of money owed—was a cry from beyond the grave. It told of increasing desperation and anguish, of a futile search for something, anything, that would halt the inexorable progress of the virus. When one drug didn't work, Ezirike had tried another and then another. The virus continued its attack. The boy began to vomit and bleed. He went into shock. Convulsions, finally. Then death.

About a week later, a patient who had been in the hospital at the same time as the boy, but who had been discharged fully recovered, was readmitted with a fever. The pattern repeated itself over and over again. Somehow, Ezirike must have believed that he could control the situation. Maybe it was pride, maybe it was fear; more likely it was ignorance. He just didn't realize the nature of the beast that was now loose in his tiny hospital. Whatever his motivation, he delayed for three weeks before appealing for help. Seventeen patients had to die and he himself had to become fatally infected before it finally sank in that perhaps he couldn't handle the crisis on his own.

After reviewing the charts, we concluded that the poor nephew was probably infected in the hospital, possibly by an injection or an IV drip, during his first admission. As to who the index case was, we were never able to say for sure. The records were inadequate and staff fear too great to piece the story together accurately.

To see whether the infection had spread beyond the doomed hospital, we went around to other health facilities in the vicinity. We talked to the doctors and nurses and pored over charts, looking for evidence of additional cases. We asked about patients who'd recently died, and we examined the records to try to determine the cause of their final illnesses. We bled the staff to see whether they had become infected. The virus had extinguished itself from the human population of the hospital by killing most of its victims and chasing other potential victims away in fear.

As the trail grew cold, we decided to survey hospitals in the rest of the Owerri area. One visit was to a small but well-run private clinic. The doctor, who was the owner, had practiced in the U.S. Midwest for some years. He sat up immediately when we told him about our investigation.

"Yes," he said, "I think I know what you are looking for. Come with me. I have a patient upstairs you should see."

We went up the narrow staircase. The doctor escorted us into a private room where we found a man in his late thirties lying in bed. He was bundled up under the covers. He was febrile and very weak but not bleeding. His throat ached horribly, and, when we examined it, we noticed yellowish exudate on the tonsils—all signs of Lassa. He also complained of severe abdominal and back pain—again symptoms compatible with Lassa fever. He told us that his business kept him on the road. Perhaps that is where he acquired his infection. We took some blood from him. Before leaving, we showed the staff how to nurse him safely without infecting themselves. It was only when we'd got back to Atlanta and put the specimen up for culture that we were able to establish for certain that the man indeed had Lassa. (Fortunately, his recovery was uneventful, and none of the staff treating him came down with the illness.)

We found another case in the main hospital of Owerri: a young woman who had aborted a dead fetus. Lassa is very severe in pregnant women, and the baby usually dies before it is born. The mother does better if she is in the first six months of pregnancy, or if the fetus aborts. Maternal death soars dramatically in the third trimester, particularly if the uterus is not emptied. This woman was quite ill, very much alone, and scared. She would not speak to us.

As soon as the nurses understood what we'd come about, they were thrown into panic. Now that they realized what the young woman might have, they wanted nothing to do with her. They wouldn't go anywhere near her. Her family, too, must have shunned her, because they had already vanished. She was completely alone in the world. Since she was lying on a miserable cot on the floor, we suggested that she be transferred to a general ward, where she could be better looked after. When no one else offered to help her, Joe and I carried her ourselves. But then we still couldn't find any nurse to care for her.

We did our best to convince the nurses that they were in no danger at all if they took some simple precautions and made sure not to come into direct contact with her blood. They listened to us and said they understood. But I'm afraid that they still weren't persuaded. I had the sense that once we were gone they would continue to have nothing at all to do with her.

Again we took serum. Again we sent it to Atlanta for culturing.

While all this was going on, wonder of wonders, the government vehicle we'd been promised in Lagos actually turned up. Wale was expecting someone to bring us money for our operational expenses. But there was no money.

Where was the money?

No one knew. The driver swore ignorance. Wale railed at him, but it did no good. So we sent him packing back to Lagos.

We next turned our attention to determining how the two surgeons, Doctors Ikeji and Anamba, had become infected. We knew that they'd come from Aba, a busy market town in the south of the state. We drove to Aba and located the chief medical officer of the town. He said that he was delighted to see us. We told him we wanted to go to the hospital. No, he said, first we had to see his superior. Though we weren't much interested in seeing him, we complied.

After we were introduced to the superior, a heated discussion ensued between him and the medical officer, the upshot of which was that lunch tokens were to be distributed to all of us. We protested vigorously that we did not want lunch. We wanted to get to the hospital. After much debate, we prevailed, but in the process we succeeded in sacrificing the good will of the medical officer. His only interest in our mission, it seemed, was the free lunch.

We drove around Aba, but at first were unable to gain access to the hospital where the surgeons had worked. Not to waste time while Nasidi went off to initiate tortuous negotiations for access, we turned our attention to a survey of all the other hospitals and clinics in the town, talking to the nurses and physicians and taking their blood, searching for evidence of Lassa fever. While we failed to find any other suspected Lassa cases, we did find ribavirin. That suggested that people were on the alert for Lassa. When a surgeon showed the drug to us, we asked where he'd purchased it.

"The market," he said casually. "Where else?"

We looked at the packaging. It was made in China.

The market in Aba was mobbed; people seemed to bring a

great deal of passion to their haggling. Whatever you wanted was available for a price: plastic pots, cooking pots, rush mats, drums, rice, onions, newly butchered meat swarming with voracious flies. And ribavirin. If they didn't have what you wanted, then the vendor would urge you to come back in half an hour. It was impossible to figure out how they could mysteriously procure the article you were after in so short a time. When it came to drugs like ribavirin, some obliging entrepreneur would produce for you whatever you asked for in no time at all, with perfectly faked packaging to make it look like the real thing. Fake drugs are a major industry in many developing countries.

We made another attempt to gain access to the hospital that we believed to be the source of the infection for Aba. It was located at the end of a narrow lane heaped with mud and refuse and filled with potholes. When we finally managed to reach the hospital, we discovered the doors bolted. The hospital was empty; everyone had gone. We were seeing the same thing all over again.

Wale and Nasidi networked. Next day they somehow succeeded in rounding up the brother of one of the dead surgeons. He, too, like the people in Aboh Mbaise, was convinced that the whole thing was a plot by competitors who would resort to anything—even juju and poison—to shut down the hospital and kill his brother. As a result, the family had refused to allow anyone to enter, including even Ministry of Health officials. They believed that, once they opened up the hospital, the conspirators would somehow take advantage of the situation. It was all that Wale and Nasidi could do to persuade him and his relatives that we had no interest in harming them. Finally, the brother relented and took the padlocks off the door.

Unlike the hospital in Aboh Mbaise, this one had opened

for business only two years previously. Its clientele was mostly poor and drawn from the nearby market area. Because it kept its rates low, the hospital was always filled. The building was constructed like a prison, with balconies facing out over a central covered well and concrete-block rooms radiating off of it. Inside, there were two tiny operating rooms, each about eight by ten feet in area. One contained a converted gynecological couch, which doubled as the operating table. A large porcelain sink sat in a corner. Light was supplied by a single flyblown fluorescent strip hanging off its wires from the ceiling. On the floor we noticed a couple of gas burners with cooking pots on them. Presumably these were used for sterilization. Hanging over a rack were a few tattered surgical gloves. Everything wore a look of desolation.

Once we'd actually got inside the hospital, the brother was very cooperative. He even invited two physicians who'd been employed at the hospital to join us. Once they began to speak, they couldn't stop. Their stories came spilling out. Oh yes, they began, there have been several deaths at this place . . .

The first victim was the hospital matron. She died only a few weeks before, in early January. She was an active, healthy woman, with no history of illness. But without any warning, she developed a fever and a sore throat, and failed to respond to the usual treatment. Her death followed quickly. It sounded like Lassa to us.

There were others like her, including a nurse and one of the patients.

And what about the two surgeons whose deaths we were investigating? They were why we were in Aba to begin with. At least here we had the advantage of having plenty of documentation available. We began pulling out the records of recent surgical procedures as well as charts for all patients admitted in the last few months. What we were looking for was a single event that would link the two surgeons, something that would have occurred about ten to twenty days before their deaths. Since they had died on the same day, and indeed had been transferred to Enugu together, we assumed that they'd been infected together. The female surgeon, Anamba, had done most of the operations. That made sense: operations were a highly probable source of infection.

That still left the third surgeon, the doctor who ran the hospital. Had he become infected performing surgery as well?

"No," replied one of the doctors, shaking his head. "He did not like to operate. He did not go to the theater. He stayed on the wards and looked after the patients there."

What about the rest of the staff? Was anyone else ill at the time the two surgeons died?

"Oh, yes, " the doctor said. "One of our nurses was very ill, but she has gone back to her village. No one knows where it is."

This evoked our curiosity.

"What did she do here at the hospital?"

"She was a theater nurse," the doctor explained. "Her name was Peace Uba."

Now we had a clue. Perhaps there was some link between the nurse and the surgeon. When none of the operating notes yielded any information, we asked to see the register of the operating theater. What we were looking for was an emergency operation that involved both Peace Uba and Anamba. Then we found it. In the middle of February, just about twenty days before the surgeons' deaths, the register indicated that an emergency procedure had been performed. We looked for notes in hope of further elaboration, but could not find them. However, as soon as we began to interview the staff, their memories came flooding back. Oh yes, they said, they remembered the patient. He was a young man who had been in the hospital for some time. He was admitted from another hospital with what was called a "failed appendectomy." He'd been getting better without any special treatment, except for the usual injections of antibiotics and other drugs. Then, after more than a week, he developed a fever again. When his condition continued to deteriorate, his doctors assumed that it must be a recurrent abdominal problem and rushed him back into the operating theater to open him up.

The more we probed, the more details we obtained. Everyone, it seemed, recalled the case because of the way the patient had bled on the operating table. It was uncontrollable. No matter what anyone did, the bleeding simply could not be stopped. There was blood everywhere. Anamba was having so much difficulty that she called for Dr. Ikeji, the hospital head.

We checked the register again. This was the only time that month that he had been in the operating theater at all. Now we knew how he had become infected. Despite Dr. Ikeji's help, the young man died later that night, after returning to the ward. We asked for the name of the nurse who was assisting at the operation. It was Peace Uba.

After reviewing the young man's case carefully, we reached two conclusions: that he had had Lassa and that he'd most likely been infected in the hospital, probably by a shared needle. We needed to know more. We decided to round up the staff and interview and bleed them to see whether they were also infected.

The next morning, when we reached the hospital, we discovered that its central hall, ordinarily the gloomiest of places, had been quite transformed. To our astonishment, we were greeted by over two hundred nervous, giggling girls, most of them in their late teens or early twenties. While we were told they were nurses, they described themselves as students. Joe and I questioned the girls and took notes, Nasidi bled them, and Wale sorted and stored the specimens.

Every girl answered our questions in much the same way. They admitted that they had little in the way of education or professional training, but even so, they still performed all the jobs that nurses usually do. They all said their age was eighteen. They gave injections, distributed drugs, cared for patients, and cleaned up after them. But when it came to the young man we were interested in, practically none of them remembered him. I was getting tired, dehydrated in the heat, and depressed.

Then I talked to another girl. I asked the usual questions. Have you been ill in the last four weeks? I asked. And if so, what kind of illness did you have?

"Yes," the girl replied shyly. "I had a heart attack."

She was also eighteen.

"A what?"

I was dumbfounded. A heart attack in an eighteen year old? As far as I could see, she looked in the peak of health.

"Describe it to me," I said.

"I had a pain here." She put her fist to her chest.

I was suspicious. One of the symptoms of Lassa fever is chest pain, which may be due to pericarditis, an inflammation of the sac surrounding the heart. I asked her to tell me more. Was she admitted to hospital? I asked.

"Oh yes," she said. "I was in the same bed as Peace Uba."

I caught my breath.

What did she mean, the same bed? It wasn't clear whether she meant the same ward, or whether it really was so crowded in the ward, that they'd had to share a single bed. But another thought occurred to me before I could pursue this.

"Did you have anything to do with the operation on the young man who was bleeding?"

"Oh yes," she said. "I cleaned up the cloths."

After hearing her story, I nodded to Nasidi, who slipped the needle into her vein and took blood for Lassa antibodies.

Later that evening, we sat in the hotel lounge in Owerri and sipped cold beers. One question preyed on all of us: Where was Peace Uba?

Nasidi made up his mind to find her. The next day he began his search. It didn't take him long. Around lunchtime, he reported back to us.

"I know where to find her," he said. "Let's go."

He wouldn't tell us how he did it, but his sources turned out to be reliable. Peace's family, he said, were simple folk, subsistence farmers, surviving in the African bush on what they could grow. Peace was their big hope—an educated girl, a girl who, until Lassa had struck, was looking forward to a bright future as a nurse. Nasidi let slip that she was supposed to be beautiful.

We had to drive for many miles, deep into the bush of southern Nigeria. How Nasidi knew how to get to where we were headed was beyond me. At last we came to a small farm and stopped the truck. We climbed out and walked down a grassy bank to a little house. Nasidi knocked on the door. For several moments he just stood there. He pressed his ear against the door. I could see by his expression that he believed someone was inside. Then the door opened and several people emerged. They huddled in conference with their visitor. Some agreement seemed to have been reached. Then Nasidi came back to fetch us.

"She is here," he said, "and her family assures me that they'll cooperate with us."

Peace Uba didn't appear immediately. Instead, we were treated to a warm-up in the form of several members of her family. We asked them the routine questions and drew their blood. I suspect that they hadn't had so much excitement in years.

Finally, the object of our search came out herself. She was a tiny, nervous girl, but very pretty. She had gone to some trouble to make herself look nice, which undoubtedly explained her delay. In any case, she walked a few oddly lurching steps in our direction and then shyly took a seat beside Nasidi.

He was grinning from ear to ear. He couldn't help himself. Nasidi liked pretty girls a lot.

But it soon became clear that something was very wrong. When he turned toward her to speak, she didn't respond. She kept staring at us without so much as glancing at Nasidi. He looked nonplussed. What was this? Were his charms failing him?

He spoke again, touching her lightly on the arm. She gave a start. There was a nervous expression on her face. Her smile, which only moments before we'd found so fetching, seemed empty.

Nasidi told us he had heard she was stone deaf. It looked as though that was the case.

Deafness is a complication from Lassa, and it can be total and permanent. Then we asked her to walk. Slowly, she rose from her seat and took a few steps forward. She began to stagger; it was a classic ataxic gait, meaning that her legs were no longer responding to the commands of the brain, with the result that she had no sense of balance. This was another terrible complication of Lassa. While the deafness might persist for the rest of her life, it was possible that her unsteady gait would disappear in time. After taking her blood, we completed our notes and spent what remaining time we had trying to reassure Peace's family.

It was sad. We had reconstructed the story of how Lassa had come to Aba and how it had infected the three surgeons and the two nurses who had worked in its hospital. But while we had established the diagnosis, we hadn't succeeded in penetrating the mystery that the disease presented. Just how much of it was there in this part of the world? From the sampling of the population we took, it seemed relatively uncommon. But how was it transmitted? What was its source? And then there was another question: When would it reappear and who would it carry off next time?

In our search for Lassa, we'd traced a circuitous route, beginning in Enugu, where we found the disease had come and gone; then continuing on to Owerri, to eat cola nuts with bureaucrats; resuming our investigation in Aboh Mbaise, where one surgeon and sixteen patients had died in a single hospital; going on to Aba, where the virus had killed two more surgeons and emptied yet another hospital; and finally ending up in a small village to find Peace Uba.

Now it was time to see what we could find out about Azikiwe's family, which was what had prompted our investigation to begin with.

The first place we looked for his family was Port Harcourt on the south coast. Wale had heard that several relatives had fled here after the funeral. However, we failed to find any of them. Maybe they'd gone into hiding; in any case, they didn't want to be found. So we decided to head to Ekpoma and Ishan. Our route took us north, toward Benin City. On our way, we came to a fairly large town at a major road junction called Onitsha. It rang a bell.

Then it occurred to me what it was. In 1974, three cases of Lassa fever had been recorded in Onitsha. One was a nineteen-year-old Nigerian boy, and the other two were German missionary physicians. The first German had become infected after he cared for the boy. He bled profusely, had multiple seizures, then lapsed into coma and died. The second missionary also became infected. He was taken to Enugu teaching hospital, the same hospital where the surgeons from Aboh Mbaise and Aba had been treated. He fared better than they did, however, and went on to recover.

Mysteriously, investigators failed to discover anyone else in the area who'd come down with Lassa and then recovered. Was this some rare virulent strain that killed nearly all people who were infected, insuring that there would be virtually no survivors? The disease had many mysteries, and this was one of them.

We passed through Onitsha without stopping—we had no time—and went directly on to Benin City, where we had an appointment with a top health official. Shown into a large office, we were introduced to the official, who made sure that we understood that he wasn't just some ordinary bureaucrat. No, he was a prince. Then we went through the motions that had by now become familiar to us. First, he listened politely while we tried to explain just how serious a problem he had on his hands, and then he gave us every assurance of his government's cooperation.

Then nothing happened.

We ended up setting out for Ekpoma alone. Later we learned that the chief minister of the state had gone on television to let the local people know that the Lassa fever outbreak was due to juju.

This was something we were getting used to. Not surprisingly, witchcraft loomed large in Ekpoma. Wherever we went, we could sense the fear of witchcraft. The house where Azikiwe's parents lived in Ishan was locked, and we could not get in. However, Wale had been there earlier, and he had obtained good histories and specimens from surviving family members. So we already knew that they'd all had tested positive. What we needed to do now was find out how many other cases there had been in the vicinity of the house. We needed resources to trap and bleed rodents. Catching a rat is not a major challenge; most people can do it. What made it so tricky was that we needed to catch the rats alive, so that we could take blood and liver samples. And we had to be sure that whoever handled them knew how to avoid getting infected with Lassa virus—which meant that we would have to do it ourselves.

We then embarked on a survey of the local community. It was important to find out how much Lassa fever there was around. The city of Ishan was set out so that most of its inhabitants lived on the main street. To each house was attached a lot of about one third to a half an acre, where families could grow enough produce to meet their needs. As we went from house to house, we encountered the same suspicious responses. No one was willing to talk. Even a simple smile or expression of welcome was hard to come by. Eventually it became clear to us that nothing was going to happen unless we had the sanction of the chiefs. Our trouble was that it was difficult to figure out who exactly the chief was. In the past, the identity of the chief would be well established, and his word was law. But in Ekpoma, the situation was much more fluid; migration, modernization, and increased communication with the outside world had altered the attitudes of communities, eroding the power and prestige of the traditional tribal hierarchies. Now, when we asked, it appeared that there was more than one chief, and it was uncertain at any given time under whose jurisdiction a certain family fell. It was even less clear whose orders carried any weight. A chief might assure us that he was the one in control, but we never had any way of confirming the truth of this.

It didn't leave us with much of a choice. Without any official sanction, we could only continue to go from door to door, asking questions and trying to get blood samples. Usually people are very helpful, even when you just turn up unannounced on their doorstep. They will even answer amazingly personal questions. This experience was different. We could see fear in the looks that greeted us. Our questions met with grudging responses when they were answered at all. And there was no question of drawing blood samples. As soon as one person refused, everyone else around them—and there were always people around—followed their example. We did very badly.

The whole business was sinister. Our every move was tracked; we were watched from behind closed doors and through parts in flimsy curtains. We felt like interlopers, like sources of the contagion ourselves. Since Azikiwe and his family had most likely contracted Lassa at the father's funeral, we were anxious to find out as much as we could about how funeral rituals were conducted. After all, there was every reason to suppose that these practices could only spread the virus. But we couldn't find out anything; the rituals were conducted in such secrecy that no one dared talk about them. Wale, however, did turn up some tantalizing information.

When people died, the bodies were taken to a local morgue, where they were kept refrigerated until the families had enough time to gather together for the funeral. Once the clan has assembled, the body was then returned to them. While we had some evidence that blood contact must be a part of the funeral ritual—how else to account for the engineer's exposure to the disease?—we had no idea how this contact had occurred. Wale said that he'd heard a rumor that the hearts of the deceased were removed. Was this true? And if it was, what happened to the hearts? And what happened to the people who handled them? In spite of an almost total lack of cooperation, it became increasingly clear that there had been a great many deaths. Invariably the symptoms of the disease that carried them off were the same: sore throat, fever, and bleeding. No other virus but Lassa (or Ebola) could produce symptoms like these.

We decided we might do better if we split into two teams. Wale and Nasidi went off in one direction, while I linked up with a microbiologist from the University of Benin. Meanwhile, Joe was still off searching for the index case, who was in hiding. I'd expected Wale and Nasidi to be away for a while, but they reappeared so quickly that I knew something had gone awry. One look at them and I could see that they were terrified by whatever experience they'd undergone.

"What is it?" I asked. "What's happened?"

They threw anxious glances behind them, as if they still weren't certain they were free and clear.

"Machetes," Nasidi managed to get out.

"What?"

"We were chased with machetes," Wale clarified. "They didn't even give us time to find out what we wanted."

It didn't matter; by this point everyone in Ekpoma knew what we were about.

Even after we'd succeeded in locating Azikiwe's family, they were no more communicative than anyone else in the area—

with one exception: Azikiwe's sister, Valerie. According to her account, the suspected index case was a cousin, who was in her late teens or early twenties. She'd fallen ill in late December. During her illness, she'd come into close contact with her aunt, Azikiwe's mother, as well as other members of the family. In January and February, two other cousins—a six-year-old boy and a forty-three-year-old woman—took sick and died. What Valerie could not tell us was whether these two victims had had any contact with the rest of the family. It doesn't appear as if Azikiwe knew about their deaths when he returned home for his mother's funeral.

We decided to try to find the suspected index case. It soon became apparent that this wasn't going to be easy. We were told that while she'd recovered from her illness, she was now considered a pariah, stigmatized as a witch, because she'd brought so much trouble on the family. Some members of the family had even beaten her, causing her to flee.

And where was she now? Valerie heard that she'd taken refuge with a distant and more sympathetic family member. But where exactly she was hiding out no one seemed to know.

With the tenacity of detective-movie gumshoes, we managed to ferret out her whereabouts. Apparently, she was holed up in a nearby village at the home of her uncle. When we reached the village in question, we did succeed in locating the uncle, only to discover that it was the wrong uncle. The uncle we wanted was living in another village not far away. So we continued our odyssey.

In the next village, we resumed our search. You have to rely on the directions people give you; there are no addresses and few street names. This time, we found the right uncle but not the girl. He told us that she wasn't there. Understandably, she had no wish to be exposed. Her life could be in danger if she were—at least that was what her uncle said. I suspected that he, a wizened old man in his late sixties who spoke a little English, might not be telling us the truth. So we persisted. Wale patiently explained our purpose, assuring him that we only wanted to speak to her about her illness and possibly take a blood specimen.

Finally, he succeeded in convincing him. The uncle smiled warily and then led us into his small house. We found ourselves in a crowded sitting room. The uncle invited us to sit. A few moments later, his wife entered the room. She proved a much tougher customer. She said that there was no way that she was going to allow us to see the young woman. She seemed quite adamant.

Wale wasn't about to give up, not after we'd come this far. Once again, he was obliged to make our case, explaining why it was so important that we have a chance to speak to the girl. I could see by the expression on his face that we had won the uncle over. After a several minutes, the uncle and aunt retreated into a corner to deliberate. A compromise was reached. The uncle said that, while we would be permitted to talk to the girl, we could forget about taking a blood sample. Wale, being the diplomat he is, agreed to their conditions. Better, he thought, to accept incremental progress than none at all.

A few minutes went by while we waited. Then the girl was brought in. She was thin and pale. It was clear that she was terrified. She kept casting furtive glances around the room, all the while avoiding our gaze. When we were able to calm her down, we began to question her about her illness. The symptoms she described suggested that she'd had a milder case of Lassa fever, which undoubtedly explained why she had recovered. She admitted that she'd been in contact with several family members, though she didn't seem to remember all of them. After some hesitation, she went on to tell us about the ordeal that had followed her illness. It was with difficulty that she was able to recount how certain members of her family had hounded her and beaten her until she'd had to flee for her life.

Bruised and bleeding from her wounds, she made her way through the bush until she reached the safety of her uncle's house. Not content with the punishment that had already been inflicted on the poor girl, someone in her family had gone to the juju man and had a curse placed on her. Now she was even more afraid. She was a virtual prisoner. She couldn't leave this house and despaired of ever escaping.

After talking to her for several minutes, we believed we'd succeeded in convincing her that we weren't acting as agents of her family or any juju man. Wale decided to up the ante and ask her if we could take a sample of her blood to test for antibodies to Lassa. Grudgingly, she agreed. But just as Wale was about to plunge the needle into her vein, she shrieked and fled from the room. We had to start all over again. It took us another hour to bring her back into the room and calm her down before Wale was able to take a small specimen. When the blood specimen was tested in Lagos, it proved to be highly positive for antibody to Lassa virus. The type of antibody we found is called IgM, which signifies a relatively recent infection. What the test couldn't tell us, though, was where she may have been infected. Rodents were ubiquitous, and people commonly caught and ate them, so there were thousands of opportunities for the virus to be transmitted.

It wasn't only machete-wielding villagers who were responsible for bringing our work to a crashing halt. We were told that the U.S. Agency for International Development (USAID) would provide us with the resources to conduct surveillance and control programs. Somehow, though, nothing happened. We learned later that the USAID representative, who had assured us of support, later mentioned in confidence that no money would be allocated to Lassa fever work. Apparently, Lassa did not enjoy a high priority when it came to the distribution of U.S. funds to developing countries. This was not a triumph for the U.S. State Department.

For the next two years, we sought funding, writing proposal after proposal to undertake the studies that we believed were essential if we were ever going to find out to what extent Lassa had spread in southern Nigeria. We wanted to carry out rodent surveys. We wanted to know in particular how Lassa fever had managed to get into downtown Aba, a city of one million, when Lassa was supposed to be an exclusively rural disease. We also needed to find out the role that rituals like funerals were playing in the spread of the disease. If Lassa was spread mainly as a result of high-risk practices—like exposure to blood in funerals or the reuse of needles in hospitals—then we had a very different situation from what it would be if the disease was being spread by a natural infectious process. Only by understanding the way in which Lassa is transmitted could we hope to curb it and protect the population. This is exactly the sort of thing that epidemiologists are trained to do. But while we'd acquired some success in combating viruses, we were not quite so lucky when it came to fighting superstition or the mindless attitudes of bureaucrats, who seemed to have better notions of what to do with "their" money than help save lives.

As to Wale, he remains our good friend. He is working at the WHO office in Zimbabwe. Each year he writes the same message: "Another Lassa outbreak. Lassa is alive and well in Nigeria, but nobody will take any notice."

These epidemics seem to be regarded as nothing out of the ordinary, no more cause for alarm than a thunderstorm. After all, Nigeria also experiences annual yellow fever outbreaks that carry off hundreds and, sometimes, thousands of victims. And yellow fever has been vaccine-preventable since the 1940s.

from The Hot Zone
by Richard Preston

Richard Preston's 1994 book includes this account of Preston's visit to Mt. Elgon's Kitum Cave, rumored to be the home of Ebola and its equally frightening cousin, the Marburg virus.

R obin's wife, Carrie MacDonald, is his business partner, and she often accompanies him on safaris with clients. The MacDonalds also bring along their two small sons, if the client will allow that. Carrie is in her twenties, with blond hair and brown eyes and a crisp English accent. Her parents brought her to Africa from England when she was a girl.

We traveled in two Land Rovers, Carrie driving one and Robin driving the other. "We always take two vehicles in this country, in case one breaks down," Carrie explained. "It happens literally all the time." Carrie and Robin's two boys rode with Carrie. We were also accompanied by three men who were members of the MacDonalds' safari staff. Their names are Katana Chege, Herman Andembe, and Morris Mulatya. They are professional safari men, and they do most of the work around the campsite. They spoke very little English and had résumés as long as one's arm. In addition to those people, two friends of mine had joined the expedition. One was a childhood friend named Frederic Grant, and the other was a woman named Jamy Buchanan; both are Americans. I had prepared a written list of instructions for my friends in case I broke out with Marburg, and I had sealed the document in an envelope and hidden it in my backpack. It ran for three pages, typewritten, single spaced, describing the signs and symptoms of a filovirus infection in a human being, as well as possible experimental treatments that might arrest the terminal melt-down. I had not told my friends about this envelope, but I planned to give it to them if I came down with a headache. This was a sign of nervousness, to say the least.

Robin turned into the opposite lane in order to pass a truck, and suddenly we were headed straight for an oncoming car. Its headlights flashed and its horn wailed.

Fred Grant grabbed the seat and shouted, "Why is this guy coming at us?"

"Yeah, well, we're going to die, so don't worry about it," Robin remarked. He dodged in front of the truck just in time. He blurted out a song:

> *Livin' and a-lovin'*
> *And, a-lovin' and a-livin'—Yah!*

We stopped and bought roasted ears of corn from a woman standing by the side of the road with a charcoal brazier. The corn was hot, dry, scorched, and delicious, and it cost five cents. It was called a mealy.

Robin chewed his mealy as he drove. Suddenly he grabbed his jaw and swore violently. "My tooth! Bloody hell! A filling came out! This arsehole of a bloody dentist!" He rolled down his window and spat corn into the wind. "Well, carry on. Three fillings, and they've *all* come out now. Carrie sent me to the man. Said he was a good dentist—hah!"

He floored his Land Rover until it hovered behind Carrie's Land Rover. The two vehicles were roaring down the highway as if they were attached to each other. He leaned out the window and hurled his gnawed mealy at his wife's Land Rover. It bounced off her rear window. She didn't seem to notice. We passed a sign that said: REDUCE ROAD CARNAGE— DRIVE SAFELY.

Toward sunset, we stopped in the town of Kitale, at the base of Mount Elgon, to buy Tusker beers and charcoal. Kitale is a market town. The main market is situated along the highway leading into town, near an old train station built by the English. The highway is lined with towering blue-gum trees. Under the trees, on pounded dirt and among mud puddles from fresh rains, people set up stands for selling umbrellas and plastic wristwatches. Robin turned his Land Rover into the market and drove slowly through the crowds. A man shouted in Swahili, "You are driving the wrong way!"

"Where are the signs?" Robin shouted back.

"We don't need signs here!"

We parked and walked through the town, and instantly we were surrounded by pimps. One guy wore a white ski parka and said, "Do you want to go Kigawera? Yes? I will take you there. Come with me. Right now. Beautiful girls. I will take you there." That might be the neighborhood where Charles Monet's girlfriends had lived. It was rush hour, and crowds flowed on foot under the gum trees, past an endless line of small shops. Mount Elgon brooded over the town and the trees, rising to an undefined height, its profile buried in an anvil thunderhead, bathed in golden light. An edge of the mountain razored diagonally upward into the cloud. A silent flash traveled around the mountain, followed by another flash—chain lightning, but no thunder reached the town. The air was cold, heavy, wet, and filled with the sound of crickets.

In our explorations on mud roads around Mount Elgon, we saw signs of the recent trouble: burned, empty huts that had once belonged to Bukusu farmers. Someone had warned me that we would hear gunfire at night, but we didn't. Sickly banana trees leaned around the abandoned huts. The huts stood in fallow fields, strewn with African weeds and shoots of young saplings. We made a camp in the same meadow where Charles Monet had camped. The cook, Morris Mulatya, dumped a sack of charcoal on the ground and built a fire, and put a metal teapot on it to heat water for tea. Robin Mac-Donald sat down on a folding chair and removed his sneakers. He rubbed his feet with his hands and then drew his knife from its sheath and began paring bits of skin from his toes. Not far away, at the edge of the forest that ringed our campsite, a Cape buffalo eyed us. Robin eyed the buffalo. "That's a male," he muttered. "Those are bastards. You've got to watch them. They'll *lift* you. The Cape buffalo have killed more human beings in Africa than any other animal. Except hippo. Those swine have killed more."

I knelt in the grass and organized a row of boxes that contained space suits, decontamination gear, and lights. Smoke from the campfire curled in the air, which was filled with the *clink-clank* noise of safari tents being erected by the MacDonalds' staff. Carrie MacDonald worked around the campsite, getting things organized, speaking Swahili to the men. A nearby stream tumbled out of a glade. Robin looked up, listening to birds. "Hear that? Those are turacos. And there's a wood hoopoe. And there's a gray mousebird; do you see that long tail?"

He wandered down to the stream. I followed him. "I wonder if there's any trout in here," he said, staring into the water. "This could be good for fly fishing."

I put my hand into the water. It was ice-cold and bubbly but gray in color, clouded with volcanic dust, not the kind of water that would sustain trout.

"Talk about fly fishing. Did you ever hear of fly fishing for crocodiles?" Robin said.

"No."

"You put a piece of meat on a chain. A piece of meat *this* big. And the flies are all *over* the place! Now there's some fly fishing! They stink, those crocodiles. You'll be standing in shallow water, and they'll swim up on you. And the water is muddy. And you can't see them. And unless you can smell them, you don't know they're there. And then—*pfft!* They drag you down. End of story. You're history, my man. Talk about Nature. The whole thing, if you think about it, is full of killers, from the river to the sea."

A young man in a beret and military fatigues knelt on one knee in the grass, holding a Russian assault rifle, watching us with mild interest. His name was Polycarp Okuku, and he was an *askari*, an armed guard.

"*Iko simba hapa?*" Robin called to him. Any lions around here?

"*Hakuna simba.*" No lions left.

Poachers from Uganda had been coming over Mount Elgon and shooting anything that moved, including people, and now the Kenyan government required that visitors to Mount

Elgon be accompanied by armed guards. The Swahili word *askari* used to mean "spear bearer." Now it means a man who carries an assault rifle and who walks in your shadow.

Kitum cave opens in a forested valley at an altitude of eight thousand feet on the eastern slope of the mountain. *"Whoof!"* MacDonald said as we grunted up the trail. "You can smell the Cape buffalo around here, eh? *Mingi* buffalo." *Mingi:* many. Lots of buffalo. Buffalo trails crossed the human trail on diagonals. The trails were wider, deeper, straighter, more businesslike than the human trail, and they reeked of buffalo urine.

I was wearing a backpack. I picked my way across muddy spots in the trail.

Polycarp Okuku yanked a lever on the barrel of his assault rifle, *clack, ta chock.* This action cocked the weapon and slotted a round into the firing chamber. "Especially in the rainy season, the Cape buffalo like to travel in herds," he explained.

The sound of a machine gun being cocked brought Robin to attention. "Bloody hell," he muttered. "That toy he's carrying isn't safe."

"Look," Okuku said, pointing to a clump of boulders. "Hyrax." We watched a brown animal about the size of a woodchuck run silkily down the rocks. A possible host of Marburg virus.

The valley was cloaked in African olive trees, African cedars, broad-leaved croton trees, *Hagenia abyssinica*, trees drenched in moss, and whiplike young gray Elgon teaks. Here and there grew an occasional podocarpus tree, with a straight, silvery shaft that thrust upward to an incredible height and vanished in the shifting green of biological space. This was not lowland rain forest, where the crowns of trees merge into a closed canopy, but an African montane rain forest, a particular kind of forest with a broken canopy, penetrated by holes and clearings. Sunlight fell in shafts to the forest floor, washing over glades where nettles and papyrus sparkled with wild violets. Each tree stood in a space of its own, and the branches zigzagged against the clouds and sky like arms reaching out for heaven. From where we stood, we could see farms on the lower slopes of the mountain. As the eye moved from the lowlands to the uplands, the farms gave way to patches of shrubby trees, to fingers and clumps of larger trees, and then to an unbroken blanket of primeval East African rain forest, one of the rarest and most deeply endangered tropical forests on the planet.

The color of the forest was a silvery gray-green from the olive trees, yet here and there, a dark-green podocarpus tree burst through the canopy. A podo tree's shaft is lightly fluted and goes straight up, without branches, sometimes spiraling as it goes, and there may be a slight swing or curve in the shaft, which gives the tree a look of tension and muscularity, like a bent bow. High up, the podo tree flares into a vase-shaped crown, like an elm tree, and the downhanging limbs are draped with bundles of evergreen leafy needles and are spangled with ball-shaped fruit. The podos were hard to see in the thickets near Kitum Cave, because they did not grow large in that valley, but I noticed a young podo that was seven feet thick and close to a hundred feet tall. I guessed it had begun to grow in the time of Beethoven.

"What's missing here is the game," Robin said. He stopped and adjusted his baseball cap, surveying the forest. "The elephants have been all shot to shit. If they hadn't been shot, man, you'd see them all over this mountain. *Mingi* elephant. This whole *place* would be elephant."

The valley was quiet, except for the remote *huh, huh* of colobus monkeys that retreated from us as we climbed. The mountain seemed like an empty cathedral. I tried to imagine what it must have been like when herds of elephants could have been seen moving through a forest of podo trees as large as sequoias: only ten years ago, before the trouble, Mount Elgon had been one of the earth's crown jewels.

The mouth of Kitum Cave was mostly invisible from the approach trail, blocked by boulders cloaked in moss. A choir of African cedar trees grew in a row over the mouth of the cave, and a small stream trickled down among the cedars and rained over the boulders, filling the valley with a sound of falling water. As we got closer, the sound of the waterfall grew louder, and the air began to smell of something alive. It smelled of bat.

Giant stinging nettles grew in clumps among the boulders, and they brushed against our bare skin and caught our legs on fire. It occurred to me that nettles are, in fact, injection needles. Stinging cells in the nettle inject a poison into the skin. They break the skin. Maybe the virus lives in nettles. Moths and tiny flying insects drifted out of the cave mouth, carried in a steady, cool flow of air. The insects floated like snow blown sideways. The snow was alive. It was a snow of hosts. Any of them might be carrying the virus, or none of them.

We stopped on an elephant trail that led into the cave, beside a wall of rock that was covered with diagonal hatch marks made by the elephants tusking the rocks for salt. The forests of Mount Elgon were home to two thousand elephants, until the men with machine guns came over from Uganda. Now the Mount Elgon herd has withered to one extended family of about seventy elephants. The poachers set up a machine-gun nest at the mouth of Kitum Cave, and after that the surviving elephants had learned their lesson. The herd stays out of sight as much as possible, concealed in valleys higher on the mountain, and the smart old females, the grandmothers, who are the bosses of the herd and who direct its movements, lead the others to Kitum Cave about once every two weeks, when the elephants' hunger for salt overcomes their fear of being shot.

Elephants had not been the only visitors to Kitum Cave. Cape buffalo had gouged footprints in the trail leading into the cave. I noticed fresh, green splats of buffalo dung, and waterbuck hoofprints. The trail itself seemed to consist of a bed of dried animal dung. Other than the elephant herd, many different kinds of animals had been going inside Kitum Cave—bushbuck, red duikers, perhaps monkeys, perhaps baboons, and certainly genet cats, which are wild catlike animals somewhat larger than a house cat. Rats, shrews, and voles go inside the cave, too, either looking for salt or foraging for food, and these small mammals make trails through the cave. Leopards go inside the cave at night, looking for prey. Kitum Cave is Mount Elgon's equivalent of the Times Square subway station. It is an underground traffic zone, a biological mixing point where different species of animals and insects cross one another's paths in an enclosed air space. A nice place for a virus to jump species.

I unzipped my backpack and withdrew my gear and laid it on the rocks. I had assembled the components of a Level 4 field biological space suit. It was not a pressurized suit—not an orange Racal suit. It was a neutral-pressure whole-body suit with a hood and a full-face respirator. The suit itself was made of Tyvek, a slick, white fabric that is resistant to moisture and dust. I laid out a pair of green rubber gauntlet gloves, yellow rubber boots, a black mask with twin purple filters. The mask was a silicone rubber North respirator mask with a Lexan faceplate, for good visibility, and the purple filters were the kind that stop a virus. The mask had an insectile appearance, and the rubber was black and wet looking, sinister. I placed a roll of sticky tape on the rocks. A plastic shower cap—ten cents apiece at Woolworth's. Flashlight, head lamp. I stepped into the suit, feet first, pulled it up to my armpits, and fed my arms into the sleeves. I stretched the shower cap over my head and then pulled the hood of the suit down over the shower cap. I zipped up the front zipper of the suit, from crotch to chin.

Generally you need a support team to help you put on a field biological suit, and my traveling companion Fred Grant was acting in this capacity. "Could you hand me the sticky tape?" I said to him.

I taped the front zipper of the suit, taped the wrists of my gloves to the suit, taped the cuffs of the boots to the suit.

Polycarp Okuku sat on a rock with his gun across his knees, gazing at me with a carefully neutral expression on his face. It was evident that he did not want anyone to think he was surprised that someone would put on a space suit to go inside Kitum Cave. Later he turned and spoke at length in Swahili with Robin MacDonald.

Robin turned to me. "He wants to know how many people have died in the cave."

"Two," I said. "Not in the cave—they died afterward. One was a man, and the other was a boy."

Okuku nodded.

"There's very little danger," I said. "I'm just being careful."

Robin scuffed his sneaker in the dirt. He turned to the *askari* and said, "You explode, man. You get it, and that's it—*pfft!*—end of story. You can kiss your arse good-bye."

"I have heard about this virus," Okuku said. "There was something the Americans did at this place."

"Were you working here then?" I asked. When Gene Johnson and his team came.

"I was not here then," Okuku said. "We heard about it."

I fitted the mask over my face. I could hear my breath sucking in through the filters and hissing out through the mask's exhaust ports. I tightened some straps around my head.

"How does it feel?" Fred asked.

"Okay," I said. My voice sounded muffled and distant to my ears. I inhaled. Air flowed over the faceplate and cleared it of fog. They watched me fit an electric miner's lamp over my head.

"How long are you going to be in there?" Fred asked.

"You can expect me back in about an hour."

"An hour?"

"Well—give me an hour."

"Very well. And then?" he asked.

"And then? Dial 9-1-1."

The entrance is huge, and the cave widens out from there. I crossed a muddy area covered with animal tracks and continued along a broad platform covered with spongy dried dung. With the mask over my face, I could not smell bats or dung. The waterfall at the cave's mouth made splashing echoes. I turned and looked back, and saw that clouds were darkening the sky, announcing the arrival of the afternoon rains. I turned on my lights and walked forward.

Kitum Cave opens into a wide area of fallen rock. In 1982, a couple of years after Charles Monet visited the cave, the roof fell in. The collapse shattered and crushed a pillar that had once seemed to support the roof of the cave, leaving a pile of rubble more than a hundred yards across, and a new roof was formed over the rubble. I carried a map inside a plastic waterproof bag. The bag was to protect the map, to keep it from picking up any virus. I could wash the bag in bleach without ruining the map. The map had been drawn by an Englishman named Ian Redmond, an expert on elephants who once lived inside Kitum Cave for five months, camping beside a rock near the entrance while he observed the elephants coming and going at night. He wore no biohazard gear and remained healthy. (Later, when I told Peter Jahrling of USAMRIID about Redmond's camp-out inside Kitum Cave, he said to me, in all seriousness, "Is there any way you could get me a little bit of his blood, so we can run some tests on it?")

It was Ian Redmond who conceived the interesting idea that Kitum Cave was carved by elephants. Mother elephants teach their young how to pry the rocks for salt—rock carving is a learned behavior in elephants, not instinctive, taught to children by their parents; this knowledge has been passed down through generations of elephants for perhaps hundreds of thousands of years, for perhaps longer than modern humans have existed on the earth. If the elephants have been tusking out the rock of Kitum Cave at a rate of a few pounds a night, the cave could easily have been carved by elephants over a few hundred thousand years. Ian Redmond figured this out. He calls it speleogenesis by elephants—the creation of a cave by elephants.

The light began to fade, and the mouth of the cave, behind me, became a crescent of sunlight against the high, fallen ceiling. Now the mouth looked like a half-moon. I came to a zone of bat roosts. These were fruit bats. My lights disturbed them, and they dropped off the ceiling and flitted past my head, giving off sounds that resembled Munchkin laughter. The rocks below the bats were slubbered with wet, greasy guano, a spinach-green paste speckled with gray blobs, which reminded me of oysters Rockefeller. Momentarily and unaccountably, I wondered what the bat guano would taste like. I thrust away this thought. It was the mind's mischief. You should avoid eating shit when you are in Level 4.

Beyond the bat roosts, the cave became drier and dustier. A dry, dusty cave is very unusual. Most caves are wet, since most caves are carved by water. There was no sign of running water in this cave, no streambed, no stalactites. It was an enormous, bone-dry hole in the side of Mount Elgon. Viruses like dry air and dust and darkness, and most of them don't survive long when exposed to moisture and sunlight. Thus, a dry cave is a good place for a virus to be preserved, for it to lie inactive in dung or in drying urine, or even, perhaps, for it to drift in cool, lightless, nearly motionless air.

Marburg-virus particles are tough. One would imagine they can survive for a fair amount of time inside a dark cave. Marburg can sit unchanged for at least five days in water. This was shown by Tom Geisbert. One time, just to see what would happen, he put some Marburg particles into flasks of room-temperature water and left the flasks sitting on a countertop for five days (the counter was in Level 4). Then he took the water and dropped it into flasks that contained living monkey cells. The monkey cells filled up with crystalloids, exploded, and died of Marburg. Tom had discovered that five-day-old Marburg-virus particles are just as lethal and infective as fresh particles. Most viruses do not last long outside a host. The AIDS virus survives for about twenty seconds when exposed to air. No one has ever tried to see how long Marburg or Ebola can survive while stuck to a dry surface. Chances are the thread viruses can survive for some time—if the surface is free of sunlight, which would break apart the virus's genetic material.

I came to the top of the mound, reached out with my gloved hand, and touched the ceiling. It was studded with brown oblong shapes—petrified tree logs—and whitish fragments— pieces of petrified bone. The rock is solidified ash, the relic of an eruption of Mount Elgon. It is embedded with stone logs, the remains of a tropical rain forest that was swept up in the eruption and buried in ash and mud. The logs are dark brown and shiny, and they reflected opalescent colors in the beam of my head lamp. Some of the logs had fallen out of the roof, leaving holes, and the holes were lined with white crystals. The crystals are made of mineral salts, and they looked evilly sharp. Had Peter Cardinal reached up and touched these crystals? I found bats roosting in the holes among the crystals—insect-eating bats, smaller than the fruit bats that clustered near the cave's mouth. As I played my head lamp over the holes, bats exploded out of them and whirled around my head and were gone. Then I saw something wonderful. It was the tooth of a crocodile, caught in the rock. The ash flow had buried a river that had contained crocodiles. The crocodiles had been trapped and burned to death in an eruption of Mount Elgon.

I shuffled across razorlike slices of rock that had fallen from the roof, and came to a fresh elephant dropping. It was the size of a small keg of beer. I stepped over it. I came to a crevice and shone my lights down into it. I didn't see any mummified baby elephants down there. I came to a wall. It was scored with hatch marks—elephant tuskings. The elephants had left scrapes in the rock all over the place. I kept going down and came to a broken pillar. Next to it, a side tunnel continued downward. I wormed into the passage, on my knees. It circled around and came out in the main room. I was boiling hot inside the suit. Drops of moisture had collected on the inside of my faceplate and pooled in the mask under my chin. My footsteps kicked up dust, and it rose in puffs around my boots. It felt strange to be soaking wet and yet wading through dust. As I was climbing out of the passage, my head slammed against a rock. If I hadn't been wearing protective gear, the rock would have cut my scalp.

It seemed easy to get a head wound in the cave. Perhaps that was the route of infection: the virus clings to the rocks and gets into the bloodstream through a cut.

I proceeded deeper until I came to a final wall in the throat of the cave. There, at knee level, in total darkness, I found spiders living in webs. They had left their egg cases scattered about, hanging from the rock. The spiders were carrying on their life cycle at the back of Kitum Cave. That meant they were finding something to eat in the darkness, something that was flying into their webs. I had seen moths and winged insects pouring from the mouth of the cave, and it occurred to me that some of them must be flying all the way to the back. The spiders could be the host. They could catch the virus from an insect in their diet. Perhaps Marburg cycles in the blood of spiders. Perhaps Monet and Cardinal were bitten by spiders. You feel a cobweb clinging to your face and then comes a mild sting, and after that you don't feel anything. You can't see it, you can't smell it, you can't feel it. You don't know it's there until you start to bleed.

So much was happening that I didn't understand. Kitum Cave plays a role in the life of the forest, but what the role is no one can say. I found a crevice that seemed to be full of clear, deep water. It couldn't be water, I thought, the crevice must be dry. I picked up a stone and threw it. Halfway down in its flight, the stone made a splash. It had hit water. The stone spun lazily downward into the crevice and out of sight, and ripples spread across the pool and died away, throwing reflections of my head lamp onto the wall of the cave.

I climbed over fallen plates of stone back to the top of the rubble pile, playing my lights around. The room was more than a hundred yards across, larger in all directions than a football field. My lights failed to penetrate to the edges of the room, and the edges descended downward into darkness on all sides. The mound of rubble in the center made the cave resemble the curving roof of a mouth. As you look into someone's mouth, you see the tongue in front, lying under the roof of the mouth, and you see the tongue curving backward and down into the throat: that is what Kitum Cave looked like. Say *"Ahh,"* Kitum Cave. Do you have a virus? No instruments, no senses can tell you if you are in the presence of the predator. I turned off my lights and stood in total darkness, feeling a bath of sweat trickle down my chest, hearing the thump of my heart and the swish of blood in my head.

The afternoon rains had come. Fred Grant was standing inside the mouth of the cave to keep himself dry. The *askari* sat on a rock nearby, bouncing the machine gun on his knees, looking bored.

"Welcome back," Grant said. "Was it good for you?"

"We'll find out in seven days," I said.

He scrutinized me. "There appear to be splatters on your face shield."

"Splatters of *what?*"

"Looks like water."

"It's just sweat inside my mask. If you'll bear with me a moment, I'm going to get this suit off." I took a plastic laundry tub—part of the gear we had carried up to the cave—and left it under the waterfall for a moment. When the tub was partly full, I carried it over to the elephants' pathway, at the entrance, put it on the ground, and poured in most of a gallon of "bloody Jik"—laundry bleach.

I stepped into the tub. My boots disappeared in a swirl of dirt coming off them, and the Jik turned brown. I put my gloved hands into the brown Jik, scooped up some of the liquid, and poured it over my head and face mask. Using a toilet brush, I scrubbed my boots and legs to remove obvious patches of dirt. I dropped my bagged map into the Jik. I dropped my flashlight and head lamp into the Jik. I took off my face mask and dunked it, along with the purple filters. Then my eyeglasses went into the Jik.

I peeled off my green gauntlet gloves. They went into the Jik. I stepped out of my Tyvek suit, peeling the sticky tape as I went. The whole suit, together with the yellow boots, went into the Jik. It was a stew of biohazard gear.

Underneath my suit, I wore a set of clothes and a pair of sneakers. I stripped to the skin and put the clothing into a plastic garbage bag—a so-called hot bag—along with a splash or two of Jik, and then put that bag into another bag. I washed the outsides of both bags with bleach. From my backpack, I removed a clean set of clothing and put it on. I put the biohazard gear into double bags, adding Jik.

Robin MacDonald appeared noiselessly in his sneakers at the top of the rocks at the mouth of the cave. "Sir Bat Shit!" he called. "How did it go?"

We walked down the trail, lugging the hot bags, and returned to camp. The rain intensified. We settled down on chairs in the mess tent with a bottle of scotch whisky, while the rain splattered down and hissed through the leaves. It was three o'clock in the afternoon. The clouds thickened to the point where the sky grew black, and we lighted oil lamps inside the mess tent. Peals of thunder rolled around the mountain, and the rain turned into a downpour.

Robin settled into a folding chair. "Ah, man, this rain never stops on Elgon. This happens all year round."

There was a stroboscopic flash and a bang, and a lightning bolt whacked an olive tree. The flash outlined his face, his glasses. We chased the scotch with Tusker beers and played a round of poker. Robin declined to join the game.

"Have some whisky, Robin," Fred Grant said to him.

"None of that for me," he said. "My stomach doesn't like it. Beer is just right. It gives you protein, and you sleep well."

The rain tapered off, and the clouds momentarily lightened. Olive trees arched overhead in squiggles, their feet sunk in shadows. Water drops fell through the halls of trees. Mouse-birds gave off flutelike cries, and then the cries stopped, and Mount Elgon became silent. The forest shifted gently, rocking back and forth. Rain began to fall again.

"How are you feeling, Sir Bat Shit?" Robin said. "Are you getting any mental symptoms? That's when you first start talking to yourself in the toilet. It'll be starting any day now."

The mental symptoms were starting already. I remembered slamming my head into the roof of the cave. That had raised a bump on my scalp. There would be microscopic tears in the skin around that bump. I had begun to understand the feeling of having been exposed to a filovirus: I'll be okay. No problem. The odds are very good that I wasn't exposed to anything.

The emergence of AIDS, Ebola, and any number of other rain-forest agents appears to be a natural consequence of the ruin of the tropical biosphere. The emerging viruses are surfacing from ecologically damaged parts of the earth. Many of them come from the tattered edges of tropical rain forest, or they come from tropical savanna that is being settled rapidly by people. The tropical rain forests are the deep reservoirs of life on the planet, containing most of the world's plant and animal species. The rain forests are also its largest reservoirs of viruses, since all living things carry viruses. When viruses come out of an ecosystem, they tend to spread in waves through the human population, like echoes from the dying biosphere. Here are the names of some emerging viruses: Lassa. Rift Valley. Oropouche. Rocio. Q. Guanarito. VEE. Monkeypox. Dengue. Chikungunya. The hantaviruses. Machupo. Junin. The rabieslike strains Mokola and Duvenhage. LeDantec. The Kyasanur Forest brain virus. HIV—which is very much an emerging virus, because its penetration of the human species is increasing rapidly, with no end in sight. The Semliki Forest agent. Crimean-Congo. Sindbis. O'nyongnyong. Nameless São Paulo. Marburg. Ebola Sudan. Ebola Zaire. Ebola Reston.

In a sense, the earth is mounting an immune response against the human species. It is beginning to react to the human parasite, the flooding infection of people, the dead spots of concrete all over the planet, the cancerous rot-outs in Europe, Japan, and the United States, thick with replicating primates, the colonies enlarging and spreading and threatening to shock the biosphere with mass extinctions. Perhaps the biosphere does not "like" the idea of five billion humans. Or it could also be said that the extreme amplification of the human race, which has occurred only in the past hundred years or so, has suddenly produced a very large quantity of meat, which is sitting everywhere in the biosphere and may not be able to defend itself against a life form that might want to consume it. Nature has interesting ways of balancing itself. The rain forest has its own defenses. The earth's immune system, so to speak, has recognized the presence of the human species and is starting to kick in. The earth is attempting to rid itself of an infection by the human parasite. Perhaps AIDS is the first step in a natural process of clearance.

AIDS is arguably the worst environmental disaster of the twentieth century. The AIDS virus may well have jumped into the human race from African primates, from monkeys and anthropoid apes. For example, HIV-2 (one of the major strains of HIV) may be a mutant virus that jumped into us from chimpanzees—perhaps when hunters butchered chimpanzees. A strain of simian AIDS virus was recently isolated from a chimpanzee in Gabon, in West Africa, which is, so far, the *closest* thing to HIV-1 that anyone has yet found in the animal kingdom.

The AIDS virus was first noticed in 1980 in Los Angeles by a doctor who realized that his gay male patients were dying of an infectious agent. If anyone at the time had suggested that this unknown disease in gay men in southern California came from wild chimpanzees in Africa, the medical community would have collectively burst out laughing. No one is laughing now. I find it extremely interesting to consider the idea that the chimpanzee is an endangered rain-forest animal and then to contemplate the idea that a virus that moved from chimps is suddenly not endangered at all. You could say that rain-forest viruses are extremely good at looking after their own interests.

The AIDS virus is a fast mutator; it changes constantly. It is a hypermutant, a shape shifter, spontaneously altering its character as it moves through populations and through individuals. It mutates even in the course of one infection, and a person who dies of HIV is usually infected with multiple strains, which have all arisen spontaneously in the body. The fact that the virus mutates rapidly means that vaccines for it will be very difficult to develop. In a larger sense, it means that the AIDS virus is a natural survivor of changes in ecosystems. The AIDS virus and other emerging viruses are surviving the wreck of the tropical biosphere because they can mutate faster than any changes taking place in their ecosystems. They must be good at escaping trouble, if some of them have been around for as long as four billion years. I tend to think of rats leaving a ship.

I suspect that AIDS might not be Nature's preeminent display of power. Whether the human race can actually maintain a population of five billion or more without a crash with a hot virus remains an open question. Unanswered. The answer lies hidden in the labyrinth of tropical ecosystems. AIDS is the revenge of the rain forest. It is only the first act of revenge.

No problem, I thought. Of course, I'll be all right. We'll be all right. No problem at all. Everything will be all right. Plenty of people have gone inside Kitum Cave without becoming sick. Three to eighteen days. As the amplification begins, you feel nothing. It made me think of Joe McCormick, the C.D.C. official who had clashed with the Army over the management of the Ebola Reston outbreak. I remembered the story of him in Sudan, hunting Ebola virus. At the end of a plane flight deep into bush, he had come face to face with Ebola in a hut full of dying patients, had pricked his thumb with a bloody needle, and got lucky, and had survived the experience. In the end, Joe McCormick had been right about the Ebola Reston virus: it had not proved to be highly infectious in people. Then I thought about another Joe McCormick discovery, one of the few breakthroughs in the treatment of Ebola virus. In Sudan, thinking he was going to die of Ebola, he had discovered that a bottle of scotch is the only good treatment for exposure to a filovirus.

The Masque of the Red Death
by Edgar Allan Poe

Poe's story speaks for itself.

The "Red Death" had long devastated the country. No pestilence had ever been so fatal, or so hideous. Blood was its Avatar and its seal—the redness and the horror of blood. There were sharp pains, and sudden dizziness, and then profuse bleeding at the pores, with dissolution. The scarlet stains upon the body and especially upon the face of the victim, were the pest ban which shut him out from the aid and from the sympathy of his fellow-men. And the whole seizure, progress and termination of the disease, were the incidents of half an hour.

But the Prince Prospero was happy and dauntless and sagacious. When his dominions were half depopulated, he summoned to his presence a thousand hale and light-hearted friends from among the knights and dames of his court, and with these retired to the deep seclusion of one of his castellated abbeys. This was an extensive and magnificent structure, the creation of the prince's own eccentric yet august taste. A strong and lofty wall girdled it in. This wall had gates of iron. The courtiers, having entered, brought furnaces and massy hammers and welded the bolts. They resolved to leave means neither of ingress or egress to the sudden impulses of despair or of frenzy from within. The abbey was amply provisioned. With such precautions the courtiers might bid defiance to contagion. The external world could take care of itself. In the meantime it was folly to grieve, or to think. The prince had provided all the appliances of pleasure. There were buffoons, there were improvisatori, there were ballet-dancers, there were musicians, there was Beauty, there was wine. All these and security were within. Without was the "Red Death."

It was toward the close of the fifth or sixth month of his seclusion, and while the pestilence raged most furiously abroad, that the Prince Prospero entertained his thousand friends at a masked ball of the most unusual magnificence.

It was a voluptuous scene, that masquerade. But first let me tell of the rooms in which it was held. There were seven—an imperial suite. In many palaces, however, such suites form a long and straight vista, while the folding doors slide back nearly to the walls on either hand, so that the view of the whole extent is scarcely impeded. Here the case was very different; as might have been expected from the duke's love of the *bizarre*. The apartments were so irregularly disposed that the vision embraced but little more than one at a time. There was a sharp turn at every twenty or thirty yards, and at each turn a novel effect. To the right and left, in the middle of each wall, a

tall and narrow Gothic window looked out upon a closed cor-
ridor which pursued the windings of the suite. These windows
were of stained glass whose color varied in accordance with
the prevailing hue of the decorations of the chamber into
which it opened. That at the eastern extremity was hung, for
example, in blue—and vividly blue were its windows. The
second chamber was purple in its ornaments and tapestries,
and here the panes were purple. The third was green
throughout, and so were the casements. The fourth was fur-
nished and lighted with orange—the fifth with white—the
sixth with violet. The seventh apartment was closely shrouded
in black velvet tapestries that hung all over the ceiling and
down the walls, falling in heavy folds upon a carpet of the
same material and hue. But in this chamber only, the color of
the windows failed to correspond with the decorations. The
panes here were scarlet—a deep blood color. Now in no one
of the seven apartments was there any lamp or candelabrum,
amid the profusion of golden ornaments that lay scattered to
and fro or depended from the roof. There was no light of any
kind emanating from lamp or candle within the suite of
chambers. But in the corridors that followed the suite, there
stood, opposite to each window, a heavy tripod, bearing a brazier of fire that projected its rays through the tinted glass and
so glaringly illumined the room. And thus were produced a
multitude of gaudy and fantastic appearances. But in the
western or black chamber the effect of the fire-light that
streamed upon the dark hangings through the blood-tinted
panes, was ghastly in the extreme, and produced so wild a
look upon the countenances of those who entered, that there
were few of the company bold enough to set foot within its
precincts at all.

It was in this apartment, also, that there stood against the western wall, a gigantic clock of ebony. Its pendulum swung to and fro with a dull, heavy, monotonous clang; and when the minute-hand made the circuit of the face, and the hour was to be stricken, there came from the brazen lungs of the clock a sound which was clear and loud and deep and exceedingly musical, but of so peculiar a note and emphasis that, at each lapse of an hour, the musicians of the orchestra were constrained to pause, momentarily, in their performance, to harken to the sound; and thus the waltzers perforce ceased their evolutions; and there was a brief disconcert of the whole gay company; and, while the chimes of the clock yet rang, it was observed that the giddiest grew pale, and the more aged and sedate passed their hands over their brows as if in confused reverie or meditation. But when the echoes had fully ceased, a light laughter at once pervaded the assembly; the musicians looked at each other and smiled as if at their own nervousness and folly, and made whispering vows, each to the other, that the next chiming of the clock should produce in them no similar emotion; and then, after the lapse of sixty minutes, (which embrace three thousand and six hundred seconds of the Time that flies,) there came yet another chiming of the clock, and then were the same disconcert and tremulousness and meditation as before.

But, in spite of these things, it was a gay and magnificent revel. The tastes of the duke were peculiar. He had a fine eye for colors and effects. He disregarded the *decora* of mere fashion. His plans were bold and fiery, and his conceptions glowed with barbaric lustre. There are some who would have thought him mad. His followers felt that he was not. It was necessary to hear and see and touch him to be *sure* that he was not.

He had directed, in great part, the moveable embellishments of the seven chambers, upon occasion of this great *fête;*

and it was his own guiding taste which had given character to the masqueraders. Be sure they were grotesque. There were much glare and glitter and piquancy and phantasm—much of what has been since seen in "Hernani." There were arabesque figures with unsuited limbs and appointments. There were delirious fancies such as the madman fashions. There was much of the beautiful, much of the wanton, much of the *bizarre*, something of the terrible, and not a little of that which might have excited disgust. To and fro in the seven chambers there stalked, in fact, a multitude of dreams. And these—the dreams—writhed in and about, taking hue from the rooms and causing the wild music of the orchestra to seem as the echo of their steps. And, anon, there strikes the ebony clock which stands in the hall of the velvet. And then, for a moment, all is still, and all is silent save the voice of the clock. The dreams are stiff-frozen as they stand. But the echoes of the chime die away—they have endured but an instant—and a light, half-subdued laughter floats after them as they depart. And now again the music swells, and the dreams live, and writhe to and fro more merrily than ever, taking hue from the many tinted windows through which stream the rays from the tripods. But to the chamber which lies most west-wardly of the seven, there are now none of the maskers who venture: for the night is waning away; and there flows a rud-dier light through the blood-colored panes; and the blackness of the sable drapery appals; and to him whose foot falls upon the sable carpet, there comes from the near clock of ebony a muffled peal more solemnly emphatic than any which reaches *their* ears who indulge in the more remote gaieties of the other apartments.

But these other apartments were densely crowded, and in them beat feverishly the heart of life. And the revel went whirlingly on, until at length there commenced the sounding of midnight upon the clock. And then the music ceased, as I have told; and the evolutions of the waltzers were quieted; and there was an uneasy cessation of all things as before. But now there were twelve strokes to be sounded by the bell of the clock; and thus it happened, perhaps, that more of thought crept, with more of time, into the meditations of the thoughtful among those who revelled. And thus, too, it happened, perhaps, that before the last echoes of the last chime had utterly sunk into silence, there were many individuals in the crowd who had found leisure to become aware of the presence of a masked figure which had arrested the attention of no single individual before. And the rumor of this new presence having spread itself whisperingly around, there arose at length from the whole company a buzz, or murmur, expressive of disapprobation and surprise—then, finally, of terror, of horror, and of disgust.

In an assembly of phantasms such as I have painted, it may well be supposed that no ordinary appearance could have excited such sensation. In truth the masquerade license of the night was nearly unlimited; but the figure in question had out-Heroded Herod, and gone beyond the bounds of even the prince's indefinite decorum. There are chords in the hearts of the most reckless which cannot be touched without emotion. Even with the utterly lost, to whom life and death are equally jests, there are matters of which no jest can be made. The whole company, indeed, seemed now deeply to feel that in the costume and bearing of the stranger neither wit nor propriety existed. The figure was tall and gaunt, and shrouded from head to foot in the habiliments of the grave. The mask which concealed the visage was made so nearly to resemble the countenance of a stiffened corpse that the closest scrutiny must have had difficulty in detecting the cheat. And yet all this might have been endured, if not approved, by the mad revellers around. But the mummer had gone so far as to assume the type of the Red Death. His vesture was dabbled in *blood*— and his broad brow, with all the features of the face, was besprinkled with the scarlet horror.

When the eyes of Prince Prospero fell upon this spectral image (which with a slow and solemn movement, as if more fully to sustain its *rôle,* stalked to and fro among the waltzers) he was seen to be convulsed, in the first moment with a strong shudder either of terror or distaste; but, in the next, his brow reddened with rage.

"Who dares?" he demanded hoarsely of the courtiers who stood near him—"who dares insult us with this blasphemous mockery? Seize him and unmask him—that we may know whom we have to hang at sunrise, from the battlements!"

It was in the eastern or blue chamber in which stood the Prince Prospero as he uttered these words. They rang throughout the seven rooms loudly and clearly—for the prince was a bold and robust man, and the music had become hushed at the waving of his hand.

It was in the blue room where stood the prince, with a group of pale courtiers by his side. At first, as he spoke, there was a slight rushing movement of this group in the direction of the intruder, who at the moment was also near at hand, and now, with deliberate and stately step, made closer approach to the speaker. But from a certain nameless awe with which the mad assumptions of the mummer had inspired the whole party, there were found none who put forth hand to seize him; so that, unimpeded, he passed within a yard of the prince's person; and, while the vast assembly, as if with one impulse, shrank from the centres of the rooms to the walls, he made his way uninterruptedly, but with the same solemn and measured step which had distinguished him from the first, through the blue chamber to the purple—through the purple to the green—through the green to the orange—through this again to the white—and even thence to the violet, ere a decided movement had been made to arrest him. It was then, however, that the Prince Prospero, maddening with rage and the shame of his own momentary cowardice, rushed hurriedly through the six chambers, while none followed him on account of a deadly terror that had seized upon all. He bore aloft a drawn dagger, and had approached, in rapid impetuosity, to within three or four feet of the retreating figure, when the latter, having attained the extremity of the velvet apartment, turned suddenly and confronted his pursuer. There was a sharp cry— and the dagger dropped gleaming upon the sable carpet, upon which, instantly afterwards, fell prostrate in death the Prince Prospero. Then, summoning the wild courage of despair, a throng of the revellers at once threw themselves into the black apartment, and, seizing the mummer, whose tall figure stood erect and motionless within the shadow of the ebony clock, gasped in unutterable horror at finding the grave-cerements and corpse-like mask which they handled with so violent a rudeness, untenanted by any tangible form.

And now was acknowledged the presence of the Red Death. He had come like a thief in the night. And one by one dropped the revellers in the blood-bedewed halls of their revel, and died each in the despairing posture of his fall. And the life of the ebony clock went out with that of the last of the gay. And the flames of the tripods expired. And Darkness and Decay and the Red Death held illimitable dominion over all.

Acknowledgments

Many people made this anthology.

At Thunder's Mouth Press and Avalon Publishing Group: Thanks to Will Balliett, Sue Canavan, Maria Fernandez, Linda Kosarin, Dan O'Connor, Neil Ortenberg, Susan Reich, David Riedy, Michelle Rosenfield, Simon Sullivan, Mike Walters and Don Weise for their support, dedication and hard work.

In Maine: Jennifer Willis oversaw editorial research and scheduling. Taylor Smith oversaw rights research.

Thanks to the publishers, agents and other literary representatives who helped us to obtain permission to publish selections.

Finally, I am grateful to the writers whose work appears in this book.

Permissions

We gratefully acknowledge everyone who gave permission for written material to appear in this book. We have made every effort to trace and contact copyright holders. If an error or omission is brought to our notice we will be pleased to correct the situation in future editions of this book. For further information, please contact the publisher.

bibliography

The selections used in this anthology were taken from the editions listed below. In some cases, other editions may be easier to find. Hard-to-find or out-of-print titles often are available through inter-library loan services or through Internet booksellers.

Brodkey, Harold. *This Wild Darkness*. New York: Henry Holt, 1996.

Clynes, Tom. "Dangerous Medicine." Originally appeared in *National Geographic Adventurer*, May/June 2001.

Desowitz, Robert. "How the Wise Men Brought Malaria to Africa." Originally appeared in *Natural History*, October 1976.

Drexler, Madeline. *Secret Agents: The Menace of Emerging Infections*. Washington, D.C.: Joseph Henry Press, 2002.

Gawande, Atul. *Complications: A Surgeon's Notes on an Imperfect Science*. New York: Picador, 2002.

McCormick, Joseph B. and Susan Fisher-Hoch. *Level 4: Virus Hunters of the CDC*. Atlanta: Turner Publishing, Inc., 1996.

O'Reilly, Brian. "Death of a Continent." Originally appeared in *Fortune*, November 13, 2000.

Poe, Edgar Allen. *Poetry Tales and Selected Essays*. New York: Library of America, 1996.

Preston, Richard. *The Hot Zone*. New York: Random House, 1994.

Rampton, Sheldon and John Stauber. *Mad Cow U.S.A.* Monroe, Maine: Common Courage Press, 1997.

Wills, Christopher. *Yellow Fever, Black Goddess: The Coevolution of People and Plagues*. Reading, Massachusetts: Helix Books, 1996.